My Brother's Keeper

My Brother's Keeper

AFRICAN CANADIANS AND THE AMERICAN CIVIL WAR

Bryan Prince

DUNDURN
TORONTO

Project Editor: Shannon Whibbs
Copy-Editor: Britanie Wilson
Design: Laura Boyle
Cover Design: Jennifer Gallinger
Cover Image: "Reading the Emancipation Proclamation." Print from steel engraving by James W. Watts from a drawing by Henry Walker Herrick. Entered according to Act of Congress 1864 by Lucius Stebbins in the clerk's office of the District Court of Connecticut. Image courtesy of Library of Congress Prints and Photographs Division, Washington, D. C. Reproduction Number LC-USZ62-5334.
Printer: Webcom

Library and Archives Canada Cataloguing in Publication

Prince, Bryan, 1951-, author
    My brother's keeper : African Canadians and the American Civil War / Bryan Prince.

Includes bibliographical references and index. Issued in print and electronic formats.
ISBN 978-1-4597-0570-8 (pbk.).--ISBN 978-1-4597-0571-5 (pdf).-- ISBN 978-1-4597-0572-2 (epub)

1. United States--History--Civil War, 1861-1865--Participation, Black Canadian. 2. United States--History--Civil War, 1861-1865--Blacks--Canada. 3. Blacks--Canada--History--19th century. 4. Canada--History--1841-1867. I. Title.

E540.C25P75 2015   973.7089'96071   C2014-906776-3
                                                  C2014-906777-1

1   2   3   4   5   19   18   17   16   15

  Canada

We acknowledge the support of the **Canada Council for the Arts** and the **Ontario Arts Council** for our publishing program. We also acknowledge the financial support of the **Government of Canada** through the **Canada Book Fund** and **Livres Canada Books**, and the **Government of Ontario** through the **Ontario Book Publishing Tax Credit** and the **Ontario Media Development Corporation**.

Care has been taken to trace the ownership of copyright material used in this book. The author and the publisher welcome any information enabling them to rectify any references or credits in subsequent editions.

J. Kirk Howard, President

The publisher is not responsible for websites or their content unless they are owned by the publisher.

Printed and bound in Canada.

VISIT US AT
Dundurn.com | @dundurnpress | Facebook.com/dundurnpress | Pinterest.com/dundurnpress

DUNDURN
3 Church Street, Suite 500
Toronto, Ontario, Canada
M5E 1M2

Indeed I tremble for my country when I reflect that God is just, that his justice cannot sleep forever. Commerce between slave and master is despotism. Nothing is more certainly written in the book of fate that these people are to be free.

— *Thomas Jefferson*

Contents

PREFACE

Hundreds of blacks from the Canadas — Canada East (now Quebec) and Canada West (now Ontario) — joined their British North American brethren in what would later become the Dominion of Canada to fight in the American Civil War. Some were born there and many more fled there, seeking refuge from slavery and from laws that oppressed the spirit and the body. Some lived in Canada for much of their lives, some only briefly before returning to the country of their birth or, in some cases, to distant, foreign shores. No matter the length of time spent in Canada, these men and women were acutely aware of the inhumanity of slavery from both their own experiences and from the constant reminders in the form of refugees who came into their midst. When the time came for blacks to put on a uniform and attempt to help remove the chains, many unselfishly and courageously answered the call. On the following pages we will be introduced to some of those who went to the front, and to others who remained behind; regardless, all of these men and women were touched by slavery and liberty, by family and community, by the horrors of war and the possibilities of freedom....

CHAPTER 1

One Soldier's Story

His cough was getting worse — a nagging, painful reminder that happy endings were sometimes dearly bought. It was now coming from so deep within his lungs that his body convulsed. In the autumn months, the cough was accompanied by chills and a fever.[1] Besides that, the wound on the side of his face never seemed to completely heal and, as the old folks would say, "his flesh was falling away." His emaciated features made him appear just a slight shadow of the dashing figure he had once cut. Proudly dressed in the regimental blue uniform of the 1st Michigan Colored Infantry, later renamed the 102nd Regiment, United States Colored Infantry (USCI) under the banner of the United States Colored Troops (USCT), his comrades-in-arms had addressed him as "Corporal" Solomon King. Memories from long ago, conjured up from the vantage point of a distant land — sixteen years and Charleston, South Carolina made for increasingly hazy recollections of his companions whom he had known in Canada West, prior to when he crossed the Detroit River and enlisted on October 1, 1863.

They were part of more than fifty thousand blacks, whites, and natives from Canada who fought in the American Civil War, predominantly for the Union, and a significant number for the Confederacy.[2] More accurately, these people came from what was then British North America, with the province of Canada — consisting of Canada East and Canada West — being a part of those British colonies, which included Nova Scotia, New Brunswick, Prince Edward Island, and British Columbia.

On a narrower focus, Solomon was one of hundreds of blacks from Canada West who joined the Union army. Not all of them had been born in Canada. In fact, a majority were like him, originally from the United States but who came to the British colony to escape slavery and the oppressive laws that supported it. Some stayed temporarily; others made it a more lasting home, at least until the war against slavery promised to change the world that they knew. The direction of their individual and collective futures hinged on the political outcomes dictated by the victor on the battlefield. Though slavery was now behind them, these throngs turned to face it again and be a part of the fight for a glorious cause in a war whose roots were entangled with their own.

In Solomon's case, his beginnings were as one of the more than 30 slaves on the 640-acre cotton plantation of John Ebenezer Phares in the East Feliciana Parish of Louisiana where he was born in 1843 or 1844.[3] Like many of his fellows, he was uncertain of the exact date. Years later, upon opening an account at Freedmen's Bank, where he was asked to list all members of his family, Solomon gave the Christian names of his mother, Eliza, his two brothers, Cornelius and William, and his sisters, Mary and Amelia. When asked to name his father, who was not a part of his son's life, the mulatto Solomon simply put the surname "Parker."[4] The Christian name was either forgotten or, in his mind, inconsequential, or both.

Eliza was in her mid-twenties and the mother of two-year-old Amelia at the time of Solomon's birth. Her mistress, John Phares's first wife, had died in the 1820s when Eliza was still a child. Her master remarried, was widowed again, remarried, then widowed, and married yet another time.[5] With stepchildren, half-siblings, and perhaps new servants added to the mix, the dynamics of the household were in a constant state of change, leaving an extra element of uncertainty with house slaves like Eliza. One of the few constants, which presumably lent some comfort through Eliza's youth, were the elder Phares daughters, Mary and Martha, who were both close to her own age.

After Mary was wed to William King, an Irish-born immigrant who was the rector of the nearby Matthews Academy, a male preparatory school for Louisiana College, she brought Eliza and her infant daughter Amelia into the marriage with her as part of the inheritance from her late mother's estate. Interestingly — and sadly — the same arrangement did not follow when Solomon was born, and he remained the property of John Phares. Perhaps the only logical explanation was that John Phares wanted to take every possible step to ensure that all of his seven children and his surviving widow were treated equitably in the distribution of his estate after his death. In his will, dated November 10, 1845, he ignored any semblance of humanity toward Eliza and included one-year-old Solomon in the bequest to his second daughter, Martha, who was then married to Andrew Jackson Brame.

State of Louisiana

East Feliciana Parish, Know all men by these presents that I have this 18th day of April 1848 delivered up to Wm King the following named negro slaves; to wit: Eliza a black woman age thirty years and Amelia a girl aged six years, said negroes being inherited by said Wm King through his wife from her mothers' interest in the property of John E. Phares, deceased and the title to said negroes is perfect in the said Wm King. Given under my hand and seal the day and year above written

D. L. Phares
Exe of est J.E. Phares

The marriage of Mary Phares to William King subtly initiated a profound alteration to the direction of everyone's lives — black and white alike — who were within their sphere of influence. King was keenly aware of the evils of slavery, both those that were suffered by the enslaved, and those that were inescapably absorbed by the master class. As a teacher and observer of young Southern men, he was disturbed to see many of their personalities gradually transform as they embraced a feeling of

Reverend William King, founder of the Elgin Settlement and Buxton Mission. *Buxton National Historic Site & Museum (BNHS&M).*

superiority over their darker-hewn fellow beings. King, a man of deep religious convictions, was alarmed at witnessing their lack of ambition, excessive use of liquor, and their penchant for fighting; wishing to start a family, he feared for his own children's salvation.

Ironically, William King found himself in what he considered to be an irreconcilable moral dilemma. As the director of the Academy, with over ninety students boarding there, he constantly had trouble hiring capable and reliable staff. After many issues with drunken, dishonest, and inept help, King desperately needed a cook and acquiesced to the request of a black man named Talbert to purchase him, thereby allowing Talbert to take a job with a master that he could be comfortable with. King justified it in his own mind that he would be a kind master and would give this slave his freedom when the opportunity arose. King intended to do the same with Eliza and Amelia, who came into his wife's possession about the same time.

King wrote of being tortured with owning slaves and of praying for guidance. He concluded he would go to Edinburgh and study for the ministry in the New College of the Free Church of Scotland. But first, he had to make plans for his wife, their then-infant son, Theophilus, and their slaves. He purchased a farm near his father-in-law and placed his slaves in a house there, instructing them to care of the land and live off of the proceeds of their own labour. The purchase price of this land included two female slaves, each with an eight-year-old child — Fannie, a forty-seven-year-old who spent years of her life anguishing over six of her older children who had been sold away from her in Virginia; her youngest son, Peter; Mollie, a Creole cook; and Mollie's daughter, Sarah. The spiral into becoming an entrenched slave-owner quickly continued when King purchased twenty-two-year-old Jacob, another male who would be critical in helping to work the land.[6] At the time, no one knew that Jacob would eventually mean so much more. With John Phares supervising his daughter and son-in-law's slaves in their absence, the newborn Solomon could remain in his mother's care — at least for the time being.

With his slaves now working for their own support, and after making an initial trip to Edinburgh alone, William King was prepared to take his wife and son to Scotland while he completed his studies. But personal tragedy soon struck viciously and repeatedly. First Theophilus, who was nearly three years old, caught fever while still in the early stages of their journey, and died within days. In January 1846 John Phares died, thereby activating his will, which included the bequest to his daughter, Mary King, of five more slaves: Ben, Emeline, Robin, Isay, and Old Steven. This same last will and testament formally threatened to physically remove Solomon from his mother, Eliza, and made him the legal property of Martha Brame. The news of her father's death coupled with the excruciating sorrow of having lost her son proved too much for Mary, and she followed her father into death the following month, leaving Johanna, their five-month-old daughter, in her father's care. Johanna died on May 9, 1846, within weeks of her mother, and was placed in the same tomb. According to Louisiana law, the timing of this series of deaths dictated that John Phares's slaves would go to his children, including Mary King and Martha Brame. Upon her death, Mary's slaves would go to her only surviving child, Johanna. Upon the death of this child, Johanna's slaves would go to her only surviving parent, William King, which meant that this divinity student and avowed abolitionist quickly became the owner of fourteen slaves.

Upon completing his ministerial studies, King returned to the United States with an unwavering resolve to free his slaves and take them to Canada where their liberty could be assured. When he came back to Louisiana he discovered that two of his slaves, Jacob (who had taken the surname "King") and Eliza (who had taken the surname "Phares") had married in a slave ceremony in his absence, and together had a son who they named Cornelius, a half-brother to Solomon and Amelia. When William King called all of his slaves together to inform them that they would be going to Canada and that they would be free, he was puzzled that he did not receive the jubilant reaction that he expected. They had become so accustomed to their present condition that they were unable to grasp the concept of freedom. When the new reality of their future began to dawn on them, a panicked and tearful Eliza ran to Reverend King and implored him to buy her son Solomon from his sister-in-law, who had inherited him, as she could not bear to leave him behind. A cash-strapped and hesitant King eventually caved in to her hysterical lamentations and negotiated a deal with Martha Brame and her husband.[7] A few months later, Reverend King wrote to a colleague to inform him of the circumstances surrounding the purchase of Solomon. He optimistically and naively predicted:

> Such is the nature of Slavery and the laws which support it, but I trust its' days are nearly numbered, the North and the West are rising up in real earnest to rid themselves of the evil, Men of all creeds & political parties are uniting their forces against the system. It cannot always remain in a Christian Community, the gospel alone will destroy it.[8]

Of course, the gospel alone did not end slavery — rather, it would take four years of bloody warfare.

With Solomon now reunited with his mother, sister, stepfather, and half-brother, the entire group, now comprised of fifteen individuals, would always have a special familial bond forged in slavery. This bond was soon to be strengthened in freedom as they were delivered to the port at Bayou Sara on the Mississippi River to meet with their owner and begin the trip northward to Canada. The scene and the emotions as they

Bill of Sale for young Solomon King.[9] *Courtesy of BNHS&M.*

bid goodbye to familiar people and landscapes, and to the closest thing that they had to a home before they boarded a boat and pushed off, can only be imagined.

Solomon, who had been too young to experience the horrors of slavery despite narrowly missing it first-hand, was constantly surrounded by other people's memories. He and the fourteen other slaves who once belonged to William King were the nucleus of the Reverend's envisioned colony for former slaves, christened the Elgin Settlement and Buxton Mission, commonly known as "Buxton." Shortly after their arrival in Canada in November 1849, Solomon's mother, Eliza, and Jacob King wasted little time in officially solemnizing their marriage in the Presbyterian Church in nearby Chatham on January 21, 1850.[10] Unfortunately their time together would be short as they were plagued by illness. Eliza died in July 1853 and Amelia also quickly disappeared from the records, presumably to a childhood grave. Jacob was troubled with a persistent fever for three years that rendered him unable to work steadily and was reliant on his young son, Cornelius, to help provide for him.[11] Following the death of their mother, the extraordinary connection that existed among this group of freedmen was vividly demonstrated in 1861: seventeen-year-old Cornelius assisted and lived with then-sixty-year-old Fanny and her elderly husband, and

1856 sketch of the buildings of the Buxton Mission. *Courtesy of BNHS&M.*

Log home of Reverend William King, where Solomon King spent his first days in Canada. *Courtesy of BNHS&M.*

Solomon lived with Robin Phares, another of the original fifteen. Further illustrating the connection between these ex-slaves, and the new community in which they lived, Peter and Sarah, the pair of eight-year-old children who along with their mothers were originally purchased as a part of a farm, were taken in by a neighbouring widow and her family.

Buxton was an all-black settlement, with its inhabitants having fled from many parts of the United States. At its height on the eve of the Civil War, the population of Buxton was about 1,200 living on nearly 9,000 acres. Scores more had come for a time before moving on. Some came directly from slavery, some via the Underground Railroad, some led exclusively by their own wits and sheer determination. Others came from the Northern states, escaping laws that threatened their livelihoods, assaulted their peace of mind, and that refused to guarantee their freedom. A handful of others filtered in from various parts of Canada. What they all had in common was slavery in their backgrounds and the heart-wrenching experiences that accompanied such a past. Reminders of the horrors to the south were reawakened with each new arrival.

Another poignant symbol that encouraged the inhabitants never to forget the past they had escaped was the peal of a beautifully ornate bronze bell that hung near the village square at Buxton, a gift from the African-American community in Pittsburgh, Pennsylvania. After learning of the ideal of Buxton in its earliest days, those citizens wished to express their pleasure and their support. The letter, dated November 23, 1850, that accompanied the bell is as touching over a century and a half later as when it was first written:

> To the Coloured Settlers at Raleigh, C. West
>
> Dear Brethren, —
>
> We have heard with great pleasure from Dr. Burns and the Rev. Wm. King of your settlement at Raleigh. We rejoice that you have met with Christian friends who cheer and encourage you in your efforts to improve your social condition.

You are now in a land of liberty, where the rights and privileges of freemen are secured to you by law. Your future position in society will depend very much on your own exertions. We sincerely hope that by your industry and good conduct you will put to silence those who speak evil of you, and show yourselves worthy of the respect and confidence of the members of the "Elgin Association" who have nobly advocated your cause.

We feel a deep interest both in your temporal and spiritual welfare. As a lasting memorial of our kindness, we send to the Rev. W. King, a Bell for the Academy, that when we shall be mouldering in our coffins, will call your children to the house of instruction. While your children are brought up under the blessings of a Christian education, we trust that in the land of your adoption you will not forget the God of your Fathers. Love and serve him; remember the Sabbath day to keep it holy, and when the bell, with its solemn tones, calls you to the House of God, remember your brethren who are in bonds; and let your prayers ascend to God, that he may, in his own good time, break every yoke and let the oppressed go free; that he may turn both the hearts of Masters and Servants from the bondage of Satan to the service of the one living and true God.

J.C. Peck

J.B. Vashon

On behalf of the committee

The reply of appreciation from the people of Buxton was equally moving:

To the Coloured Inhabitants of Pittsburgh

Dear Brethren: —

We have received your letter dated the 23rd Nov., and the bell presented to the Rev. W. King for the Academy at Raleigh. We are delighted at all times to hear from the friends that we have left in a land of pretended freedom, and although separated in body, we are present with you in spirit; and we fondly hope that our prayers often meet before the throne of God for mutual blessings. We will endeavour to observe and practice the advice which you have kindly given us, by loving and serving God and obeying the laws of our Sovereign. We will not cease to implore the Divine Blessing on that Government which has given us liberty not only in name but in reality. The bell has been raised to the place erected for it, and for the first time the silence of our forest was broken on last Sabbath morn, by its joyful peals inviting us to the house of God. We would return to you our sincere thanks for this memorial of your kindness, and we trust that while its cheerful peal invites us to the house of prayer, we will then remember our brethren who are in less favourable circumstances; and our constant prayer will be that the Bible, the gift of God to man, may no longer be withheld from you by the unrighteous acts of professed Christian legislators; that the power of the oppressor may be broken, and that those who have long been held in bondage may be set free.

It would be another fifteen years before the final phrases of the letter to Pittsburgh came to pass — "that the power of the oppressor may be broken, and that those who have long been held in bondage may be set free." After the first shots were fired on Fort Sumter, South Carolina, on April 12, 1861, thus beginning the Civil War, black men from all over the United States as well as Canada and all of British North America wished to join the Union Army. Even though President Lincoln made it clear that the war was not to end slavery, but rather to save the Union, they were convinced that it was a war for freedom.

Throughout 1863, and for the next two years, black regiments were formed across the individual states, both north and south. Early in that first year, Reverend King called a public meeting in Buxton to explain the details of the Emancipation Proclamation: that slaves in the parts of the South that were in rebellion to the Union had been declared free and that the young men of the Settlement now had the opportunity to enter the army and assist in freeing those still held in bondage. Reverend King was well aware that many of the men before him still had brothers, sisters, and parents who were enslaved. Emboldened by love and by duty, forty men immediately volunteered to enlist, and thirty more later followed. Among them were two of the once-little boys, now young men, whom Reverend King had once owned: Cornelius King, who travelled across country to Providence to join the 14th Rhode Island Heavy Artillery, and his older brother Solomon, who had shed his original surname "Phares" and adopted "King," the married name of his late mother and of his former owner, who had proudly watched him grow into manhood. Solomon, like a great many of his colleagues, decided to enlist closer to home and made the fifty-mile trip southwest to Michigan to enlist in the coloured regiment being formed there. According to Reverend King's memoirs, Solomon was more than a soldier. He also credited him with returning to Canada periodically and taking more recruits to the United States. That was risky enough, as his actions ran afoul of the Foreign Enlistment Act, which, under penalty of law, forbade British subjects from participating in foreign wars, but he also, on more than one occasion, went into the slave state of Kentucky to find recruits.[12]

As the initial euphoria gradually gave way to reality, the business of preparing for war proved far from glamorous. Solomon later blamed his declining health on his experiences in the Union army, which proved little short of a nightmare. Intermittent fever began to plague him shortly after he and his comrades crossed the Detroit River from the Canadian side and enlisted on that autumn day in 1863. Conditions in the barracks assigned to them in Detroit were reprehensible and Solomon took ill there.[13] A Detroit newspaper informed its readers: "There is not a barn or a pigsty in the whole city of Detroit that is not more fit for the habitation of a human-being than the quarters at Camp Ward."[14] There were leaks in the roof, no flooring, large cracks in the wall that allowed snow to blow in, beds made of straw, and poor ventilation that allowed smoke from the stoves to linger in the air.[15]

Letter from Cornelius King to his father, Jacob, shortly after enlisting in the 14th Rhode Island Colored Infantry. *Civil War survivors pension application for Jacob King, National Archives Record Administration (NARA).*

The following year, he spent much of March and April in the General Hospital and was not able to rejoin his company, who had been deployed to Annapolis, Maryland in April, to report for active duty until May 12, 1864. In June he was again sick with intermittent fever and was finally reduced in rank to private, losing the prestigious designation of corporal that officials had bestowed upon him from the regiment's organization. Unbeknownst to him, Cornelius was also suffering from fever at the same time. Solomon's younger brother had lied about his age at the time of enlistment. While he had sworn that he was the legal age of eighteen, and old enough to enlist, he was in fact at least a year younger. Although recognized as having the same rank of private as all 122 of his colleagues within his company, Cornelius was one of two musicians in that same group. Perhaps he thought that he would be somewhat safer than the ordinary soldier, but disease had a longer range than a musket ball and had ways of attacking far behind the front skirmish lines.

Cornelius became another victim, when, unable to rally, he died on June 29, 1864 in the Battalion Hospital in Plaquemine, Louisiana, the state of their birth. Cornelius had been desperate to earn money to send back to his ailing father in Canada.

For the duration of the war, Solomon was often incapacitated between short periods when his health rallied enough to resume his duties.[16] During 1864 he was periodically treated at the Regimental Hospital in Beaufort, South Carolina, as well as at the Regimental Hospital of the 54th Massachusetts between April 6th and 25th, 1865, which gave temporary treatment to members of the 102nd. Medical prescriptions that included tincture of iron and sulphate quinine gave little relief.[17]

Some of his lingering health problems were only indirectly attributed to sickness. As his company was on the march to Columbia, South Carolina in the spring of 1865, near the end of the war, the soldiers were unable to find any water to drink. Solomon finally refused to march any further. Perhaps another factor that contributed to Solomon's temporary defiance was that as of the end of February 1865, he had still not received any pay from the time of his enlistment in October 1863. In addition to that indignity, he was charged as owing $1.50 to the U.S. government for a screwdriver, a wiper, a cartridge belt, and a belt plate.[18] Lieutenant Molena exhibited no sympathy and seized Solomon's rifle and struck him on the head with the barrel of the gun, knocking the private senseless. When Solomon finally came to, he forced himself to rejoin the march but never fully recovered from the head wound for the duration of the war.[19] He did, however, complete his tour of duty and was mustered out in Charleston, South Carolina on September 30, 1865.

The end of the war signalled the arrival of a season of great optimism for all blacks on the continent. Many had once left loved ones behind and now there was an opportunity — albeit one fraught with monumental challenges — to try to find them. Others looked to economic opportunities in the industrialized Northern states. Some were attracted to the comfort of the sizeable black communities scattered across the United States. Many of those who had found a new life in Canada could not resist the lure of the country they had once left behind — no matter how many years may have intervened, home was, and is always, home.

It was not necessarily always something that drew people to the United States, but in some cases it was the dawning realization that things would never be quite the same again in Canada. Now that American slavery no longer existed, discrimination and racial intolerance, while somewhat understated, was again becoming more pronounced. Just as the lives of those who experienced war were profoundly changed, so too were the souls of the black communities. Just as blacks had once trickled, or occasionally flooded, into Canada to escape slavery and oppressive laws in the U.S., many now made the exodus in reverse. Also, hundreds of young black men joined thousands of young white men from across British North America who had been part of the Union Army. Of those, far too many had died in combat or of disease, each leaving a gaping hole in the fabric of their communities.

In Solomon's case, there was little to return to. Of the close-knit group of fifteen slaves who had first come to Canada, few of them remained. His mother and sister Amelia had both died shortly after coming to Canada. His stepfather, Jacob, had remarried, started another family, and joined a sizeable group of neighbours who moved to work in the lumber and salt manufacturing industries in Saginaw, Michigan.[20]

And there was an even more compelling, personal reason for Solomon to remain in the south. He confided to one of his fellow soldiers that he had met a girl when their company was on maneuvers in the south. He had promised her that he would return. It was his intention to keep that pledge with the ultimate goal of marrying her.[21]

Life had been very different for Sarah Richardson, the woman who would become his wife. Like so many individual stories related to slavery, both Solomon's and Sarah's were vaguely familiar and dramatically unique. Taken together with the too-often forgotten, heart-wrenching narratives of the millions of children of Africa who had been held in bondage, it was inevitable that any emotional, legal, or philosophical arguments about the institution of slavery must be put aside and settled by a bloody resolution.

Sarah was like so many women who, when faced with tragedy, drew incredible strength from some invisible reservoir that has been largely ignored by their contemporaries and inexplicably unrecognized or relegated to footnotes in the pages of history. Explanations were impossible and unnecessary, only to be observed with wonder and admiration.

She had been a slave much longer than her husband. Indeed, she had been for most of her life. She was born in St. John's Parish, South Carolina on the Eutaw Plantation.[22] Her original owner was the prominent William Sinkler, who owned cotton plantations bordering the Santee River, with its picturesque banks complemented with giant cypress trees. Visitors to the main house approached by a long avenue, shaded with oak trees that were covered in Spanish moss. The building sat on a tall, brick basement and was supported by arches that spanned a covered passageway, which in turn was covered by a wide piazza that encircled the home. A large central stair was a focal point of the interior, and the four largest first-storey rooms each had a fireplace.[23]

Following the fashionable practice of naming slaves after classical or mythological figures such as Caesar, Scipio, Pompeii, Jupiter, or Venus, her father had been given the name "Hercules"; her mother was called the less pretentious, more mortal "Margaret." Although only identified by their Christian name, Hercules and Margaret had the surname "Richardson," which suggests that they or their ancestors were once owned by the neighbouring white family of the same name, who had intermarried many times over with the Sinklers.

Sarah was a cook for the family, a life-long occupation she had in slavery and later in freedom. During her time at Eutaw, she settled into the daily rituals. As the master's family assembled in the hall at 8:30 a.m., Sarah would help prepare and serve breakfast, which consisted of hot cakes, waffles, biscuits, and toast. The Sinkler's family prayers followed at 9:30, after the tables had been cleared. The kitchen slaves then prepared for dinner as the Sinkler females, with greyhounds and terriers running alongside and a slave riding ahead to open gates, enjoyed a horse-drawn carriage ride in the countryside, while the males went off to hunt partridges, foxes, or the occasional wildcat. The mid-day meal was not eaten until 3:30 p.m. or later. Supper, which was similar to breakfast, except that cold meat was included, was taken after 8:00 p.m. Hominy grits, made from ground corn mixed with seasoned boiling water, was the family's favourite dish and was served at all three meals. The kitchen slaves cleared the supper dishes as their owners relaxed to music from a guitar and a piano.[24]

Eutaw Plantation Home where Sarah King was enslaved. *Call Number: HABS SC, 38-EUTA.V,6-. Repository: Library of Congress Prints and Photographs Division (LOC).*

Outbuilding on the Eutaw Plantation. *LC-J7-SC- 1401 [P&P]. LOC.1-7.*

William Sinkler, the patriarch of the family, had a passion for horseracing — the sport of Southern gentlemen. He kept a suite at the grand Charleston Hotel so he could be near the Washington Race Course to witness his horses and jockeys, clad in the red and white silks of his Eutaw Plantation, regularly win. He also had his own track at his Eutaw plantation. His slave, Hercules, who had a remarkable talent with horses and trained winner after winner, was singled out "as one of the most faithful colored grooms in the State."[25] Among his secrets for training a superior racer was rubbing the horse down with whiskey and allowing it to drink some. Each day before it was time to exercise, the horse was given twenty eggs to eat.[26]

There was always a great deal of action about the house. Even though there were only four bedrooms in the house, there were five slaves who served as chambermaids.[27] Christmas season was a special time for all, and for three afternoons each year the slaves gathered on the piazza of the great house on the Eutaw Plantation to celebrate and to entertain the gathered Sinkler relatives. The music for dancing was provided by slaves playing a fiddle, drums, and bones.[28]

Colonel Richard Irvine Manning II, Sarah King Richardson's master. *Courtesy of Manning descendant and genealogist "ss847."*

28

As had been the case with Solomon King's mother, Sarah moved to a new household when a daughter of her master, Elizabeth Allen Sinkler, commonly called "Eliza," married Colonel Richard Irvine Manning. Both of her new owners were part of South Carolinian aristocracy: Richard was a senator, and both Richard and Elizabeth were closely related to four past and two future governors of the state.[29]

The family inhabited what they fondly referred to as "the old Castle" in Clarendon County, South Carolina until 1859 when they purchased a home and a 4,100-acre farm in Sumter County. They christened that home "Homesley," which they considered to mean "A Home For All."[30] The ninety-five individuals who lived in twenty-eight different slave houses on the plantation perhaps described it differently.[31]

The Mannings and their slaves were close to the dramatic firing of the cannon on Fort Sumter that launched the War Between the States. Colonel Manning, although opposed to the secession of his home and neighbouring Southern states, formed and outfitted a company of soldiers, "the Manning Guards," and joined the Confederate army.[32] Colonel Manning's service would be short-lived, however, as he died in October 1861 of typhus fever that he had contracted in July while in the service, leaving Eliza and the slaves to raise the children and run the farm.[33] The members of the South Carolina Senate expressed their condolences by unanimously adopting a resolution to address the fact that:

> ... death, ever busy, and striking at shining marks, has called from the sphere of human existence, in the vigor of his energy and usefulness, the Hon. RICHARD I. MANNING, Senator from Clarendon.... A pure patriot; a sound statesman; a beloved husband, father, son and brother; one in every relation of life well worthy the example of us all.[34]

All of the slaves, including those who may indeed have had a genuine affection for their late master and had joined in the grieving, would suddenly have had additional terrors present themselves — the spectre of being sold away from loved ones in the division of the property resultant from the settling of the estate. That chill was re-enforced on March 15, 1862, when appraisers put a value to all of Manning's slaves from both of his plantations. From the Homesley Plantation: Sarah; her mother, Margaret; her brother, Hercules; her sisters, including Lucy and Ellen; and her young daughters, Jane and Mary, were examined by five men and evaluated:

Margaret (Nurse) $350
Lucy (Seamstress) $1000
Sarah (Cook) $1000
Jane $250
Mary $150
Elijah $75
Ellen $500
Harriet $175
Toinette $75
Hercules (House Servant) $800[35]

But perhaps they were in a much better position than the other 141 slaves on the two Manning plantations, given that they held the prestigious position of house slaves. The Manning children also had a special affection for Margaret, who they referred to as "Mauma," and they later recalled that the other slaves of the house were their childhood friends and their parents trusted them to care for their children.[36] During the war, the Manning family developed an even deeper appreciation for Margaret and the other "loyal" slaves who protected them from the black Union soldiers, some of whom came from Canada, who posed a special terror.[37]

The war years touched Sarah in a variety of intimate ways. Her father, also named Hercules, died early in the second year of hostilities. The February 5, 1862 front-page contents of the flowery obituary that appeared in the *Charleston Daily Courier* is a unique, albeit paternalistic, compliment to a "good and faithful servant." Years later, slaves would recall a moving and melancholy tradition they would follow when one of their fellows was near to death. They would position the dying person's bed to face the open door "so the chariot would have no hindrance when it came and the spirit of the newly dead would be free to go." The black population joined together to stay awake and await the coming of the chariot.[38]

> We are sorry to announce that "Old Hercules" the well know trainer of Albine during her triumphant career, has recently depart this life, full of years and full of honors. His crowning glory was his beating with Albine, during the last season in Carolina, every horse in succession, in the stable, (regarded previously as invincible, of those fine specimens of kind and hospitable Virginia gentlemen, "the Doswells" — father and sons).
>
> Hercules, like old Charles and Cornelius, was for a long time, a conspicuous figure on our Course, busy in his vocation, always receiving from the passing crowd, the notice and respect due to him from all who knew his worth, as a faithful, upright, civil, humble man. We have no doubt that having, whilst here on earth, done his duty in that state of life, in which it please God to place him, he has gone where he has already heard falling on the dull, cold ear of Death, these encouraging words: "Well done, good and faithful servant, enter thou into the joy of thy master." No richer award could be granted him, for we verily believe no man ever shuffled off our mortal coil, purer and better, more fitted for Heaven, and to be admitted to the glorious company of just men made perfect, than Hercules beloved master, the late WILLIAM SINKLER!
>
> We are preparing a memoir of old Hercules, detailing his long career on the Turf, with notices of the different horses he brought to the post from time to time. This will be very interesting to our young Turfmen. We will put it on record as soon as completed.

The most intensely personal experience of the war was the loss of William Thompson, Sarah's lover and the father of her three children. Thompson was a slave on an adjoining plantation belonging to a neighbour and relative of her master, both of whom were named Richard Manning. Slaves were not allowed to marry in that section of the state unless they belonged to the same master, so the couple were powerless to make their union official in anyone's eyes other than their own. When war broke out, William Thompson accompanied his master when the latter joined the confederate army. Sarah never heard from him again, and in her words "it was supposed that he was killed and died."[39]

When the Emancipation Proclamation, which declared that all slaves held in states that were in rebellion "shall be then, thenceforward and forever free," came in to effect on January 1, 1863, Charles Sinkler, Eliza Manning's brother, called all of the slaves on the Belvidere Plantation and told them that although Abraham Lincoln had declared that they were free, they would be better off to quietly stay in their own comfortable homes.[40] According to Sinkler's daughter, her father promised to divide most of his provisions among the slaves, which he did.[41] In later years, ninety-seven-year-old Jane Hollins, a former slave of Charles Sinkler, enthusiastically confirmed her affection for her master to a WPA interviewer.[42] While it is not recorded if Sarah Richardson's mistress, Eliza Manning, did extend the same sentiments, it does appear that her slaves remained loyal to her.

In the final days of the war, 55th Massachusetts, whose members included several of Solomon King's Canadian neighbours, was among the regiments that passed through the area of the Sinkler and Manning plantations. The Sinkler family was horrified at the sight of armed blacks in uniform as they came onto the property and began to distribute the goods of the household to the slaves.[43] Rumours abounded of decisive Confederate victories — that France had recognized the Confederacy, that the North had declared war on Mexico. Conversely, stories of emboldened slaves who refused to work, or who were seizing or destroying the property of their owners were plentiful. That on-again, off-again series of events was dictated by the immediate presence of Union troops who told them that they were free, or of Southern patrols who warned them that they were slaves for life — that the Yankees had no right to tell them otherwise. The patrollers promised to appear every two or three days to ensure that their orders would be followed and threatened to kill anyone who disobeyed. Outrageous reports of Yankee soldiers, exasperated at the conduct of blacks, joining with the citizens of Savannah to massacre four thousand of the unruly Africans, were fleeting delusions.[44]

The reality was that General Hartwell commandeered Eutaw Plantation as his headquarters. The Sinkler women were forced to move into the upper story of the house and the General and his staff took over the lower level. One of the outbuildings was converted into a hospital to treat Northern soldiers who were wounded in guerilla warfare with Southern scouts that was common in the surrounding countryside. In the evenings a band would play in the avenue leading up to the mansion. The plantation's slaves would dance, all the while trying to grasp what their newfound freedom meant.

Corporal Alfred Brett, a Canadian who belonged to Company A of the 4th Massachusetts Cavalry, was among the white Union regiments whose easy and humorous manner ironically gave comfort to the women in the area who were greatly alarmed by the black soldiers. Brett assured a trio of women that "he was only fighting for his pay, that he did not care which side whipped." He pledged to safeguard the women until the Colored Troops passed — a promise he kept, although he did take the liberty of substituting a broken-down horse for their beautiful one, which he commandeered.[45]

In those closing days of the war, the recruiting of men continued for new regiments or to fill the ranks depleted by combat or disease. Sarah's brother, Hercules, and other relatives and fellow slaves enlisted in the 104th United States Colored Infantry. Major Martin Delany, who lived in Chatham, Canada West before the war, and Captain Abram W. Shadd, from the fringes of the Buxton Settlement, were officers and recruiters. Delany was the highest-ranking African-American soldier in the Civil War and had dutifully impressed Abraham Lincoln, who called him "a most extraordinary and intelligent man." He had also been involved in recruiting various regiments, including the 14th Rhode Island Heavy Artillery, in which Cornelius had enlisted. His oldest son, Touissant, was reported as having attended school in Buxton, and it was Martin Delany who, through the pages of Frederick Douglass's anti-slavery newspaper, *North Star*, had first brought wide-spread attention to William King and his fifteen slaves as they made their way toward Canada.[46] Shadd occasionally attended Reverend King's Presbyterian mission church at Buxton, and several members of the Shadd family had been involved in recruiting when Solomon King was doing the same. Both men would have known Solomon well. Each would know countless more from their adopted country to the north.

As for Solomon King, he remained in Charleston for the rest of his life with the short exception of a time one summer when he went north to wait on tables. There were times when he had the strength to carry on a life that had periods of normalcy. In January 1874 he drew on his military past and was elected first lieutenant of a coloured militia, The Stevens Light Infantry, named after the anti-slavery hero and congressman, Thaddeus Stevens.[47] His most regular employment working on the wharves of Charleston harbour was frequently too demanding for his frail health. He worked

Daniel E. Huger house where Sarah King worked after the Civil War. *HABS SC, 10-CHAR, 265—3. LOC.*

as a stevedore for Rommel and Company and as a longshoreman for the Morgan Steamship Company, where he was known as "Captain King," as he was in charge of a crew that loaded cotton bales onto ships.[48]

His wife, Sarah, was not very good at remembering dates, but rather divided time into pieces. Just as more learned people delineated the grand scheme of history into B.C. and A.D., or as common folk used a dramatic event in their own lives as a point of reference, she divided her own history by President Lincoln's Emancipation Proclamation, or, as she termed it, "before freedom came" and "after freedom came." Her marriage to Solomon at the Morris Street Baptist church in Charleston, South Carolina occurred during the latter. In later days she never forgot the name of the minister, Reverend Jacob Legare, who officiated at the ceremony, but could not recall the entire date, only that it was May 16th, "two years after freedom."[49]

The couple would have five children together to add to the three that Sarah had by her previous partner, who South Carolinian law and custom would not allow her to marry. Only two of the five children first mentioned would survive to adulthood — Eliza King, named after Solomon's mother, and Hercules King, named after Sarah's father. Margaret, who was named after Sarah's mother, only lived to be two and a half. Lucia Evelyn, named after Sarah's sister, lived just past her third birthday. William King, named after the man who gave Solomon and his family their freedom, lived less than two weeks.[50]

The family's burdens were heavy, even more so when Solomon was unable to work and they had to rely on Sarah's tiny income as she worked as a domestic in the households of wealthy people — a job that she had been raised to do as a child. By 1878, times had gotten so difficult that Sarah had to take some of the children and move into one of those homes. By early summer of 1880, Sarah could no longer care for her husband. It was a melancholy irony that Solomon was spending his final days at what people referred to as "the old Confederate hospital" on Trapman Street in Charleston.[51] It was an unattractive building, despite the wooden-columned piazzas with eighteen rooms above-ground and a large basement that once served as a temporary morgue for soldiers. Among them were wounded and dying young Southern men who had fought at Battery Wagner against Solomon's

Canadian colleagues in the 54th Massachusetts, the first black regiment organized in the North.

Now it was an apartment building owned by Sarah Gardner, an enterprising thirty-seven-year-old African-American widow raising four children, who supplemented her rental income working as a washerwoman. She rented out twenty-two other rooms in the building to other black families or to individual tenants. The adults worked as washerwomen, house servants, a dressmaker, a cooper, barber's assistant, butcher, farm hand, and several general labourers. When the census taker arrived on June 2, 1880, he recorded that of the fifty people who lived under the roof, two were ill or disabled — the landlady's five-year-old son Henry had a fever, and thirty-nine-year-old Solomon King was suffering under the nineteenth-century death sentence of consumption.[52]

Thirty-nine years of age — far short of the three score and ten that had been spoken of elsewhere — still Solomon seemed an old man. The

Former Confederate and later coloured hospital on Trapman Street, Charleston, South Carolina before it became an apartment building, where Solomon King spent his final months and died. The image above was taken in 1886 after an earthquake. According to legend, ghostly apparitions of the dead Confederates who had been buried on the grounds regularly rose from their graves at night to march again. Also, according to the September 9, 1875 *Charleston News and Courier*, the Committee on Epidemics, Public Hygene, &C. responded to complaints that the building was dilapidated, dirty, "unduly crowded," and that some of the constantly changing tenants burned fires in the corridors for warmth.

war and its aftermath steadily robbed him of his health just as surely as it had once taken whatever fragments may have remained of his youth. But he had done his part and had been a tiny piece of something historic, something important, something lasting far beyond his own time, which now was running short.

The Buxton of his youth was just a microcosm of the larger Canadian community that had done its part by sending some of its finest sons to Southern battlefields. What can be said of the contributions of one small settlement can be expanded to include the whole. But Solomon knew it best from the people and the places that he had been closest to. The opportunities afforded to the people in the settlement left them uniquely qualified to help the newly freed blacks and to contribute to the reconstruction in the United States. Seven hundred children of former slaves and free blacks had gone to the mission school that Solomon had attended by the time the Civil War ended. Many went south and served as teachers in the schools for freedmen. Among those who received their early education were five doctors of medicine and divinity, two state senators, one member of congress, two surgeons in the U.S. Army, one speaker of a state legislature, two judges, six lawyers, one president of a university, twelve principals of public schools, and three newspaper editors. Many others held less prominent positions, but the knowledge of worth and independence that they had acquired was no less valuable. Solomon King was in that number, an ordinary person making his way through an extraordinary life.

CHAPTER 2

Canada and the Civil War

Toronto, March 25, 1860

My dear Parker,

I look with the most interest upon Canada because it seems to me she is to be the great & reliable ally of the northern states in the coming struggle with slavery. When the lines are finally drawn what an immense moral aid it will be to the north to have such a foundation as that of Canada, especially Canada West, at her back.

— Samuel Gridley Howe[1]

During the days of the Civil War, Canada's role as a safe haven for American refugees took an ironic twist as whites from both the Union and the Confederacy looked north for a sanctuary.

The institution of the army draft, which began at different times and in different states in 1862, initiated floods of "skedaddlers" flocking into Canada. The South issued the first conscription act on April 16, 1862, legislating that all white men between the ages of eighteen and thirty-five were eligible for three years' service. The Northern draft (which began as three hundred thousand men) followed later that year, with each state being issued a quota based on proportional population. All able-bodied men between eighteen and forty-five could be called by random selection of their names. To meet those quotas, different states began to offer bounties as an enticement for men to volunteer, thereby avoiding the unpleasant situation of forcing unwilling men to enlist. Wealthier states, as well as those that had county government and/or organizations who would help raise money to top off the bounty, were at an advantage and lured recruits away from other states. Wealthier men could pay a three-hundred-dollar fine for avoiding the draft, a supposed penalty that led to many paying that same amount to a less fortunate man taking his place as a "substitute."[2] Many Canadian men, both black and white, would take advantage of such a financial opportunity.

The *Kingston Daily News* of July 24, 1863, attacked the draft dodgers through its columns, calling their act "cowardice, one of the meanest and lowest and most useless, elements of human character." It begrudged the fact that these men "with nimble heels but feeble courage" would work for lower wages, thereby putting British subjects out of work. These displaced workers were then compelled to travel to the United States — with proof of British citizenship to avoid being drafted there in their pockets — to take jobs that the skedaddlers had left behind.

Frederick Douglass, editor of one of the leading anti-slavery newspapers of the time, took a barely concealed delight in reprinting "A 'Skedaddler's' Story," which featured a letter dated August 15, 1862 from Montreal, from one brother to another, to inform the latter of the former's hasty flight to Canada. Prompted by the receipt of an official order that he had been drafted, the New York resident gave his wife one hour's notice that he was leaving, kissed her and the children goodbye, and departed in the middle of the night. He had anticipated being drafted and had gone to the trouble of having his doctor complete a request for exemption on the medical grounds that his patient suffered from a liver complaint. The brother sarcastically confided in the letter that the army agents were unsympathetic to the pleas of sick people, but that Uncle Sam "might ease up a little when they had lost a leg or an arm, or were incurables in the hospital."[3] He decided to employ an alternative plan.

The new scheme suggested he proceed across New York State, trying to avoid the officers who patrolled the various railroad stations and other means of transport and departure — scenes reminiscent of officials watching for escaping slaves, except now their target was draft-dodgers. This particular man on the run formulated the story that, although he was heading to the Suspension Bridge at Niagara Falls, it was only because it was the easiest and nearest route that would allow him quick passage to Detroit, albeit through the foreign country of Canada. Should that border crossing be denied to him, he was quite prepared to risk the treacherous crossing of the Niagara River about a mile beyond the rapids.

As he continued toward Buffalo by train, he perceived that the conductor was suspicious, and therefore modified his plans, changing directions toward a small, less guarded port on the St. Lawrence River, a couple hundred miles north. Several more harrowing adventures awaited him as he skillfully manipulated mistrustful adversaries who were on the watch for skedaddlers and who anticipated the reward money that would follow the capture of their unpatriotic prey. He ultimately found a First Nations man with a leaky canoe who agreed to take him across the river. Gale force winds hampered their progress, but the fact that three would-be captors were pursuing them inspired him to keep rowing and bailing. The fact that he was quite willing to shoot his aboriginal companion inspired his canoe-mate to do the same. Hours later, they reached Cornwall, which he described as being in Canada East.

Many held deserters in equal contempt to draft dodgers. In a letter to President Lincoln, Henry Wilson offered a solution to put a speedy end to it, noting that there "are thousands in Canada who would return" to their regiments if they received a pardon and were only penalized with loss of pay for the time they had been absent. Wilson made a distinction for those who had enlisted, received a large bounty, and then deserted. For them, he recommended that they "be arrested, tried and shot without mercy."[4]

Samuel Small, a twenty-four-year-old sailor from Hastings, Peterborough County in Canada West, offered President Lincoln a less bloody solution. Upon learning about the secession of South Carolina (whose conduct caused him to be "much Incensed"), and believing that war would be inevitable, Small took up his pen and addressed a letter "To the Honourable Thomas Lincoln" to share a secret that he had been keeping from the world for twelve years:

To wit, an Invention by which I can take one thousand cavalry and reduce the Whole South Teritory [sic] to complete Submission in three months. The nature of the Discovery is to shock by the power of Mercury any Army or Fleet that may be brought together into a State of stupification so that they can easily be made Prisoners, bound and Secured without doing them any material Injury. You may not doubt it in the least as I have tried it on Animals such as Bears, Deer &c. with full effect. If this will not Suit then I will venture to say As A Field General or Officer you will not find my Superior in the World.

Specifically requesting that the President communicate by persons rather than by mail, Small left his address, and, under his signature, his alias — A. Napoleon. The records show no response from "Thomas Lincoln."[5]

The *Halifax Morning Chronicle* of Nova Scotia carried an almost admiring article of the Confederate warship, *Tallahassee*, in their August 19, 1864 edition. Fresh from capturing, burning, and bonding thirty-three Federal boats in less than two weeks, *Tallahassee* entered the Halifax harbour to take on coal. The ship was described as an iron steamship that was extremely fast and maneuverable, and which was armed with "formidable swivel guns." The ship's captain, they believed, was the nephew of Jefferson Davis. He was allowed to take on a large quantity of coal but was informed that he must leave the harbour within twenty-four hours. The *Chronicle* also made note that reports in Northern newspapers of cruelty to crewmembers of captured ships were untrue — in fact, according to the *Tallahassee's* officers, "upon the contrary, the comfort of the captured persons is invariably attended to …"*

August 24, 1864 Toronto C.W.
John B. Castleman CSA

By virtue of authority vested in me & having complete confidence in your courage & fidelity you are appointed

* Reprinted in *The Charleston Mercury*, September 1, 1864.

to special service ... with Capt. Thomas Hines for an expedition against the U.S. prisons in the North West States ... To you & Captn Hines is left the selection of such confederate soldiers in Canada as are probably suited for use in so perilous an undertaking. You are expected to take with you all those whose courage & discretion you are willing to rely.

Your obedient servant
Jacob Thompson[6]

Confederate prisoners of war who escaped Union prisons sometimes found a safe-haven in Canada. Henry Lane Stone wrote in his 1919 autobiography *Morgan's Men: A Narrative of Personal Experiences* that he stayed in Windsor and Kingsville for four months during the winter of 1863–1864. He wrote of Confederates who escaped from the Johnson's Island prison camp and took advantage of the extreme cold by crossing Lake Erie, which had completely frozen over. When Stone himself reached Windsor and signed the registry in a hotel there, he was quite amazed to read that nearly every other signature was boldly signed by other Southerners, along with their company, regiment and brigade of the Confederate States Army.

There was a constant worry about Confederate offensives that might be launched from Canada, and rumours ran rampant. One newspaper reported a number of suspicious vessels on Lake Erie, which might have the objective of liberating "over two thousand rebel officers on Johnson's Island, Sandusky Bay," who, once free, would burn the city of Buffalo. The Canadian government responded that every effort would be made to arrest and punish any such attempt.[7]

Robert Cobb Kennedy was an escapee who became the only person who was captured and hung for the 1864 Confederate plot to burn New York City. He was a Louisiana officer during the war, who was captured and sent to Johnson's Island Military Prison. He escaped on October 4, 1864 and fled to Canada. There, he met with other Confederate officials who planned raids into the North from the safety of Canada. Kennedy went to New York and attempted to burn down the American Museum there. He safely fled to Canada following this, but was later captured while trying to return to the United States at Detroit. He was tried and convicted, then hung at Fort Lafayette in New York on March 25, 1865.[8]

There was at least one case where a Southerner did not come to Canada voluntarily. Margaret Preston, a property owner in Kentucky whose husband, William, had sided with the Confederacy as an army officer and an envoy to Mexico, visited Halifax along with her children. Upon returning to the United States onboard the steamer *Africa* and attempting to land at Boston, the family was seized by the Provost Marshal and deported back to Canada. In a frantic letter written from the Bahamas to Francis P. Blair Sr., who had influence with the Lincoln administration, William Preston, who in a previous administration had been U.S. Minister to Spain, tried to explain that although he had made the mistake of siding with the south, his wife and children should not be punished. He was unsure of his family's whereabouts, believing that they might be in Montreal, and begged that they be restored to him. Appealing to Blair's merciful side, Preston said that he had already lost his own property and thought it unfair that his wife, who incidentally was the daughter of Kentucky's largest slaveholder, as well as a friend of Mary Todd Lincoln, would also lose hers by confiscation of rebel property. Although he admitted to an error in his own judgment, he justified it as "a cause to which I was devoted by birth, by kindred, and by a conviction of right." He asked if Blair, who he had known in peaceful times and who had maintained relationships with other Southerners, would let him know if his wife and children were not only to suffer the penalty of banishment but also a life of destitution.[9] A powerful family, the Prestons reached out to influential people for assistance during their personal challenges. At one time, Margaret Preston had written to Mary Todd and Abraham Lincoln to ask for a pass so she could travel unmolested by Union troops. In a difficult spot because of his wife's love for Margaret, Lincoln was apparently unable or unwilling to intercede on her behalf. At any rate, Margaret and her children remained in Montreal for the remainder of the war and were joined on two occasions by her husband. They were comfortable there, surrounded by other Southerners and friends, including the family of Confederate President Jefferson Davis.[10]

Many Canadians were perplexed at the pro-Southern sentiment that existed in their provinces. Part of the answer could be explained by anti-black feelings that were still pervasive. The *Sandwich Maple Leaf* newspaper of May 2, 1861 expressed some of those sentiments when it reported:

> A dark cloud hung over Windsor Monday morning as 200 negroes of all ages and colours arrived from Chicago and other parts of Illinois. 300 more were to arrive last night and more to follow. All because a family of 5 from there were sent back south a week or two ago. We wish that slave owners whose slaves made the free states would leave them in peace because we do not want them!

Lewis Chambers, a former Maryland slave who had been called to the ministry in Chatham and had served at many places in Canada West, including Dresden, McGee's Ferry, Botany, St. Thomas, and Ingersoll, was then stationed at the British Methodist Episcopal (BME) Church in London and would have fit into the category of unwelcome guests. A puzzled Chambers wrote to George Whipple of the American Missionary Association: "I do not know what the people in Canada meane for the most of them seame to be in favour of the south there is something wrong."[11]

Reverend James Proudfoot, a friend of blacks who fought against segregation in London, Canada West, schools, noted the overwhelming pro-Southern sentiments that permeated the city as well as a country-wide fear that the North was encouraging a servile insurrection "with all its horrors." He also blamed the prevailing anti-black feelings of the inordinate influx of Americans who resided there — in his opinion far more than could be found in Toronto or Hamilton. However, Reverend Proudfoot took the side of the blacks and expressed that he was among those friends who "always trusted, that in God's Providence, this war would end in the freedom of the blacks" and that it was perfectly proper that they should fight for their own freedom and that the Union should employ them in the army to that end.[12]

P. Jertius Kempson of Fort Erie had similar feelings that he expressed in a letter to Abraham Lincoln, assuring the President that he had "our earnest and most constant prayers that you may entirely succeed in ridding the Great and Glorious Union of the foul canker worm of Slavery." He said that although popular sentiment of both Englishmen and Canadians was with the south, there were many exceptions and his own "cheeks flushed with shame" at the thought of it. And, on another note, would you mind "giving me a line or two in autograph, that I may be able to leave to my children & my children's children, as a heir loom in remembrance of the great apostle of Liberty."[13]

Other Canadians went even further. Augustus Watson wrote to Lincoln advising him that the time was right for a United States annexation of the British provinces. His plan was to organize a group of Canadian agents throughout the provinces who, along with the support of sympathetic newspapers, would arouse the will to help stamp out slavery by combining the numeric, moral, and military strength of this new, larger Union. This organization of Freemen would be called "Order of the North Star."[14]

From the earliest days of the war there was conjecture that England and therefore all of British North America might side with the South. There was also a fear of being invaded and annexed by the North. Either eventuality raised some difficult challenges as Canadians braced themselves for military encounters. In the southwestern corner of the Niagara peninsula, Samuel Amsden, the captain of the Volunteer Militia, as well as the editor of the town of Dunnville's *Independent* newspaper, ran an advertisement dated December 28, 1861 under the provocative heading:

> WAR! WAR! WAR! WAR! — TO THE COLORED POPULATION — All the male inhabitants of Dunnville and the surrounding country desirous of joining Her Majesty's Loyal Volunteer Militia, can do so by calling at my office, where the service roll is now lying for signatures.[15]

American newspapers were quick to take note of the not-too-subtle suggestion in the article that Canadian blacks might be called to take up arms against the Union army. The *New York Tribune* asked its readers:

"Would'nt [sic] it be curious to see these fugitives from the blessings of slavery employed by England the great abolition power, in a war for the establishment of Jeff Davis negro despotism? 'Tis a queer world."[16]

The *Chicago Post* took that thought even further:

> But would it not be more queer to see these fugitive slaves marching upon Chicago, Detroit, and Cleveland, and shooting down the people who had induced them to escape from slavery, and who afforded them facilities to evade the laws and defy the process of courts. Just think of black regiments of British troops occupying the Western Reserve, or quartered in Knox college, and levying contributions upon a people who had made the freedom of the negro paramount to their constitutional obligations to their white brethren of the Union.[17]

For some time, those musings were not as far-fetched as they would appear in historical retrospective.

But not all sentiment was against the North, and white Canadians flocked across the border to enlist. *The Christian Recorder*, a Philadelphia-based newspaper that was the official organ of the African Methodist Episcopal Church, reported on April 27, 1861 that a Canadian gentleman informed them that there was a fervent pro-North feeling aroused in Canada and that six-hundred men from Quebec, many of them from Montreal, were travelling to Boston to enlist. Some joined various regiments of the Union army because they believed in the cause. Some were opposed to slavery. Others believed that it wasn't right for the American slaves to come to Canada. Some went for adventure. Some went for money — privates could get thirteen dollars per month, twenty-five dollars per month if they had a team of horses. Some answered advertisements and were paid handsomely for joining as substitutes for the wealthy who wanted to escape the draft and could legally pay someone to take their place.

Barnett D. Hotchkiss was one of the young men who left Canada to fight against slavery. Hotchkiss was the youngest son of a missionary who himself spent a decade before the war as a missionary to fugitive slaves.

As a nine-year-old, he accompanied his parents and three siblings from Pennsylvania, where the children had been born and raised to that point, to Amherstburg; they then travelled again to the Refugee Home Society grounds in Rochester Township, Essex County where his father, who was originally from Vermont, preached, and his mother, who was born in Connecticut, taught school. It was quite an adjustment for the family as they tried to settle in among the refugees. It was also dangerous and disheartening for them in the early years, particularly when opponents made a violent statement by burning the Hotchkiss home to the ground.[18]

Much to his father's chagrin, Barnett D. Hotchkiss left his family in Canada at the age of 18 and travelled to Warren, Pennsylvania where he joined the 10th Pennsylvania Reserve Infantry, later renamed the 39th Pennsylvania Volunteers on May 7, 1861, as a musician.[19] In a letter to the American Missionary Association, Reverend Hotchkiss wrote that his son, "who is young and hasty" was going to the south "in defense of freedom." The father bemoaned: "I expect thousands of our young men will be ruined & slain and Slavery, that plague spot, will be left to curse master & Slave and nation, after all, God only knows."[20] Three years later, on March 1, 1864, Barnett re-enlisted into the 16th Pennsylvania Cavalry. He survived the war and was mustered out with his company on August 11, 1865. His elder brother, David Jr., who had enlisted in New Haven in the 6th Connecticut Infantry on September 12, 1861, had a shorter time in the service, being discharged just over a year later due to disability.

Canadian Militia Colonel Arthur Rankin, who was elected the Essex County member of the Legislative Assembly, offered to raise a lancer regiment for the Union army that would be composed of men from Canada. The offer was accepted and Rankin was given a commission. However, there was a great outcry throughout Canada over the fact that he would not only serve in the U.S., but also that he would recruit fellow Canadians, and Rankin was forced to withdraw. In an attempt to explain his position, he stated in December of 1861, "... when I proffered my services to the President, I did so in the spirit of a friendly neighbor, not as a dissatisfied or discontented subject of her Britannic Majesty...." However, as tensions increased between England and the United States, Rankin resigned his commission in the Union Army, stating that he would have fought "with the zest and earnestness not inferior to that of any citizen of the republic ..." but "... under no circumstances could I be induced to occupy an attitude of hostility to my own country."[21]

Other officers of the Canadian militia also occasionally ignored British and Canadian laws by offering assistance to the Union. On June 17, 1863, A. Dingman, the brigadier-general of the volunteers, sent a telegram from Belleville, Canada West to Lincoln to let him know that should Washington be in peril of being invaded, the Fifteen Battalion would rush to its aid to "drive Lee back to Richmond."[22] The appreciative president responded the next day, telling Dingman that he did not believe that the capital was in danger.[23]

Martin Doxtator, from the banks of the Thames River in Middlesex County, Canada West, who was one of many who not only offered but actually gave his support to the Union, had quite a different background. His tribe signed a treaty on June 2, 1840, in which they were identified as "the First and Second Christian parties of Oneida Indians" who lived in New York State but who decided to sell their collective lands because they were "disposed to migrate to Upper Canada or elsewhere beyond the limits of said State."[24] Ironically, the treaty was signed by William Henry Seward, then-governor of New York and later secretary of state for the Lincoln administration.

Colonel Arthur Rankin, who attempted to recruit a Canadian regiment of lancers for the Union Army. *Frederick Neal*, The Township of Sandwich, Past and Present. *(Sandwich: Record Printing Co, 1909), 70.*

Other members of the Oneidas decided to move to a section of Michigan Territory, which later became the state of Wisconsin. Although many miles separated the groups, they maintained close ties, which helps explain why Doxtator travelled to Wisconsin to join the 3rd Wisconsin Infantry, a regiment that included several other Oneidas. He enlisted into Company C on September 3, 1864 and was wounded in Savannah during General Sherman's famous "march to the sea," before being mustered out on June 3, 1865. Doxtator applied for a pension on November 5, 1887 and, according to *The Toronto Mail*, October 23, 1890, it was granted retroactive to the time of his application until his death on March 28, 1920.[25]

Deserters from the Canadian forces were a problem throughout the war. This was a particular issue along the Detroit River. Captain Hall received a letter from one of his officers complaining about the Windsor detachment "where the inducements to desert are too much for the 'virtue' of any British Soldier." Despite the genuine attempts of the officers to thwart the schemes of the Crimps who were on both sides of the border, their efforts were often futile. The report took aim at the American authorities, who were felt to be complicit in the activities. The letter writer asked to be granted authority to remove any of the soldiers who were suspected of planning to cross the river, and felt that "any detachment near Detroit will melt away."[26]

Some of the inducements that tempted the "virtue" of the deserters mentioned above were made clearer in another letter from Windsor that same week. Officer Heary Sabin wrote to his colonel that two "professional" women, one of whom was Minnie Sherwood, whose fame had caused her name to appear in the newspapers, lured the men with their charms to cross the Detroit River. They had a house in Windsor and were supported by "Yankee officers." They met the Canadian men at night, provided a change of clothing for them, "and try to get them off in Every way." The desertion rate was getting so extensive that Provost Marshal White from Detroit, seeking to line his own pockets, offered to either catch the deserters or give the names to Canadian officials so he could collect the standard reward of fifty dollars. After having his proposal accepted, the provost marshal then shared the story of the two most recent deserters. They had stolen a leaky boat from Walkerville,

Canada West and one used a board for a paddle while the other bailed out the water. By the time they approached the Detroit shore, they were up to their waists in water, and had it not been for White being at the wharf and throwing them a life buoy, they would have drowned. The two wet and shaken men promised White that they would enlist with him in any regiment that he chose, as long as they could get a decent bounty. The devious White told them that the Michigan bounty had dried up but that he could get them six or seven hundred dollars if they would enlist in New York; in order to do so, however, they would have to be disguised and take the train through Canada West to get there. All the while, White planned on turning them over to Canadian authorities once they got to Windsor. The men agreed. However, before they could put the plan into motion, another officer recruited the two men. An incensed White then determined to get the men drunk and have them carried back, a revenge that's opportunity had not yet arrived. In the meantime, White had intercepted a letter exchange between a Canadian deserter and three of his comrades who also wanted to defect that detailed some of their plans. The trio was to go to the Walkerville distillery at 8:00 p.m. and watch for a light signal from the other side of the river, after which a boat would be delivered to them by two men who would ferry them across. Thus forewarned, both the Canadians and Americans hid several soldiers in the vicinity to thwart the scheme. Unfortunately, the three would-be deserters became suspicious, did not climb into the boat when it arrived, and eluded their would-be captors.[27]

Privates Hacket and Flin of the 63rd Regiment in London deserted the Canadian militia and went to Detroit to enlist in the Union army. They came to profoundly regret that decision as they both awaited hanging in January 1863 for a breach of discipline.[28] According to James Conolly, a lieutenant-colonel in Montreal, some American agents specifically targeted soldiers in Her Majesty's forces. Conolly spoke from first-hand information when he shared the contents of a letter he had received from a soldier, who claimed that he had deserted from the Royal Canadian Rifles and enlisted in the Union army in August of 1861 during a fit of intoxication. In the two years that followed, he had been involved in bloody battles at Chickahominy and Bull Run, in which he witnessed thousands of casualties. Sickened by it all, the private passionately expressed his grief, warned others not to follow his tragic path, and pleaded for a pardon, promising to return to his Canadian regiment if allowed to do so.[29]

It wasn't only Americans who tried to get Canadian soldiers to desert. Courtrooms in Canada East were particularly busy in the last year of the war. Showing the different currencies in use, and the various punishments levied by different judges, Charles Pullen, Patrick Tierney, Thomas Murray, and John Cook were all sentenced in Quebec courts to six months in the penitentiary and a fine of forty pounds. In Montreal, James Dailey, John Murphy, and Ed Mitchell each received six months and ten-pound fines. St. John's courts sentenced Louis Blanchet to six months and Philip Welcome (alias Bienvenue) to eighteen months and a twenty-dollar fine. In Montreal, Michael McDonnell, Patrick Collins, and Francois Poliquin received four months and forty pounds, while Mathew Hawkins, Charles Smith, and Edward Kelly each got six months and were levied forty pounds. James Moody's fine was the same, but his sentence was one year.

Silas W. Knowlton of Nelsonville received six months and a one-hundred-dollar fine for violating the Foreign Enlistment Act. Heary Sabin's fine for the same offence in Beauharnois was fifty pounds, with no time in jail. Charles Hammond received eighteen months in Montreal, while Peter Russhaw (alias Pierre Rochon) received six months and a ten-pound fine, and Charles Bezeau received six months and a two-hundred-dollar fine.

On September, 29, 1864, a Quebec court sentenced five men to one year in the penitentiary for actually enlisting into the U.S. army. In their case, each received an unconditional pardon on April 20, 1865. Some of the others who were charged in this series of sentences relating to the Civil War also did not serve their entire sentences. Thomas Murray was released on May 16, 1865 after signing a document pledging that he would "go to sea." After three months, John Cook was released on the same conditions. Patrick Tierney was released four days later after paying his fine. All of the others were released at various times in 1865 after the war ended. Many received unconditional pardons.[30]

In neighbouring Canada West, there was at least one charge to ensure that a witness would appear in a foreign enlistment case. A judge in Fort Erie made one Michael Nolan pay fifty dollars to assure that he would appear and testify against L.L. Hyames for attempting to seduce Robert Clarke to enlist.

Not all of the Canadians who fought in the war were willing participants. A practice called "crimping" was carried out whereby unsuspecting men were forced into the American army. The means of achieving this varied — some were kidnapped, often after having been plied with alcohol or drugged. Others were enticed to the U.S. with promises of jobs, only to find themselves enlisted once they were over the border. Still others, like sixteen-year-old Alfred Broissoit of Montreal (who had been forcibly intoxicated and carried into the states by an unscrupulous recruiting agent), were swindled out of the bounty that enlistees were given. These agents, who were motivated by money, often kept the lion's share of the bounty. Fifteen-year-old John Bland Allison from Niagara awoke to find himself on Lake Erie, aboard the U.S. naval ship *Michigan*.[31]

Nervous Canadian authorities had taken steps to combat the threat of Canadians being "crimped" into the federal army. By 1864, expensive military schools had been hurriedly opened and a large force of militia was preparing to go to the American border to prevent crimping, as well as to prevent Southerners from making raids into the Northern U.S. from Canadian bases. The militia in Canada West numbered ninety thousand men, and volunteers accounted for thirty thousand. It was estimated that, if need be, nearly half a million men could be called up to bear arms. For necessary munitions, factories in Hamilton produced four hundred thousand pounds of powder for a single year's use. One hundred and twenty drill instructors were needed and their cost, along with the pay of brigadier-majors and other militia expenses, amounted to nearly three-quarters of a million dollars.[32]

Word spread through the U.S. of Canada's, and her mother country's, increasing vigilance. Washington, D.C.'s *Daily National Intelligencer* reported on October 6, 1864 that British troops with artillery had arrived in Windsor to prevent further raids from the shores. In defense of the other side of the border, heavy artillery from Boston travelled to Plattsburg, New York to guard against invasions that might occur south of Montreal.[33] By December 1864, the governor general of Canada, Lord Monck, instructed three battalions of militia who had recently been called into service, as well as numerous volunteer companies from across the province who had offered their services, that their purpose was not to wage war, but to prevent Southerners who had taken up residence there from instigating acts of aggression into the Northern states.[34] The *Toronto Globe* attempted to reassure their Union neighbours by apologizing for "the felonious doings of the Southern chivalry" who had abused their asylum, and that the people of Canada were "not the unprincipled, short sighted fools they suppose them to be."[35] The editor also called upon the legislature to take whatever necessary steps to remove those marauders from the country.

There were already plenty of reports to inspire Canadian officials to make preparations to defend their border. On September 26, 1861, the *Hamilton Spectator* carried a story that had earlier appeared in the *Essex Journal*, reporting that several U.S. soldiers, armed with bowie knives, daggers, and revolvers, descended into Gosfield Township searching for deserters. It was believed that after four American men were captured, the local people came in a mob and effected their escape. However, the raiders were not arrested and were able to beat a hasty retreat back across the border. The newspaper warned its' readers to prepare themselves for more such invasions.

Numerous stories — some true, some perhaps not — circulated about Canadians who were less than honest. The Washington *Evening Union* of August 27, 1864 carried a story of a wealthy man in New Jersey who had given a Canadian man eight hundred dollars to serve in his place. The Canadian promised to enlist and get in touch with his benefactor at the earliest opportunity. The latter was astounded when he received the promised letter, sent from Quebec, which expressed the substitute's appreciation for having been provided enough money to allow he and his wife to open a grocery store. As consolation, the patron was promised a free drink should he ever be in the neighbourhood.

In the *Chatham Tri-Weekly Planet* on September 7, 1887, there appeared a sarcastic article by an anonymous veteran who claimed that the young "brave" Canadian boys joined because they received a three-hundred-dollar bounty. He claimed that he enlisted under the name "Jim Smith":

> ... and with the price of valour in my pocket, I at once engaged in the desperate struggle — to reach the nearest Canadian town. I reached it. I enlisted again as Henry

Jackson, there was then again another desperate struggle
and I landed safe. My next venture was as Sam Jones and
so it continued till the "Cruel War" was over. I dare say
my tombstone appears in several national cemeteries.

Many Canadian families would find no humour in the musings of that
anonymous writer. Captain David Brown, formerly from Montreal, who
fought with New York's 29th Highland Guard, was killed at the Battle of Bull
Run.[36] John K. Payne of Chatham, who was enrolled in the 1st Michigan
Regiment, participated and witnessed that slaughter, as did Thomas Hood,
James Hough, Charles Miller, William Mitchell, William Parker, Charles
Birmingham, and two of their colleagues with the surnames Drew and
McCormack, all from Guelph. Two of these men were also killed.[37] A
Sergeant Marsh of London, who joined an Illinois regiment, was killed at
Fort Donelson.[38] Neither the families nor the survivors of the twenty-eight
Canadians who were awarded the U.S. Medal of Honor for distinguished
bravery in the face of enemy fire would be amused.[39] Among them were
William Pelham of Halifax, Nova Scotia, who served in the navy on the
USS *Hartford* and won a medal for assisting with caring for the wounded
and voluntarily manning a gun during a heavy firefight, which resulted in
the capture of the Confederate ship *Tennessee*.[40]

Likewise were the feelings of the families of the Confederate dead,
like Jerry Cronan who, as a member of the 10th Louisiana Infantry, died
June 2, 1864 of wounds suffered at the Battle of Spotsylvania, Virginia,
and who, in death, has the distinction of being a Canadian who fought
for the South and was buried at Arlington National Cemetery, before it
became the burial grounds for Union Soldiers.[41]

Many others, like Mount Pleasant, Brant County's William Winer Cooke,
who fought with the 24th New York Cavalry, bore the physical reminders
of the conflict. Wounded in the leg, Cooke spent considerable time in the
hospital before convalescing enough to rejoin his regiment. He survived the
war, but the lure of adventure drew him back to the U.S. army, joining the
7th Cavalry. His last conflict would be on June 25, 1876 against Crazy Horse
and his Sioux warriors at Little Big Horn in Montana, where he and some
250 fellow soldiers died with their general, George Armstrong Custer.[42]

Offbeat stories abounded of soldiers who had unique backgrounds. The *Daily Eastern Argus* from Portland, Maine reported in their January 2, 1864 edition that a sixteen-year-old Canadian girl had recently arrived in Louisville. According to that report, she had already served in the Union Army for eighteen months, had "been connected with seven different regiments, participated in several engagements, been seriously wounded twice, and had been discovered and mustered out of service eight times." Seven days later, the *Worcester Aegis and Transcript* revealed that the girl's name was Lizzie Crompton, who had been born in London, Canada West, where her parents still resided. Unable to resist further glamourizing of the story, the newspaper described her as "a beautiful, buxom girl of sweet sixteen," who had most recently been a member of the 11th Kentucky Cavalry. She was at that point confined to barracks until authorities could figure out what to do with her.

The most famous such case involved Sarah Emma Edmonds, a woman from New Brunswick. Edmonds was the fifth daughter born into a family whose father could not overcome his disappointment at not having a son, and instead assigned the masculine role to her. Edmonds eventually fled the family home, ultimately settling in Flint, Michigan, where she assumed the persona of a man, adopted the name "Franklin Thompson," and made a living as a door-to-door bible salesman.

When the war broke out, she volunteered as a nurse in the 2nd Michigan Infantry, and tended to the wounded at Bull Run, Antietam, and other battlefields. She also disguised herself as a slave so she could spy behind enemy lines. On one such occasion in March 1862, she overheard Confederate troops discuss a plan to paint logs so that they appeared to be canons, thereby fooling Union tacticians.

In the spring of 1863, Sarah fell victim to malaria and left her regiment rather than receive medical treatment, which would have revealed her sex. After recovering, she was unable to return to her regiment (still as Franklin Thompson) because she would face charges of desertion. Instead, she wrote and published a fictionalized account of her life in 1864, entitled *Nurse and Spy in the Union Army,* and donated the proceeds from the book to charities, which included the United States Sanitary Commission. She worked for that same organization for the remainder of the war.

Sarah Emma Edmonds, who disguised herself as a man to serve in the Union army. On one occasion, while acting as a spy, she coloured her skin dark and wore a wig to pass for an escaped slave. *http://commons.wikimedia. orgwikiFileSarah_Edmonds_ lg_sepia.jpg.*

When word began to spread prior to the enactment of Abraham Lincoln's intended Emancipation Proclamation, which would free slaves that were held in areas that were in rebellion against the Union and allow blacks to enlist in Northern forces, the Southern press very naturally sneered at the thought. The Richmond, Virginia *Examiner* reluctantly mentioned "Abe Lincoln's Message to the Yankee Congress" and mocked the President's abilities, which, in their opinion, were miniscule at best, and were now diminishing. The editor opined that his "brain appears to have dwindled under the pressure of events." They did give him credit for not mentioning his ludicrous proclamation to emancipate all of the slaves in the confederacy, feeling that Lincoln must be conceding that the "proclamation was simply the unmeaning utterance of idiocy." As for Lincoln's scheme for compensated emancipation, the newspaper columnist was convinced that it would assure "the free passport of its author to the Paradise of Fools."[43]

Canadian opinion on the proclamation was divided. The *Montreal Gazette* published an article laying suspicion on the President's motives, believing in part that it was an appeal to foreign countries that were sympathetic to the slaves to prevent them from recognizing the independence of the Confederate States of America. The article continued:

> We are also the more inclined to question the motives which have prompted it because it comes from men who, at the beginning of the contest, were so liberal in their offers to slaveholders, liberal beyond the point of self-respect, if they would only not secede. It comes just before the fall elections, and must exercise a decisive influence upon them. It would appeal more to foreign sympathies if it recognized emancipation as a natural right of man, instead of a punishment for secession, while the protection of slavery is in the same breath offered, as a reward for obedience to the federal Constitution. Its effect on the South will no doubt be to embitter the war; to place before the eyes of the southerner the alternative of extermination, possibly including the slaughter of blacks, before he can permit federal success stimulated by the promulgation of such doctrines.[44]

The *Toronto Leader* agreed on many of the same points. It opined that:

> The president has made a false step; he has been trifling with the public weal, he has pandered to the prejudices of a political sect, and consented to echo the shibboleth of the impracticable negro-phobiasts of the northern states. His whole previous course precludes the supposition that he has entered upon the dangerous ground of radicalism from honest conviction. The morality of the matter is not open to doubt. The welfare of the slave did not enter into that mental argumentation which must have preceded the conclusion at which the president has

arrived. It is only a few days ago that he proclaimed in
the face of the whole world that the "Union" was above
every consideration of welfare for the unfortunate negro.
Could he carry out his "idea" he would not free a single
slave. These are his words. Does he now expect that he
will restore that "Union" by declaring the slave free?[45]

The *Lambton Observer* also rained down criticism on Lincoln, accusing
him of selfish motives, and of looking "not to the emancipation of the
bondsman as a duty or principle, but as the only means which they see
open likely to enable them to obtain the end sought — the preservation
of the Union — can they expect the blessing of Providence to accompany
it?" The writer argued that he would have had more respect for the administration if they would have made the issue a civil matter and produced a
plan to pay slave owners for their slaves and to prepare the slaves for independence. Equally damning was that the Proclamation was to free slaves
in the states that were in rebellion, over which the administration had no
control, rather than order in slave states that remained loyal to the Union.[46]

Toronto Globe took issue with the *Observer*'s stance, defending
Lincoln, his Cabinet, and Congress for listening to the will of the people
who had been influenced by the abolitionists, and of acting on moral
principles that they possessed. "We say, therefore, that the proclamation
policy took its rise in the best motives that the human heart can entertain
— love to God and love to man." At any rate, although the process could
be questioned, there should be no argument against the praiseworthy
ambition that many slaves would get their freedom.[47]

CHAPTER 3

Recruiters

I am happy to learn that the cause of freedom is doing
so well, that God has heard the prayers of his people. I
know that your longing heart has been maide to rejoice
in the goodnefs of God for his kindnefs in hearing our
prayer, and aiding the cause of Liberty for you with others, have longd to see the day, a happy day to the friends
of the cause of freedom.

— Reverend Lewis C. Chambers[1]

(Written on New Year's Eve, the night before the Emancipation Proclamation came into effect.)

Although Abraham Lincoln had made it clear that the Civil War
was a conflict to save the union and not to end slavery, blacks
could not help but feel otherwise. Parker T. Smith, who was
living in Dresden in the spring of 1862, wrote to a Philadelphia friend
expressing the comments of a friend who hoped that the war would not
end before slavery was abolished. William Whipper, a wealthy black man
and Underground Railroad conductor from Columbia, Pennsylvania, who
owned land in the Dawn Settlement in Canada, told Smith, "I am satisfied

to share with my brethren in bonds, and if the war leaves me with a shirt and a pair of pantaloons, if it abolishes slavery I am satisfied."[2]

Peter Lester, from Victoria, British Columbia, was more removed from the war. Raised in Richmond, Virginia, Lester reflected that he had no great love for the country of his birth, although he admitted that he would have liked to witness the battle that had taken place near Richmond. Writing on August 14, 1862, he shared his beliefs that the end of slavery was near at hand, and that within six months the blacks would be the only ones capable of shifting the balance of power and bringing an end to the war. Lester warned that it was no time to ease up on the anti-slavery cause — indeed it should be revitalized and strengthened. A realist, Lester foresaw continued trouble after the war concluded: "Then to think that the Southern people, after they have been well flogged, will return to the Union like so many obedient children, O, what a delusion for men of sense to entertain!"[3]

Prior to the Emancipation Proclamation, blacks who had wished to fight were turned down because of their race. Blacks were considered shiftless, cowardly, and it was expected by many that they would run at the first sign of trouble. The *New York Tribune* printed an article in May of 1863, which read: "loyal whites have generally become willing that (blacks) should fight, but the great majority have no faith that they would do so. Many hope that they will prove cowards and sneaks — others greatly fear it." But as the war continued into its second year and the casualty lists grew, families grieved their dead and resented that their young men were drafted while African Americans were not called to serve. This contributed to an official change of policy within the Lincoln administration that led to black families from British North America joining in spirit with their American counterparts on the final night of 1862 to await the arrival of the New Year, when the Emancipation Proclamation would come into effect, signalling the acceptance of blacks into the Union Army. After joining in spirit to celebrate the enactment of the Proclamation, blacks in Canada prepared to demonstrate their support in the sincerest way.

But the wisdom of black Canadians possibly enlisting in the war was not without debate. Peter Lester's daughter, Sarah, wrote a letter shortly after the United States Colored Troops began forming into regiments about a controversy within the black community. In the letter, she stated that some people say that "neither the North or South is the true friend of right," and why should blacks suffer any more. She noted that the North "has enacted laws whose sentiments disgrace Christendom," but she hated the spirit that wanted blacks to stay out of the war and remain mere spectators; she likened it to avoiding a bayonet without even lifting a hand to ward off the blow.[4]

The Christian Recorder weekly newspaper, which covered both American and Canadian issues, trumpeted that the four million enslaved blacks in the south and a quarter of a million free coloured people in the North would be glad to strike a blow against slavery. In addition to them, the writer was convinced that "there are in Canada thousands of picked men who would be glad to return to the sunny South under the folds of the star-spangled banner and to the sound of martial music."[5]

Canadian newspapers also reported on preparations by blacks to enter the fight. A May 9, 1861 article in *Chatham Weekly Planet* said that John Brown Jr., who, like his father, was an intimate friend of Canadian blacks, was encamped on Beaver River between New Castle, Pennsylvania and the Ohio River with four hundred negroes, mostly from Canada, doing military drills. Later that summer, the same newspaper published a letter from Brown Jr. declining an invitation to attend an Emancipation Day banquet on August 1st because he was now in the Union Army. In parting words he urged the people to prepare for the formation of colored regiments in the war.[6] There would still be a considerable wait, but when that time came, Brown Jr. made an offer to his father's old friend, George Stearns, who was in charge of recruiting coloured soldiers, to supply a list of contacts and to travel to Windsor to raise money or recruit men.

Among the stories of runaway slaves who fled to Canada and eventually became recruiters, few are as colourful as that of Abraham H. Galloway. He was born in North Carolina to a slave woman and a white father, who recognized the boy as his son and, although he was not his master, attempted to protect Galloway as far as he was able. Upon reaching the age of twenty-one, Galloway and a friend devised a plan to escape from the Deep South — a bold plan with all of the distance involved in making it to the North. They found a ship captain whose vessel was bound for Philadelphia and made the risky move of asking for passage as stowaways amid the cargo of tar, rosin, and turpentine. However, a law to prevent slaves from hiding in the holds of ships going north dictated that the holds be smoked.

The ingenious young men came up with the plan to cover themselves from their heads to their waists with shrouds of silk soaked in oil. Within this cocoon they carried towels and a bladder of water to soak them in so that they could hold them against their nostrils. As luck would have it, the authorities neglected to smoke the hold; however, the effects of the turpentine were worse, causing blood to seep out of their pores. The pair survived the voyage and were further aided along their flight by William Still and members of the Philadelphia Vigilance Committee, who helped to forward them on to Kingston, Canada West.[7]

Abraham Galloway as he appeared in a sketch from William Still's *Underground Railroad*.

Galloway returned to his home state during the Civil War, rescued his mother from slavery, and served as a spy for General Butler and other Union officers. He also assisted with recruiting for Brigadier General Edward Wild's First Brigade, which consisted of the 1st, 10th, 22nd and 37th USCI.[8] Before that, in one of his most audacious moves, Galloway summoned a Northern recruiter to an attic where the latter was stunned to find an armed Galloway, along with several others, demanding that unless black recruits get equal pay, care for their families, schooling for their children, and promises that the Union would try to force the Confederates to treat captured blacks as legitimate prisoners of war, there would be no black enlistment. The recruiting agent, with a revolver against his head, agreed to the terms. Large-scale volunteering began immediately thereafter.[9]

In 1864, he was among five black delegates who met with President Lincoln to discuss equal rights, which included acquiring the right to vote. Galloway became one of the most active and prominent black leaders in North Carolina and beyond, both during and after the Civil War. In 1868 and 1870 he was elected state Senator. He died unexpectedly at age thirty-three in the first year of his second term in office.[10]

On November 18, 1862 — six weeks before the Emancipation Proclamation became law — Reverend Lewis Chambers wrote to George Whipple of the American Missionary Association, based in New York City: "there is a effort being maide no in london and Chatham to raise collord regiments"[sic].[11] Both London and Chatham were obvious places to be among the leading centres for black recruitment. Both had large black populations and boasted some of the most recognized and influential leaders, not only in the province, but also well beyond the Canadian borders. At the fore were Garland H. White, Doctor Martin Delany, George W. Brodie, and Mary Ann Shadd Cary.

No one on behalf of the black population in Canada, albeit with the pen of someone denied a formal education, more passionately and eloquently expressed their desire to become involved in the war than did Reverend Garland H. White. White had been the body servant, carriage driver and slave in charge of horses for Georgian Senator Robert Toombs, who was one of the most fervent pro-slavery spokespersons in

Georgia Senator Robert Augustus Toombs, the owner of Garland H. White, became an ardent secessionist and briefly served as Secretary of State for the Confederacy.

the federal government. One day, while Toombs and his slave were in Washington, D.C., White, who had learned to read, found his master's will and discovered that while one or two of Toombs's slaves were to be freed upon their owner's death, his name was not listed. Feeling betrayed upon making this discovery, he fled to Canada when the legislators prepared to return to their home states at the end of the fall session in December 1859.[12] White first settled in Chatham, Canada West, where everyone was still abuzz with grief over the martyred John Brown, who had laid the foundations in that town for an armed assault against slavery, and had recently been executed for the unsuccessful raid on the federal armory at Harper's Ferry, Virginia. White soon married and worked as both a grocer and a plasterer, but wished to resume the spiritual calling that he had received on September 10, 1859, when at the Quarterly Conference held in Washington, Georgia he was officially licensed to preach the Gospel.[13]

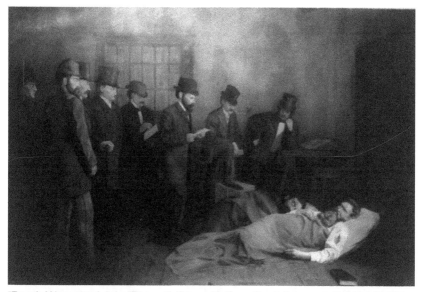

"Death Warrant of John Brown." *Reproduction of painting, copyrighted 1906 by E. Avey. LC-USZ62-36581.* A quote attributed to a Mr. Foster in *The Liberator,* March 30, 1860, stated: "It was the John Brown of Charleston Jail that the people admired, not so much John Brown of Harper's Ferry. He did his great work after his battle — was victorious in his defeat, and conquered his enemies while their prisoner. Had he fallen in battle, the direct and immediate effect of his movement would have been adverse to our cause, though ultimately it would have proved beneficial."

White, a natural leader and, from his time as Toombs's slave in Washington, an acquaintance of prominent abolitionist, New York Senator, and U.S. Secretary of State, William H. Seward, was within two years appointed as a minister to a splintered faction of the British Methodist Episcopal mission in London, in the same province. It was from that place that he wrote to Edwin M. Stanton, the U.S. Secretary of War, offering their services:

> London Canada West May 7th 1862
>
> dear sir. please indulg me the liberty of writing you a few lines upon a subject of grave importance to your & my country It is true I am now stoping in canada for awhile but it is not my home — & before I proceen

further I must inform you of your humble correspondent. My name is G.H. White formerly the Servant of
Robert Toombs of Georgia. Mr Wm H Seward knows
something about me I am now a minister, & am called
upon By my peopel to tender to your Hon thir willingness to serve as soldiers in the southern parts during
the summer season or longer if required. our offer is
not for speculation or self interest but for our love for
the north & the government at large, & at the same
time we pray god that the triumph of the north & res-
toration of peace if I may call it will prove an eternal
overthrow of the institution of slavery which is the
cause of all our trouble if you desire to see me let me
hear at an early day. I am certain of raising a good no.
in the west & in the north. I am aquainted all thro the
south for I traveled with Senator Toombs all over it
nearly. I am quite willing to spend my life in preaching against sin & fighting against the same. Mr Seward
& many other of both white & colored know me in
Washington please let me hear from your Hon soon
your most humble servant

Garland H. White

please excuse my bad writing as I never went to School
a day in my left. I learnd what little I know by the hard-
est. yet I feel that the simplist instroment used in the
right direction sometimes accomplishs much good. I
pray you in gods name to consider the condition of your
humble speaker in the distant. A man who are free from
all the calumities of your land. yet when he thinks of his
sufferring countrymen he can but feel that good might
make him instromental in your hands to the accomplishments of some humble good. as simple as this
request may seem to you yet it might prove one of the

greatest acts of your life. an act which might redown to your honor to the remotest generation — I want to see my friends at port royal & other places in the South. I now close by saying I hope to hear from you as soon as possible. I shall not be happy till I hear from you on this very important subject & not then if I am denied — So now my chance to do good as I think rest altogether with you. now may the good lord help you to make a faverorabl desition heaven bless you & your dear family is the prayer & your most obedient sirvant G. H. White minister of the gospel London Canada West[14]

Of course Garland White was unsuccessful in his early attempts to contribute to the war effort, but that was about to change.

When it did come, the rumour mill sped into action. The April 25, 1863 edition of *The Christian Recorder* reported a story that was circulating around Washington that since Massachusetts Governor Andrew had opened recruiting offices for blacks, "that all of the colored people are leaving Massachusetts and going to Canada." The correspondent opined that:

> If the colored people of that noble State, after making so much to-do in their speeches, resolutions, and demonstrations, &c., have shown themselves such contemptible cowards as that, they ought never to say freedom again while they have a hot tongue; but should rather hold their lips in confounded silence, and be as mute as soapstone statues forever. It will do more to damn our interests than twenty Copperhead Senators.

Three weeks later, the same newspaper carried a letter from an incensed man who used the nom de plume "Guerre" to vigorously deny that any blacks had left Massachusetts for Canada. He deeply resented any implication that his fellows were unpatriotic or that they did not appreciate the freedoms that they enjoyed in their state, which they believed were more plentiful than any place else in the country.[15]

However, there was some difficulty in filling the ranks at the beginning. Contributing to this was the ready availability of high-paying jobs for blacks in Boston and the resentment toward U.S. policy that all officers' positions were to be exclusively filled by whites. Governor Andrews turned to George Luther Stearns, a known abolitionist who had been a supporter of John Brown. Stearns assured the governor that he could find plenty of men in Ohio and in Canada West. With the governor's blessing, Stearns travelled first to Buffalo, where he was able to recruit about a dozen men. Thus encouraged, he crossed the Niagara River and settled in to the Clifton House hotel, where some blacks were employed. It was also a favourite haunt for Southerners seeking shelter from the war, a fact that Stearns soon learned when they started to hurl insults aimed at him and other abolitionists. After Stearns countered by proudly proclaiming his connection with John Brown, the critics were silenced and made their exit. Stearns also travelled to Toronto, where he found Southern sympathy was strong, so he had to work quietly behind the scenes. People who were willing to act as recruiting agents were soon onboard.[16]

George Luther Stearns was one of John Brown's "Secret Six" supporters and was later in charge of recruiting coloured troops. *Image from Oswald Garrison Villard's* John Brown 1800–1859 *(Boston and New York: Houghton Mifflin Co, 1910)* 396.

One of those agents was Garland H. White. In late May and early June, 1863, White, along with Sergeant S.W. Franklin, had gathered twenty-six men from Sandusky, Ohio, who, to much fanfare by a large crowd assembled at the station to cheer them on, boarded a train to Boston.[17]

Robert Shaw, a twenty-five-year-old soldier and son of abolitionist parents from Boston, was commissioned to help raise the first black regiment from the Northern states, the 54th Massachusetts Colored Infantry. He was a curious choice for such an assignment at first, only reluctantly accepting command and referring to himself as a "Nigger" colonel. His letters to his family reveal some of the recruiting operations to Canada. On February 23, 1863, Shaw wrote, "to-day three men are going on a campaign into Canada," and in a letter to his father the next day: "Our agents start for Canada tomorrow." On March 17th, Shaw informed his mother: "The regiment continues to flourish. Men come in every day. Mr. Stearns who is at home for a few days from Canada, says we can get more men than we want from there."[18] Four days later Shaw reported: "Mr. Stearns' recruits are beginning to come in too. We are picking them carefully & shall have a very sound set."

Colonel Robert Shaw was initially hesitant to accept the command of the 54th Massachusetts Colored Infantry, but relatively quickly committed himself to his job and to his men. *LC-DIG-ppm-sca-10888. LOC.*

In order to save travel expenses for men who were not physically fit, a Doctor Lincoln Ripley Stone was sent to Buffalo to examine the men. Recruiters were paid two dollars for each man who was mustered into the regiment. Alfred M. Green was among the recruiters for the 54th Mass. who had a Canadian connection. Green was the son of an AME minister, Reverend Augustus R. Green, who brought his family to Windsor, Canada West and was a part of the movement that broke away from their American connection in 1856 and formed the British Methodist Episcopal (BME) Church. The senior Green was also the editor of the *Missionary Messenger*, which was the official newspaper of the church. Alfred moved to Philadelphia and became active in the antislavery movement there. In 1860, Green was one of nine blacks to be arrested and sentenced to prison for attempting to rescue Moses Horner, a fugitive slave. Perhaps his early life in Canada helped inspire him to organize August 1st Emancipation Celebrations in observance of the anniversary of the end of slavery throughout the British Empire (including Canada) in 1834. He would also support John Brown's attempt at organizing a slave revolt and would ask Virginia Governor Henry Wise to have mercy on Brown and his captured men following the failed raid on Harper's Ferry.

An articulate and sought-after speaker, Green had immediately called for black enlistment following the firing on Fort Sumter. At the beginning of the Civil War, he helped to form two regiments of "Home Guards" to defend Philadelphia in the event of a Confederate invasion. Unsuccessful in his initial requests to allow black enlistment in the Union Army, he seized the opportunity to recruit for the 54th Massachusetts in 1863. In August of 1864, Green would himself enlist in the 127th USCI, soon becoming a sergeant-major. He continued recruiting, as well as speaking, at war meetings in the Northern states, and joined in the fight to have blacks become officers and for enlisted men to receive the same rights and pay as whites.[19]

Alfred Green's father, now BME Bishop Augustus Green, and Dr. Martin Delany from Chatham quickly took up the challenge to encourage black men from Canada to enlist. Cognizant of the neutrality law, the two men met in Windsor and agreed that although the Queen would not like her subjects to fight in a foreign war, she would surely have no objection to them sending New Testaments to their enslaved brothers. Delany then collected a number of bibles and gave them to these new "missionaries," who in turn carried them to enlist on the other side of the border.[20]

Bishop Green also became active as a recruiter, saying of the men who enlisted that they were "too brave to be slaves, and felt the odds against them to stand and fight out their liberty" at that time were now encouraged according to the poem:

He who fights and runs away,
May live to fight another day.

Bishop Green was pleased to visualize so many of the young men don the Northern uniforms, and with musket in hand go back to their old masters and march them to Union strongholds. As the war progressed, he lamented the death and destruction of war, the loss of loved ones, and the hardships of the families, but he believed that the United States had to atone for its sins and that it was God's bidding.[21]

Delany recruited for the states of Massachusetts, Rhode Island, and Connecticut, and also acted as examining surgeon to make sure that the men were physically sound. His duties required him to travel to various parts of the Union into states beyond those he recruited for. On one occasion, in September 1863, as the 1st Michigan Colored Infantry was being formed, Delany appeared at a meeting at the Lafayette Street colored church in Detroit, where heavy arguments occurred as to whether prospective soldiers from Michigan should enlist in their own state or in the Rhode Island Heavy Artillery, which had established a recruiting office in that city. Accusations had been made that the Rhode Island agents were offering high bounties in a dishonest attempt to enlist enough men to ensure that the agent would be granted an officer's commission as a reward.[22] William Webb, the chair of the meeting, spoke of the importance of men of all colours enlisting in any Union regiment to put down the rebellion. However, George De Baptist and Henry Barns of Detroit spoke adamantly that blacks from their state should only enlist in Michigan. Martin Delany dismissed any effort to limit blacks to serving in the Michigan regiment as a political move to save whites from being drafted to fill the necessary state quota. Delany expressed his belief that Rhode Island was a far better choice, because that state committed to giving blacks the rights of citizens, something that he believed Michigan would not do.[23]

Delany also found himself embroiled in other controversies that threatened his reputation. James F. Jones, who had been recruited for the 14th Regiment Rhode Island Heavy Artillery, wrote a scathing letter that was published in the Feb 13, 1864 edition of *The Christian Recorder*. Jones levelled his sights directly at two men who had recruited his regiment. Of Dr. Delany, he wrote:

> He has persuaded young men who had been taught to hold his name sacred, to go into the army by promising them bounties which they were not to get. Yea, he has even managed to filch from them that which they should and would have received but for him. The reverend M.D. has called down upon his head the curses and ill-will of many a poor man who is a member of the Fourteenth, many who have sworn to hand his name down to the rising generation as the robber of the widow and orphan, and the man that would fain fill his coffers with money due their fathers, while soldiers, fighting for the rights and freedom of the same egotistical M.D.
>
> Of all the men that took any part or interest in the formation of the Fourteenth, Dr. Martin R. Delaney is the most heartily despised, and men who once almost worshipped his name, now almost curse the very utterance of it in camp.

Jones also accused another recruiter, Joshua Highwarden, who he said had formerly "had the title of Rev. affixed to his cognomen" of being in league with Delany in cheating the recruits out of part of their bounty. The men had been told that some of the money was deducted to pay their transportation costs from Indiana and Illinois to Rhode Island, but he suspected that they had pocketed some of it for themselves.

Major Martin Delany was one of the most important black leaders of the 19th century. *LC-DIG-ppmsca-10888. LOC.*

Delany vehemently denied the charges and promised to investigate and make a full report.[24] It appears that Delany was without fault, but as with many other black regiments, the uncertainty of pay was a regular practice. Many men from the various regiments, including those from the 14th Rhode Island, had refused on principle to accept any pay rather than the seven dollars per month offered. When they had enlisted they were told that they would be entitled to the same rights and benefits as any other soldier. However, the reality was quite different. White soldiers received ten dollars per month plus three dollars a month for a clothing allowance. Blacks would receive ten dollars a month *minus* three dollars for clothing.

There had been several cases where complaining soldiers were charged with insubordination when they argued for justice. It was not until September 21, 1864, thirteen months after the men had been mustered in, that one of the captains wrote from Fort Jackson that the matter of pay had finally been settled. Although he had been forced to send several men to the brig as a result of their fight for equal pay, the captain believed that no white regiment would have remained in the service if they had been treated thusly.[25]

After being deceived in the matter of pay and by promises of equal treatment with white soldiers, recruits would have been slowly heartened by the strengthened evolution of Abraham Lincoln's resolve. Touched by the plea of a widow who had lost her husband in the slaughter that was Fort Pillow, Tennessee, Lincoln wrote to Charles Sumner, who was the senator that led the fight for black rights, to consider legislation to give the widows and children of black soldiers who had died in the service the same rights as were accorded to dependents of whites. Knowing that slave marriages were not legally recognized, the President believed that it still should not be a barrier to entitlement.[26] The time seemed right for such a move, as the public was then in shock and angered by the events at Fort Pillow on April 12, 1864, in which scores of black Union soldiers — many of whom were wounded, had surrendered, and had pleaded for mercy — were summarily executed in a variety of fiendish ways. Confederate General Nathan Bedford Forrest, who had been a slave-trader before the war, acknowledged that "the river was dyed with the blood of the slaughtered" who had dove into the Mississippi in a futile attempt to escape.

Delany's glowing reputation had been well earned. Freeborn to former slaves in Virginia and the grandson of slaves who had been stolen from Africa, Delany was able to acquire a classical education in Pennsylvania and later attended Harvard Medical School before racial prejudice forced him to withdraw. Among his many accomplishments were the founding of an anti-slavery newspaper, *The Mystery*; reporting for Frederick Douglass's newspaper, *North Star*; writing and publishing several books; starting a medical practice; and being revered as one of the most prominent abolitionist lecturers in North America. In 1856, Delany and his family moved to Chatham to escape oppressive conditions in the United States. Always a stalwart black nationalist, he spearheaded an exploration expedition to the Niger Valley in Africa to investigate and make provisions for establishing a settlement there where American and Canadian blacks could have a peaceful and just homeland.

These recruiting posters for the 3rd USCT and the 127th USCT, with black men beside a white Lady Liberty, were somewhat typical. Alfred M. Green, late of Windsor, Canada West, who recruited for 54th Massachusetts, later enlisted in the 127th regiment. *LOT 6592, no. 134. LOC and 3a24165u. LOC.*

This poster for the 22nd USCT was meant to appeal to a very different emotion. "Sic Semper Tyranus" (thus always to tyrants) were the same words that John Wilkes Booth shouted out at Ford's Theater after shooting President Lincoln. Canadians who joined this regiment included Thomas Brown, George W. Franklin, Oliver Hammond, Charles Hines, George H. Lewis, Willard Maynard, Emanuel Rickets, Robert Robertson, George Smith, Samuel Treadwell, Thomas Willard, and Charles Wilson. *LOT 6592, no. 132. LOC.*

The beginning of the Civil War interrupted those plans, but that experience ideally placed him as a person that the Lincoln administration, who feared that blacks and whites could never peacefully co-exist, could consult with concerning American colonization plans to remove blacks from their country. Two letters in *The Abraham Lincoln Papers* at the Library of Congress speak to the esteem in which Delany was held:

To The President of the United States

Sir — Doctor Martin R. Delany is a reliable man and as you cannot fail to discover a man of energy and intelligence — and any monies that may be placed in his hands will be faithfully and legitimately applied as shall be stipulated.

I have the honor Mr. President to be
Your very obedient servant
Chas. V. Dyer

To his Excellency
Abraham Lincoln
President of the US.
Washington
D.C.
Chicago April 26th, 1863[27]

And another:

Chicago May 1st 1863
Dear Sir,

The bearer of this, Dr Delany is a man (who from the short acquaintance I have had with him, & what I have read of his operations, & explorations in Africa) I think eminently qualified to conduct an enterprise of Colonization of the free colored people of this country, should that be thought the best way to dispose of them. I therefore take great pleasure in recommending him to your favorable consideration.

Yours truly.
Peter Page

Delany, whose focus had been on Africa, was not among the five black delegates that met with Lincoln in August 1862 to discuss the President's plan for colonization in Central America, which he deemed more suitable. However, a select committee of the U.S. House of Representatives on the subject did include a lengthy study on the subject, which was co-authored by Delany, Augustus R. Green, and John A. Warren, all from Canada, along with nine men from the U.S.; this study was included as an appendix in the official Report on Emancipation and Colonization.[28]

It would be almost three years later before Delany had the opportunity to meet with Lincoln, only this time it would be to discuss raising black regiments that would be commanded by black officers. After this meeting, the President, obviously impressed, wrote the following succinct and complimentary letter:

February 8, 1865

HON. E.M. STANTON, Secretary of War,
Do not fail to have an interview with this most extraordinary and intelligent black man.

A. LINCOLN

The result was that Delany became the first black major of a field regiment, the 104th USCI in the United States. Among his duties and those of his regiment was to recruit newly liberated slaves in South Carolina, where they were stationed.

Earlier on in the war, when still recruiting in the North, Martin Delany sought the help of Mary Ann Shadd Cary to assist him in recruiting. On December 7, 1863 from Chicago, Delany wrote that he had just completed a contract with the state authorities in Connecticut to have the sole right of raising black troops in the west and southwest. Five thousand men were needed to fill the state's quota, and "as many of them as can be obtained may be Black." Any slaves that could be obtained to enlist would be paid $120 cash immediately upon being sworn in and they were to obtain exactly the "same pay per month, clothing and political status as white men." Free blacks were to receive a two-hundred-dollar bounty. Delany explained the disparity in bounty for a slave or freeman as "inconsequence of all the contingencies attending the obtaining of our 'slave' brethren." Further, he would give Shadd Cary fifteen dollars for every slave or five dollars for every freedman who she could deliver to him in Chicago so that he could examine them. Delany added that he was still an agent for Rhode Island Heavy Artillery so if any men preferred that to infantry, she could supply those as well.[29]

Shadd Cary went right to work and newspapers revelled in telling her story (and often misspelling her surname):

> Mrs. Carey, a colored woman, belonging in Canada West, is acting as recruiting agent for the Thirtieth Regiment, now in camp at New-Haven. She gets her men from the refugee slaves in Canada, and brought twenty-nine good ones to the camp on a single day last week."[30]

Another wrote:

> A Mrs. Carey of Canada West, a colored woman, is engaged in the recruiting business, and reached New Haven a day or two since with twenty-nine men, who were all accepted and placed in the Thirtieth C.V. How many white women have done better?"[31]

Mary Ann Shadd Cary distinguished herself as North America's first black female newspaper editor, and as a teacher, lecturer, civil rights activist, and Civil War recruiter. *Courtesy of BNHS&M.*

Officials were so happy with her work that on August 15, 1864, by special order of Governor O. P. Morton, she was appointed as a recruiting officer for any county in the state of Indiana.[32] Historian and author Barbara Blair wrote that Shadd Cary had her base in New Albany, Indiana near the Kentucky state line, where she also organized aid to contraband families; Blair also noted that she was an agent for the Chicago-based "colored Ladies' Freedmen's Aid Society," which sent supplies to former slaves at the front lines.[33]

Many descriptions of Cary survive, one of which came from her acquaintance and fellow-recruiter, William Wells Brown:

> As a speaker, she ranks deservedly high, as a debater, she is quick to take advantage of the weak points of her opponent, forcible in her illustrations, biting in her sarcasm, and withering in her rebukes.
>
> Mrs. Carey is resolute and determined, and you might as well attempt to remove a stone wall with your little finger, as to check her in what she conceives to be right and her duty. Although she has mingled much in the society of men, attended many conventions composed almost exclusively of males, and trodden paths where women usually shrink to go, no one ever hinted aught against her reputation, and she stands with a record without blot or blemish. Had she been a man, she would probably have been with John Brown at Harper's Ferry.
>
> When the government determined to put colored men in the field to aid in suppressing the Rebellion, Mrs. Carey raised recruits at the West, and brought them to Boston, with as much skill, tact, and order as any of the recruiting officers under the government. Her men were always considered the best lot brought to head-quarters. Indeed, the examining surgeon never failed to speak of Mrs. Carey's recruits as faultless. This proves the truth of the old adage, that "It takes a woman to pick out a good man." Few persons have done more real service for the moral, social, and political elevation of the colored race than Mrs. Carey.[34]

Abraham (Abram) W. Shadd enlisted in the 55th Massachusetts and received the commission of captain before the war's end. *Courtesy of BNHS&M.*

Shadd Cary's brother, Abraham W. Shadd, was also active in recruiting, even after enlisting in 55th Massachusetts, Company B. Born in West Chester, Pennsylvania on February 24, 1844, Abraham, along with his parents and siblings, followed Mary Ann to Canada in 1853. By the time he enlisted at age 19 on May 16, 1863 at Readville, Massachusetts, he had already worked a teacher in Chatham. Well-educated, he quickly rose in the ranks. He was appointed quartermaster sergeant on June 24, 1863, was returned to his company in charge of quartermaster's department on November 19, 1863, and was promoted to sergeant on August 4, 1864. While stationed at Folly Island, South Carolina, a homesick — and lovesick — Shadd wrote to the assistant adjutant general on October 13, 1864, "most respectfully to make application for furlough for thirty (30) days to visit my home in Detroit, Michigan." Perhaps to avoid any complications, he slyly avoided any mention of his true home in Canada, or the true purpose of his visit.

The provost marshal's office immediately "approved and respectfully forwarded — for good conduct in the field" his application for furlough. Shadd, on October 29, made a hasty trip north, with $7.50 allotted for rations in his pocket. On November 17, after arriving at his parents' home in Raleigh Township, he stood before the acting pastor at St. Andrew's Presbyterian Church in Buxton and married nineteen-year-old Salina Anthony. The young groom returned to his regiment by November 28. Late in the war, on April 13, 1865, by special order ninety-three from the Headquarters of the Department of the South, Shadd was detailed on a recruiting assignment in the Charleston, South Carolina area.[35]

Recruiting became quite the family affair for the Shadd family. The late historian Norman McRae wrote that their brother Garrison also recruited, as did David Thomas Williamson, who had married one of their sisters.

David Thomas Williamson's experiences growing up are one of those remarkable stories that demonstrate the complexity of the owner/ owned relationship. He was born in Moorefield, Hardin County, Virginia in 1825. At the age of four, Williamson's mother took him to Sunday school on three different occasions, but when the anti-black laws became strictly enforced, the school was closed. Williamson and his mother were the house slaves of blacksmith and farmer John Peterz. While living there, young Williamson developed an aptitude and love for making and repairing watches. On the surface he appeared to have a good relationship with his master and family, but everything changed when a fear of being sold to a slave trader surfaced. What occurred next is best described by Diane Peterz, the master's daughter.

Williams Port, Virginia Dec 25th, 1852

We have been anxiously looking for a letter from you Davy for the last few weeks but as yet have been disappointed and thinking perhaps the letter Mr Peterz wrote you might possibly have been directed to Lower Canada instead of Upper. He has come to the conclusion to write again.

The letter I have reference to Mr Peterz wrote on the 10th of October and if you could have seen how hard it was for him to write a letter you would not blame him for getting some one to write for him. He commenced writing your letter in the forepart of the Day and never finished it till late at night. Would write a while and then rest a little and then at it again. I never felt like I wanted to write a letter so bad for any body in my life but to satisfy you he would write it himself though with so much difficulty.

We sincerely hope Davy this letter may find you well and with your mind entirely made up to return home. We were in hopes you would have been home by this time. We have prepared your winter clothes. I even had you a very pretty vest shipped and knit your winter socks. I wish you were here today to eat your Christmas dinner with us but instead of that your house is deserted your place is vacant in the family, your clock and all your things have a melancholy appearance. Little did I think that night when I set you your supper that you would be gone the next morning. Davy I never had any thing to hurt me as bad in my life. Sarah Ann's death was nothing to compare to it. We never knew how much we were attached to you until you were gone. Besides we missed you so much if you could just see Papa toiling and slugging along by himself and that tired at night that he can scarcely sit up. I frequently want him to hire some one to help but he says he can't get any person to suit him as well as you and he still thinks you will come back. If McDowel [the slave-trader] was to lay down ten thousand dollars it would not have induced us to sell you. I don't know why you should be so fraid to trust us. We never deceived you.

Mr Peterz wrote in his letter to you that he had not sold you nor would not sell you if you returned home but would set you free at the time agreed upon if you desired it. He wrote also that he would pay you back what it would cost you to come home and if you would rather he would meet you at Pittsburg or Brownsville and bring you home if you would let him know the exact time you would be there. He thought perhaps it would be best to send you a pass as he had you advertised and you might be taken up and the reward claimed.

We are all well. Pap's arm mends a little. I heard from your mother a few weeks ago. Wesley was here said she was well and that she talked of coming to see us. There has been no Coloured persons sold to the traders in this neighbourhood since you left that I know of. Nor none run off.

Our New Church is to be raised on next Tuesday. It would have been done by this time but Jim Miles got contrary about the ground. They say it will be pretty large with a gallery in it. Miles Saw Mill is nearly finished. It is build just a little above the Schoolhouse and the Church is to be rite by the Schoolhouse. I understand Ben McNaMar has been offered 8 hundred dollars for his farm more than he is to give for it which will make it 24 hundred and sixty dollars. A good price is it not. He ought to take it. Cate Smith and John Brown was married last Wednesday. A week now I believe. I have give you all the most important news. Now Davy don't fail to write as soon as you receive this. We remain your sincere friends.

Diane Peterz

p.s. Now Davy don't fail to write as soon as you receive this that we may know you got it and what you will do.

Understandably, "Davy" ignored this plea to return. He "squatted" on a farm in the marshy area just north of the Buxton Settlement, as did many other black families from the United States. He married Amelia Shadd, the sister of Mary Ann Shadd Cary and Abraham W. Shadd. The couple eventually moved to St. Catharines where he opened a watch and clock repair shop, using the skills that he had honed as a young man in slavery in a small town in Virginia. Five years after the Civil War and twenty years after he made his escape, Williamson returned to his old neighbourhood in West Virginia to renew his old acquaintances. We can only imagine the reunions that took place there.

Other friends and close associates of the Shadd family were also involved. Hezekiah "H" Ford Douglas was for a time co-proprietor of the *Provincial Freeman* newspaper with Mary Ann Shadd Cary in 1856. He wrote, travelled, and spoke against slavery and segregated institutions in Canada. On one occasion, at an anti-slavery meeting held on June 10, 1857 at the black Wesleyan church on Richmond Street in Toronto, the eloquent Douglas forwarded the following resolution: "We will use every effort, consistent with our duty as loyal British subjects, and the injunctions of our holy religion, to break his chains — and place him 'Redeemed, and disenthralled, upon the world wide platform, of a common humanity."[36]

Douglas returned to the U.S. in 1858 and became the midwestern agent for the Haytian Emigration Bureau. He enlisted in the 95th regiment of Illinois Infantry Volunteers in July 1862, becoming one of the few blacks to serve in a white regiment. Douglas believed that he was the first black soldier who had enlisted in the war. On one occasion he shared a story of having served at Fort Donelson and at Vicksburg, where he laid in a trench before the city for forty days. Because of having served honourably, he was eligible for a promotion. General Thomas, who held the necessary papers, told Douglas that before he could receive them, he must answer the question: "Are you a negro or a white man?" After first hesitating, Douglas replied, "General, I am a negro! and I would not deny my race for all the commissions in the army." General Thomas then replied, "Mr. Douglas, you cannot be promoted." He then left the army of the Mississippi and came to Kansas, where he received a commission as captain and was authorized to raise the Independent Colored Battery of Light Artillery, which entered the war in 1865 and was stationed at Fort Leavenworth, Kansas.[37] Douglas is believed to have been the only black officer to lead troops into combat during the war.[38]

Elijah Willis was another associate of the Shadd and Delany families and had been a friend of John Brown, who recruited for the 1st Michigan Colored Infantry.[39] It was reported that by birthright Willis was an African prince of a tribe called Guinea, and that "his father was captured by slave dealers and brought to Virginia where he married a slave."[40] After moving to Canada, Willis and his family lived near the Thames River in Raleigh Township, just west of Chatham.

James H. Harris was a free mulatto, born in Granville County, North Carolina, who had moved to Ohio and then to Chatham. His abolitionist fires were stoked at John Brown's Constitutional Convention, where he was a delegate. Like Mary Ann Shadd Cary, he also was appointed by Governor Morton to recruit men in Indiana for the 28th USCI.[41] It is interesting to note that Harris, like many other black leaders before the Civil War, rose to positions of prominence afterward. In Harris's case, he became a member of the state legislature for North Carolina in 1868, 1872, and 1883.

Various reports exist about Osborne Anderson, the printer's assistant for Mary Ann Shadd Cary's newspaper, The *Provincial Freeman*, and the only black from Canada who accompanied John Brown to Harper's Ferry, serving as a recruiter for several months before enlisting himself in the Union Army.[42] Anderson survived the war, but soon after fell victim to consumption and the poverty that resulted from it. While attempting to travel to the South, in hopes of restoring his health, he was recognized for his heroic past and fundraisers were held to support and pay tribute to him. Unfortunately, before he could reach his destination, he died on December 12, 1872 at the Washington home of his friend and former fellow-recruiter, Alfred M. Green.[43] Bishop Green conducted the funeral service. One of Anderson's lasting legacies is the 1861 publication of his first-hand account of one of the events that helped to spark the inevitable conflict, *A Voice from Harpers Ferry: A Narrative of Events at Harper's Ferry; with Incidents prior and subsequent to its capture by Captain Brown and his Men.*

Other Canadian men, too old to enlist, offered their support however they could. Josiah Henson, a former slave from Maryland who is associated with the title character in Harriet Beecher Stowe's novel *Uncle Tom's Cabin*, promised an advance of money to families to entice men in the Dawn Settlement in Dresden to join the army. He wrote in his final autobiography that he went to Detroit with Alexander Pool's son and son-in-law so that they could enlist; both young men later fought in several battles. Lewis N. Clarke, who was involved with Refugee Home Society in Essex County, and whose life in part was the model for Eliza Harris's husband, George, in Stowe's same ground-breaking novel, attended a recruiting meeting at the Croghan Street Baptist Church in Detroit.[44]

During the proceedings, Clarke spoke passionately about how the original purpose of the war was to restore the Union — it was now clearly a battle to end slavery. Though he had once been opposed to blacks being involved, he now "exhorted his friends to go, and share the glories of the field," and he thanked God that it would be impossible to restore the Union as it once existed. Both Henson and Clarke had earned respect for the work they did in their Canadian communities, and were widely known for their early autobiographies about their lives in slavery and in freedom.[45] Henson went on to issue four editions of his autobiography. In his final edition, published in 1881, he shared the melancholy news of how he was most acutely touched by the war: "My eldest son, Tom, went to California, and I think was killed in the Civil War, for I have not heard from him since he enlisted."

Recruiting continued throughout the war, and soldiers, as was the case with Martin Delany and Abraham Shadd, were occasionally placed on detached service to carry out the task. Nathaniel Sparrow, a thirty-four-year-old carpenter from Chatham, was among those early Canadian recruits to the 54th Massachusetts, where he held the rank of corporal; there he received a special order by the Department of War's Adjutant General's office in Washington to go on recruiting duty with the Superintendent Volunteer Recruiting Service in Boston. It is interesting to note that he was a neighbour of Garland H. White when the latter lived in Chatham.

James Peak, a twenty-three-year-old cook from St. Catharines, enlisted into 1st USCI (organized in Washington, D.C.) on June 17, 1863 at Mason's Island, Virginia. Officials saw some special leadership qualities in the young man and immediately gave him the rank of sergeant of Company E. From June until October 1863, Peak was on detached special assignment, recruiting in Baltimore, during which time he was promoted to first sergeant. However, his rise to prominence was short-lived when he was reduced to the rank of private in November, placed under arrest, and found guilty of "Charge 1st Violation of the 21st Article of War — 2nd Conduct prejudicial to good order and military discipline — 3rd Pillaging — 4th Riotous and disorderly conduct." His sentence required that he be reduced to the ranks and confined to hard labour on some government fortifications for the remainder of his term, as well as to forfeit all pay and allowances due or to become due him.

Peak served part of his arrest at Fort Norfolk before his sentence was remitted by order of General B.F. Butler. Peak was restored to duty and was to be paid starting May 4, 1864. Quickly getting back into the officers' good graces, Peak was promoted to sergeant less than three weeks later. He was wounded in action on October 27, 1864 at the second battle of Near Oaks, Virginia and remained hospitalized until the following August, during which time he was again reduced to the ranks.

Months after the war ended, and just three days before he was to be mustered out of service, Peak again faced charges. Testimony accused Peak of entering a store in Roanoke Island, North Carolina, where he proceeded to "murderously assault with his fists and an axe, the said Malachi Hubbard and when the said Malachi Hubbard cried out for assistance he the said James Peak did say 'if you do not stop your noise I'll kill.'" This testimony is dated September 26, 1865. An additional charge was levelled of "uttering threatening language" against Malachai Hubbard's wife, Louisa. Apparently there was doubt about the accusations and Peak was mustered out with his regiment on September 29, 1865. Unfortunately, Peak's side of the story, or that of other black witnesses who may have been present, do not appear in his record, making it impossible to know if racial prejudice had a part in the accusations.

Some Canadian and American newspapers took a particularly perverted enjoyment in disparaging black recruits. The *Chatham Weekly Planet* of August 20, 1863, carried a story of a black man, who the article referred to as a "darkey," and who was attached to a white regiment. After expressing his fear that he would not receive his pay unless he was "mustered in," some men from his regiment placed a large mustard plaster to his lower back. Believing that this was the standard procedure for all recruits, he reportedly wore it until the heat produced was unbearable. At that point, the soldiers declared that he was indeed then "mustered in." Unable to resist a final jab, the newspaper correspondent concluded: "if that darkey don't get his wages, it will not be because he has [not] suffered for his country."

The Growler, another Chatham newspaper, also delighted in issuing racist comments, as in their satirical article in their October 26, 1861 edition, which stated "The Southerners to be reinforced with Darkies from Chatham." Even one of the newspapers from the abolitionist heartland of Worcester, the *Massachusetts Spy*, joined in when they reported that over one hundred colored men from Canada had enlisted in black regiments in the first half of 1863. In a feeble attempt at humour, it continued: "The old classical proverb used to say: — 'The feet of the avenging deities are shod with wool.' Present appearances indicate that it is their heads that are covered with it."[46]

The United States Secretary of War, Edwin Stanton, gave permission to a Massachusetts recruiter to raise a cavalry regiment, "and a large number of the negroes for it were to be smuggled from Canada, with due regard to the 'Queen's neutrality.'"[47] However, the British Foreign Enlistment Act forbade recruiting within the borders of her colonies. This law stated that no person in this province shall "hire, retain, engage or procure … any natural born subject of Her Majesty, to enlist or to serve in any warlike or military operation of any foreign power." If convicted they were to pay a penalty of two hundred dollars, along with court costs, and may be committed to six months in the common "gaol" at hard labour.

The answer to the question of who was considered to be a British subject was particularly vague for black refugees who had come to the colonies from the United States. While some received their naturalization papers, which they were eligible for after five years' residence by swearing an oath of allegiance to the British Crown, many others did not. Through the February 27, 1864 columns of *The Christian Recorder*, Windsor's Reverend Augustus R. Green attempted to help clear the issue for blacks residing in the British provinces. Green believed that until recently it had been the case that any naturalized citizen could enjoy all the rights of citizenship, including being eligible for the draft in those provinces, if one was called for. However, he learned from the British consulate in St. Louis that those American-born people, then living in the provinces, were subject to the U.S. draft.

A case in point was that of John Johnson, a young black man from Windsor. Johnson had been born in the United States but had taken the oath of allegiance and had therefore become a British citizen. Sometime during the early war years, he had left his job as a waiter in Canada and taken a job with one of the railway companies in Michigan. When that state instituted the draft, Johnson was seized and was informed that he was then in the Union army. Officials from Windsor protested to the military department and Johnson was released. However, a few days later, the military again seized Johnson. This time, higher-up British ministers made the decision that Johnson had to serve. He was enrolled into Michigan's 102nd USCI, and even though he could have escaped back across the Detroit River, as did some of his fellows, he chose not to, not wishing to be considered a deserter.

In response to this case, Reverend Green was even more aroused to encourage Canadian blacks to enlist. Trying to find a silver lining, he, perhaps sarcastically, announced that they were in a unique and "enviable position," being allowed to serve in the army on either side of the border. This allowed them to demonstrate beyond question their worth as full citizens. He concluded: "Then let our young men prepare for the mighty contest. It may be truly said of the black man, the irrepressible; for he is here and there; in despite of all fate he will have a place assigned him higher than he would otherwise claim."[48]

A curious advertisement carried in Toronto's *Globe* in July 1863 sought to alleviate the fears of Canadians who might seek employment in the states. Under the heading 500 LABORERS WANTED, it explained that these men were needed to construct the Atlantic and Great Western Railway in Ohio from Akron to Gallion. It promised to pay $1.25 per day (with $11 per month deducted for board — added in much smaller print) and assured all that there was absolutely no danger of British subjects being drafted, there having been many Canadians already having worked there for months unmolested.[49]

Another question that hovered over the heads of runaway slaves was whether they would still be subject to the terms of the hated Fugitive Slave Act of 1850, which allowed for the seizure and return of fugitive slaves. After all, there were still slave states, such as Maryland, Kentucky, and part of Virginia, which remained loyal to the Union, and slaves from those areas were not given their freedom by the terms of the Emancipation Proclamation. Charles H. Middleton attempted to get an answer to that question by asking President Lincoln on behalf of a young man who had fled to Canada, taken out naturalization papers there, and had become

British envoy Lord Lyons (seated centre) to the left of Secretary of State William Seward, along with other diplomats from Sweden, Italy, Nicaragua, France, Russia, Hanseatic Republics, U.S., and Britain at Trenton Falls, New York in August, 1863. The year previous, Lyons and Seward negotiated a treaty to allow for British and American ships to search for slaves being transported in vessels, thereby effectively ending the Trans-Atlantic slave trade. *LC-DIG-ppmsca-23733. LOC.*

a British citizen. Middleton included in his letter that even though this young man's skin was so white that there was no outward sign of his black heritage he had still been enslaved. This seemingly irrelevant addendum was often used by abolitionists to further appeal to the sympathy of whites. The additional question was if this man was arrested and attempts were made to re-enslave him, would Lord Lyons, Britain's envoy to Washington, demand his release and, if so, what would the American response be? Lincoln forwarded the question to Secretary of State William Seward, who gave a less-than-definitive legal answer, responding that it would be an injustice for this man to be taken under the Act.[50] However, it was not until June 28, 1864 that the law was repealed by Congress.

Lincoln would naturally seek the counsel of Seward on other occasions as well. Seward was one of the most outspoken advocates against slavery and unlike many of his philosophical compatriots, he acted on the most fundamental level and allowed his Auburn home to be used as a station of the Underground Railroad. His feeling on the enactment of the Emancipation Proclamation was that "such a proclamation ought to be borne on the bayonets of an advancing army, not dragged in the dust behind a retreating one."[51] On one occasion, Lincoln requested that Seward respond to a Senate resolution that enquired if authority had ever been given to anyone to recruit Irishmen or Canadians as soldiers or sailors for the Union forces, or if anyone was inducing them to emigrate to the U.S. in order to be recruited. The secretary of state disingenuously responded that no such authority existed "by the Executive of this Government, or by any Executive Department to anyone, either in this country or elsewhere to obtain recruits either in Ireland, or in Canada."[52] Seward continued that on "two or three instances it has been reported to this Department that recruiting agents crossed the Canadian frontier, without authority, with a view to engage recruits," but immediate investigations followed and the recruits were immediately returned and the agents dismissed. While admitting that there were Canadians in the Union army, Seward protested that, "if any were obtained, they were recruited by people who were citizens of the country from which they were obtained" and those agents were "answerable to the laws of the foreign province or country where their offenses were committed." Secretary of War Stanton, one would presume with his fingers firmly crossed behind his back, echoed much the same comments — that no recruits had been obtained in Ireland or in Canada "with my knowledge or consent, and, to the best of my information and belief, none have been obtained nor any effort to obtain them."[53]

The two politicians were careful, imaginative, and somewhat evasive with their wording, very much unlike officials in New York State, who were exceedingly straightforward when unhesitatingly enlisting John Hedgeman, a Canadian farmer, into the 31st USCI and requiring him to sign the following document:

STATE OF NEW YORK,
Niagara County,
John Hedgeman being duly sworn, deposes and says, he
was born in Hamilton, Canada West and is a subject of

Queen of Grate Brittin [sic] that he is not a citizen of the United States, and was never naturalized within the United States nor did he ever declare his intensions to become a citizen of the United States, nor as [sic] he at any time assumed the rights of a citizen of the United States, by voting at any election held under the laws, or authority thereof, or of any State or Territory within the same, nor has he ever held office under such laws of any of them, nor has he ever enlisted in the Naval or Military service of the United States before this time.

Although both federal Cabinet members were less than forthcoming with the entirety of their reports, Seward was certainly correct about any agents or recruits being subject to the laws of their province. As had been the case on foreign enlistment with whites in Canada, the same was so for blacks. There were many charges related to those infringements that made their way to the courts.

Kent County constables focused almost exclusively on blacks. As the new year dawned in 1864, at the Kent County Police Court such Victorian offenses appear as: "profane swearing," "driving furiously through the streets," "selling whiskey to Indians," "releasing pigs," "driving [carriage] without bells," "Inmate of" and "frequenting House of ill fame," as well as a school teacher "unjustifiably beating Ryan's son." A nefarious trio were charged with "indecent bathing," and each were fined two dollars for their indiscretion. More serious charges, albeit with lenient penalties, included those against six Irish, Scottish, and Canadian men who were found guilty of "taring [sic] and feathering" one Daniel Morrison. Those aggressors were fined $4.50 plus costs, but received no jail time. During that time, fines for assault and battery were typically between one dollar and ten dollars; being drunk and disorderly might demand a fine up to five dollars, and disturbing the peace might be settled for one dollar. "The Queen of the West," alias Rebecca King, found out the not-too-subtle difference of the whens and wheres — the latter charge was most significant; she received the wrath of the court when she was sentenced to one month in jail for "disturbing religious worship."

The first case to make its way to the Chatham Police Court occurred in the Quarter Session on January 2, 1864. It involved two black men, Isaac Washington and Willis Hosey, for "violation of Neutrality Laws." The cases were set over to the Assizes for trial, as were the cases of William Streets, John Ramsey, Abraham Collins, and Calvin Simmons, all coloured, and Finley McGregor and Henry Winter, both white.[54] Finley McGregor was discharged on February 20, 1865 without penalty. On February 27, 1864, A.B. Coleman, whose charge was "Breech of Neutrality Law" against Alexander Leah, was put over to the quarter sessions.

J. West and a Mr. Young were both charged with enlisting on January 11, 1865, but were discharged prior to March 11, 1865.

Chatham cabinet shop owner Charles H. Ramsey's charge of attempting to enlist thirty-three-year-old Israel Fowler was dismissed on April 17, 1865. At least one woman, a Mrs. Sutton, was unique in being the only female charged, in her case for attempting to enlist George Snively of Howard Township, a man already in his mid-fifties. Her case was dismissed on April 19, 1865.

Lucien Boyd enlisted at Detroit in the 102nd USCI on January 18, 1864. However, on January 25 he was absent without leave, briefly returning until February 29, before leaving again and making the critical mistake of returning to Chatham, where he was promptly arrested for enlisting. On March 1, he was committed for trial. While awaiting his hearing, he apparently found a way to briefly return to his regiment, but finally deserted on March 26, 1864. Leaving a bad reputation wherever he travelled, the U.S. army was out not only a man but also an Austrian musket and full set of accoutrements worth $13.66.[55]

The October 20, 1864 edition of the *Chatham Weekly Planet* reported that at the fall assizes of the Chancery Court in Kent County, the defendant in the case of *The Queen v. David Lingle*, gave fifteen-dollar bounty in American greenbacks, with the promise of seven dollars more when they arrived in Lockport, New York, to two minors — sixteen-year-old Lew Lewis and seventeen-year-old Charles Jones — to join the American army. The deal was made in Windsor, where the two boys boarded a train that would carry them to Buffalo, New York. Apparently having second thoughts, Lingle (who also used the aliases "Single" and "Lingo") attempted to stop them at the Chatham station. Lingle was found guilty of promoting parties to enlist in the U.S. army and sentenced to one year in prison.

On March 30, 1865, the same newspaper informed its' readers that Lewis Howard, coloured, of Chatham, went before the police magistrate in Windsor to answer to charges of inducing John Jones, coloured, of Raleigh Township, to enlist. The October 1865 *Local Courts & Municipal Gazette* relayed the case of Chatham's James Bright, a not infrequent visitor to Police Court to answer to charges of assault, who was convicted on March 28, 1865 for attempting to procure Thomas Livingwood and John F. Russell to enlist. Bright was fined one hundred dollars and also ordered to pay additional costs fifty cents for the information and warrant, fifty cents for hearing the case, one dollar for return of conviction, two dollars for arrest and attendance of the constable, and fifty cents for the witness. In default of such payment, Bright was to be "imprisoned at hard labor in the Common Gaol for a period of six months and for such further time as the said penalty and costs remain unpaid." Unable to meet those financial penalties, Bright was assessed an additional twenty-five cents for commitment to jail and one dollar for being conveyed to the jail. Upon appeal, the lawyer for the defense attempted to shoot a quiver of arrows through every legal loophole, arguing that the original warrant was dated "at Chatham in the County of Kent," but there was both a town of Chatham and a township of Chatham, and it was unclear in which jurisdiction the police magistrate had acted. Further, although the warrant contained part of the wording of the law — that is, that it "prohibits the hiring, retaining, &c. any person to enlist or to serve in any warlike or military operation, for any foreign power" — it lacked the phrase "as an officer, soldier, sailor or marine, or in any other military or warlike capacity." He also pleaded that the statute set the fine at two hundred dollars. But his client had only been fined one hundred dollars. Judge C.J. Draper supported the arguments, including the opinion that "a judgment for too little is as bad as a judgment for too much." A much-relieved James Bright was ordered to be released.[56]

In September 1865, *The Canadian Law Journal, Volume 1* carried another case of a Chatham grocer that had earlier been published in the April 6, 1865 issue of *Chatham Weekly Planet* — that of *The Queen v.*

Andrew Smith. This black defendant received the maximum penalty for giving Samuel Denby and Daniel Ferguson $750 to enlist in a colored regiment. He was found guilty, fined two hundred dollars, and committed to jail until the fine was paid. Upon appeal, Smith's conviction and appeal was withheld.[57] In two separate charges that appear in the Police Court records, on April 1, 1865 Smith was also convicted of enlisting H.A. Johnson and Charles Mitchell. He was fined two hundred dollars for each of those offenses, a huge sum that he was somehow able to pay. However, he was also sentenced to prison for six months in both cases.

Canadian courts were still busy hearing cases of Canadians who were charged with contravening this law as the war drew to a close in the spring of 1865. Of course, in many cases the blacks who enlisted were not "natural born subjects," but rather immigrant refugees; still, a very significant number were indeed born in the colonies. At any rate, this law served as little deterrence to the recruiting and the enlisting of blacks.

Many of the black recruits enlisted as substitutes. *The Richmond Examiner* of October 17, 1864 carried a provocative article that addressed the issue of fulfilling state quotas that equated the enlistment of black substitutes, many of whom were Canadian, to the buying and selling of slaves. In the border city of Buffalo, New York, substitutes were reported to cost between $550 and $600. Blacks who were physically denied acceptance as soldiers in New York, could be sent to Massachusetts, where criteria was less stringent and prices were higher. Bounty agents who regularly expected car loads of prospective recruits refused to take orders ahead of time because the market price was increasing almost daily. A "sound Canadian" was reputed to have gone for $765. After being delivered, he was then branded to prevent him from deserting and then re-enlisting elsewhere.

Throughout the war, protective parents, some of who might agree and others who would dispute Secretaries Seward and Stanton's assertion that no Canadians had been recruited, went to great lengths to save their children from themselves. When Samuel Woods of Howard Township, Kent County learned that his nineteen-year-old son John had travelled to Detroit and enlisted, he was outraged. John, an apprentice blacksmith, believed that he was going to have the relatively safe job of shoeing horses. To his dismay, he was handed a musket and placed in a volunteer regiment. His

Bounty brokers in New York State looking for substitutes. Many of these men were unscrupulous and took large amounts of the bounty that enlistees were entitled to. *LC-DIG-stereo-1s02984. LOC.*

lamentations to be released were ignored. His father, who was described as "a real old Britisher," travelled to Detroit only to receive the same refusal. Undeterred, the elder man determined to seek the help of Lord Lyons, the British envoy to the United States, who, according to reports, had secured the release of two or three British subjects only days before.[58]

Elizabeth Nugent, a widow from Montreal, also sought the help of a British official, this time in her own country, when she asked Governor General of British North America Sir Charles Stanley Monck to intercede on behalf of her son, James; she stated that he had been born in London, Canada West, but that she considered him a "minor" even though he was nineteen years old.[59] Anne Aide, the widow of a Newfoundland ship captain, also wrote to the governor general to help have her minor son, William, who had been enticed to enlist in Burlington, Vermont, when on a trip to visit his sister in Philadelphia. At the time, her son was four months shy of his eighteenth birthday.[60] Unfortunately, both widows received bad news. After contacting Lord Lyons in Washington, the military secretary in Quebec was told that the U.S. Act of Congress, which called for the release of British subjects who were underage, had been repealed, so there was no longer much hope for their — or for anyone else's — discharge.[61]

Samuel Waller of Montreal went right to the American top when he wrote to Abraham Lincoln. Waller and his "two and twenty"-year-old son, George, who was a member of the volunteer artillery company in Montreal, had travelled to New York State to visit relatives. While there, George was enticed to join a company of soldiers under the pledge that they would not leave New York. He foolishly consented and was quickly whisked off to the front lines. His father had difficulty deciding what enraged him more — the fact that his son had been deceived or that his son had only been given the rank of private! Speaking man to man, Samuel informed President Lincoln that this was "far below his station as he's of a family who are and have always been of the highest respectability and immediately connected with some of the Nobility of the British Empire." On a more sentimental note, Samuel continued that his son would not be missed among the hundreds of thousands of troops that Lincoln already had, and that his son "is all the world to me — so that one word from Your Excellency would restore him immediately to his family and friends — and would endear your name to us forever." Unable to help himself, Samuel's weeping eyes seemed to immediately dry by his next sentence — "Unless Your Excellency would appoint him to some more suitable position."[62] Hopefully, this letter would have given the war-weary Lincoln, who was known for his sense of humour, a slight reason to smile.

Dice Williams, a black woman from Amherstburg, had to deal with an even more disturbing situation in trying to have her fourteen-year-old son, Henry Hugh Williams, released from service. According to Henry's sworn deposition, on September 13, 1864, while in Detroit, where the family had only recently moved, a coloured man named Charles Medley and an unnamed white man with red hair asked him to go with them to help with some work. Assuming that he would be paid, Henry consented. Feigning an interest in Henry's handwriting skills, the men produced a paper and asked him to write his name, which he proudly did. When they asked him to do it a second time, a suspicious Henry refused. At that response they became angry, telling the boy that he must do as he was told because he was now a soldier and therefore obliged to follow orders or go to the guard house. Terrified at the prospect, Henry complied.

The youth pictured in this recruiting poster, "Freemen to Arms," brings to mind the underage boys, such as Henry Williams, who enlisted. *Gladstone collection. LOC.*

At an early opportunity, Henry and his mother went to a notary public in Wayne County, Michigan, to make a sworn affidavit as to his age and to the subterfuge that had led him to sign what was now clearly an enlistment form. In addition to being four years too young, Henry also insisted that since the age of five he had pleurisy in his side and was unfit for military duty. In her statement, Dice Williams confirmed her son's age and his story. His age is also confirmed by the 1861 Canada West census for Amherstburg. The case was taken to the Provost Marshal's Office. The response of the investigating official was that Henry had sworn that he was eighteen years and two months and, when questioned further, gave unhesitating, mature answers. The ruling was that there was no undue influence put upon Henry to enlist. Days before his fifteenth birthday, Henry's appeal was refused and he was committed to the army. By his third week in the army, he had to be removed from duty for treatment of pleurisy. Despite all of this, he was assigned to the 102nd USCI, eventually joining the regiment then stationed at Charleston, South Carolina on March 4, 1865. He was mustered out on September 30, 1865 — two days after his sixteenth birthday.[63]

CHAPTER 4

Soldiers

The Colored Soldiers
… And their deeds shall find a record
In their registry of Fame;
For their blood has cleansed completely
Every blot of Slavery's shame.
So all honor and all glory
To those noble sons of Ham—
The gallant colored soldiers
Who fought for Uncle Sam!

— Paul Laurence Dunbar

Well over eleven hundred black men, who had been born or had sought a safe asylum in Canada, volunteered to return to the country from which many of them or their families had once fled to serve in the army and to fight for the freedom of others. They enrolled in many regiments that had been organized in many Northern states, including Michigan, Ohio, New York, Indiana, Illinois, Pennsylvania, Rhode Island, and Connecticut. They also enlisted in regiments raised in the South: Tennessee, Missouri, and Virginia.

They joined heavy artillery units, light artillery units, infantry, and cavalry, as well as the Union navy. While most men joined in units that originally had state designations in their names, most had their designation changed to a number after the federal Bureau of Colored Troops was established on May 22, 1863; for example, the 1st Michigan Colored Infantry became the 102nd Regiment, United States Colored Infantry (USCI) and the 14th Rhode Island Heavy Artillery (Colored) became the 11th United States Colored Heavy Artillery (USCHA) of the United States Colored Troops. However, the 54th and 55th Massachusetts Infantry, the 29th Connecticut Infantry, and the 5th Massachusetts Colored Cavalry maintained their state designation for the duration of the war.

The 54th Massachusetts was one of the first Colored companies formed, and their story was made famous in the movie *Glory*. This powerful film brought to life the incredible hardship that soldiers endured — black soldiers in particular.

In chilling detail, it tells the story of the July 18, 1864 suicidal charge on Fort Wagner, where the Confederate army cut them down like "wheat before the scythe." Although casualties were huge and they were forced

The 55th Massachusetts marching through the streets of Charleston while singing "John Brown's March." *Illus. in AP2.H32 Case Y. LOC.*

to withdraw, it was in some ways a victory because it resoundingly dispelled the popular belief that blacks would not fight. The hometowns of the Canadian soldiers who fought in that regiment include Georgetown, Toronto, St. Catharines, Galt, Woodstock, Fort Erie, London, Malden (Amherstburg), Windsor, Sandwich, Buxton, and Chatham.

Although the film is intensely moving and gives viewers a glimpse of the war and what soldiers faced, it can only scratch the surface of the realities of the bloody confrontations and the hardships that everyone involved — regardless of race — had to endure.

When black soldiers entered into battle, they faced the diabolical reality that if they surrendered or were captured they were often shown no quarter. Stories of atrocities abound. It was written that after being defeated and surrendering at Fort Pillow, Tennessee, blacks were shot or bayoneted. In an even more chilling account, some wounded men were locked into a building, while one poor soul was crucified to the wall with nails through his wrists, before their captors proceeded to set the building on fire. Despite facing these and many other types of horrific possibilities, these men did not forget where they came from, and thus left their families, their homes, and their communities, and joined in the struggle, each with their own histories and motivation.

Those who were most intimately involved with soldiers in the field constantly had trouble finding relief or answers about their loved ones. In June 1864, Adline Dyer of St. Catharines wrote to the U.S. War Department, beseeching them to let her know if her husband Harvey was dead or alive. She described him as a "collord man" belonging to the 14th Heavy Artillery. If he was alive, could they please let her know how he was doing.[1] Four months later, on October 11, Adline wrote a second time, asking the same question. She had received a letter from her husband on August 1, but no more since then. Being of German descent, with an uncertain hand at English spelling, she continued:

... I Wood Like Here From Him As I have A larg Family and Am a lone [illeg] Muss To Talk Care of Four Childrens I Wood like to wharie is Will you Plise to Be So kind To writ To him And Aske him To Send Me

Some Money Be Coz I Am in Nede it Very Much And
To Write To Me As Sune As he get This.

Fortunately, Harvey survived the war, but it would have been difficult to send part of his wages home as the company was paid very sporadically. At the time of his discharge in New Orleans on October 2, 1865, he had been last paid in February. Besides that, he had not yet received the one-hundred-dollar bounty that was promised when he enlisted on November 30, 1863.[2] However, the family were reunited, moved to nearby Welland, and soon added Mary, a little sister for her four brothers.[3]

The story of George M. Lucas brings sharply into focus the many hardships that some soldiers and their families had to endure. Leaving behind his family in Canada, Lucas travelled to Clifton Park, New York to enlist as a private in Company F of the 26th USCI. He was mustered in at the training camp on Riker's Island, New York on Feb 27, 1864, and the regiment was sent to the Department of the South at Beaufort, South Carolina in April, where they were to be involved in several engagements in the months that followed. Lucas was among those who participated in the Battle of Burdens Causeway, or as it became more vividly referred to, the "Battle of Bloody Bridge." The fight took place on Johns Island, which remained in Confederate hands that protected Charleston, which was the critical hub of the South. As part of a larger brigade, composed of both black and white regiments under Brigadier General John P. Hatch, Lucas and the 26th and 9th USCI made the arduous march toward Johns Island under stifling heat that greatly sapped their endurance. They were also temporarily halted when a new bridge had to be constructed to the island to replace the one that the Confederates had burned.

They continued on under the bombardment of their enemy, who held the higher ground. On the afternoon of July 7, 1864, the 26th launched an attack on the Confederate rifle pits, at first partially protected by trees, before a final charge across an open field. After heavy close-range combat with many killed and wounded, the rifle pits were taken, only to be retaken again by the enemy forces, who had been reinforced with newly arrived additional troops, forcing the 26th to retreat. The battle continued for the next two days, some of it through fog so thick that

26th USCT, in which Canadian George M. Lucas enlisted. *NARA*.

it was difficult to see, with back and forth movement from both sides. Ultimately, the Union forces were forced to retreat from the island.

In October of that same year, he received tragic news from home. On October 14, he had a literate comrade pen a letter from his station at Battery Taylor, near Beaufort, South Carolina, using the vocabulary of the army:

> I have the honor to ask for a Furlough for thirty (30) days to visit my home near Niagara Falls, state of New York. I have there a family of five small children, lately made destitute by the death of their only remaining support — a mother. They are left among strangers, and it is necessary that I should go home if possible, and make some provision for them.
>
> Most respectfully,
> Your obed't Servant
> his X mark
> George M. Lucas

The request was quickly approved by the various levels of army bureaucracy — first by the captain of the regiment, then the lieutenant-colonel, followed by the colonel, before getting final approval by Brigadier- General Rufus Saxton three days later.

The army paid for Lucas's transportation from South Carolina to his place of enrolment in New York State. However, $9.11 was deducted from his pay for the train from New York City to Niagara Falls, and an additional $7.69 from Rochester to New York on the return trip. Lucas had only a short time to comfort his children with some of the thirty-day furlough being consumed by transportation, most of it by train. However, he did what he could before returning to his post within the allotted time by November 15, 1864. Sadly, George Lucas did not survive the war, succumbing to acute dysentery on June 2, 1865 at Beaufort, where he was buried the next day.[4] It was not until over four years later, on September 30, 1869, that a "D. Palmer" made an application for George Lucas's pension on behalf of his orphaned children; Mr. Palmer was guardian for at least one of the children at the time.

Disease was the great killer of the war, much of it caused by the exposure to the elements. According to a report from the U.S. Army Medical Department, in the year ending June 30, 1864, there were 190,000 cases of blacks being treated by medical staff, and only four percent of those were for wounds or injuries. The total number of cases is staggering, considering that, by the medical department's figures, there were approximately 186,000 black soldiers in the entire war. The disease rate for blacks was almost twice that of whites, and their death rate from disease was four times higher.[5]

Among those fatalities was twenty-two-year-old Jacob Hicks from Canada, who enlisted at Goshen, New York into Company I of the 20th U.S. Colored Infantry on October 10, 1864. He died of typhoid fever on March 13, 1865 at Corps d'Afrique General Hospital in New Orleans. The sexton was directed that "his remains should be interred with the usual military honors" in the colored section of the Union military cemetery in New Orleans, Louisiana.[6]

Silas Robison of St. Catharines suffered a similar fate. A private in the 55th Massachusetts, Robison, who enlisted at Readville, Massachusetts on May 31, 1863, never got to leave the state, succumbing to "typhus fever" on July 16 of the same year. According to his compiled military service record, orders had been issued for Robison to receive a promotion to corporal, a position that he did not live to see.

Benjamin Matthews of Buxton, who enlisted in the 102nd USCI, was another who did not get to leave the state in which he was mustered. Benjamin, who worked aboard a Great Lakes ship, married his Dresden sweetheart, Nancy Jane Johnson, less than one month before he volunteered in Detroit on September 26, 1863. Hearty, robust, and capable, he was promoted to corporal two weeks later. However, the freezing conditions that the recruits had to endure soon caused him to be hospitalized, and he was unable to depart with the rest of his regiment when they began their trip to the south. The regiment was in Hilton Head, South Carolina when they received the news that Matthews's father had secured a furlough for his ailing son and had taken him back to Canada, where he died in his parent's house of the effects of consumption on January 25, 1864.[7]

Eighteen-year-old Henry Thomas from "New London," Canada went to St. Louis, Missouri on August 15, 1864 to enlist as a substitute in the 18th USCI. The examining surgeon described Thomas as five-foot, six inches tall, with brown hair, black eyes, and a "yellow complexion." He died of typhoid pneumonia on November 25 at the General Hospital in the Benton Barracks in that same state. Up to the time of his death, he had not received any pay, and, as a substitute, was not entitled to any bounty. Charged against his pay was the cost of his clothing, knapsack, canteen, and haversack, which totalled $36.84. His clothing consisted of a greatcoat, a pair of trousers, a pair of flannel "drawers," and a flannel shirt.

Yet another who died of disease was a Chatham storekeeper, Alexander Atwood. He was among the many Canadians who enrolled in the 14th Rhode Island Heavy Artillery (later renamed 11th U.S. Colored Heavy Artillery). He was born in Prairie Bluff, Alabama, thirty-five years before he enlisted on October 3, 1863. His fascinating past is among the many complex and extraordinary histories of the era of slavery. Alexander, along with his six mulatto siblings, was the child of a slave woman named Candis and their master, Henry Stiles Atwood.[8] Henry was a wealthy cotton plantation owner worth an estimated three- or four-hundred thousand dollars. On August 3, 1843, he drew up his last will and testament, which included several controversial clauses concerning his slaves. As an extra precaution, he appointed two different sets of executors in case one or more died or refused to carry out his wishes.[9] His concerns were justified by the events, including the refusal of his executors to act, which followed his death in September 1851.

Court-appointed administrators ordered the sale of the 800 bales of cotton, all perishable property of every description, 100 slaves for cash and another 175 to be sold at public auction. All of these sales were accomplished without complications. However, the special clauses related to Candis and their children were problematic. According to Henry's wishes, each of the children were to receive eight thousand dollars, with half invested in land in Indiana, Illinois, or Michigan, and half in secure mortgages or bonds, for their use. Candis was to receive two thousand dollars. Knowing that it was against the law to free slaves and allow them to remain in Alabama, Henry instructed his executors, who would have temporary ownership, to deliver all of the family who remained in Alabama to a free state. During his lifetime, Henry Atwood had already taken nine-year-old Alexander and his sister, Ann, six, to Ohio, and placed them in the charge of one Lemuel Brown, thereby practically — if not legally — giving them their freedom. At the time, Candis also had two older children whose father was black. They too would get their freedom, but not be entitled to a financial bequest.[10] All necessary expenses to remove the family to a free state, for clothing and furniture, plus provisions for six months, were to be borne by the estate, as was the final charge to the executors concerning the children — "to make such arrangements as will secure them a good English education."[11]

Henry Atwood's legal heirs, his sisters, one Sally C. Northrop, who was to be given five thousand dollars with the stipulation that none of it be allowed to "be in the control of her husband," and Hannah M. Worster (who was not even mentioned), as well as many other Southerners, were deeply troubled by a variety of issues that arose from the will, and took the matter to the Wilcox County, Alabama's Chancery Court. Sally Northrop and her two sons, who were also bequeathed the remainder of the estate, which stood to be tens of thousands of dollars, argued that the bequest of money and property to the slaves was void. Also, since the executors who were appointed as guardians for the slaves refused to act upon Henry's instructions, the Northrops requested ownership be given to them. Part of their reasoning was that since they lived in the free state of Wisconsin, they were in a logical geographic and practical position to escort the slaves there. Appearing to desire to honour Henry's wishes (with the glaring exception of the financial details) the Northrops appealed to the judge's sense of family by arguing that "they would feel bound, by the ties of blood as well as those of justice and humanity, to carry into full and complete execution what was the intention of said Atwood, deceased."

The rulings were complex. Since Alexander and Ann Atwood were already quasi-free in Ohio, it was quickly ruled that they were entitled to their inheritance. However, the presiding chancellor ruled that the slaves remaining in Alabama could not be emancipated as instructed in the will, nor were they entitled to the money allotted to them. Verbalizing the harsh reality of the time, the chancellor reminded those in attendance "that, being slaves, they must be treated as such" and that the proceeds of the estate belonged to the Northrops. Neither the Northrops nor the administrators were completely satisfied with the decisions and appealed to Alabama's Supreme Court.

The Northrops disagreed with the chancellor's ruling, insisting that although Alexander and Ann were physically in Ohio, they were not truly free and therefore the legacies of eight thousand dollars each were not valid. Their argument was that it was a "natural right" for an owner to do what he pleased with his slaves during his life, but:

> ... the right of disposition after death is the creature of society, and of law... A man may burn up his property, or may sell it and cast the proceeds into the sea, but a will directing his executors to do these things would scarcely be held good and valid. Atwood might have sold his estate, and taken the proceeds to New York, or any other free state, and there established a press for the printing and distribution among our slaves of incendiary publications to excite them to insurrection; but if he had bequeathed his estate to executors or

trustees, for the purpose of such an establishment, our courts would certainly declare it void, as being against the policy of the State.

While philosophically concurring with the latter sentiment, Franklin Beck, the court appointed administrator of the will, disagreed with the former part, arguing that the legacies left to the slaves in Alabama should not have been ruled void and that they should be carried out, opining that "the owner of property has the absolute control and dominion over it, and this dominion he can relinquish at pleasure." This control that the owner expressed in his will while alive should be considered valid after his death. Technically, the will did not emancipate the slaves while in Alabama, but rather directed the executors to take them to a free State, "that they may acquire freedom by the silent operation of the laws of that State," which were laws that Alabama had no jurisdiction to interfere with.

In his lengthy decision, Supreme Court Justice William P. Chilton made what would seem by most slaves as a clumsy attempt to display his compassionate side:

In considering the rules which apply to, and regulate this peculiar species of property, we must look upon them in the double capacity of chattels and intelligent beings. Considered in this latter capacity, our law, pervaded as it is by the spirit of Christianity, and founded on principles of humanity and benevolence, throws around them its protection.

Judge Chilton recognized that there was no ambiguity in Henry Atwood's intentions for his slaves when he wrote his will. They would be allowed to be carried out of Alabama by the executor, who would be at the mercy of his own conscience to see that the slaves also received their inheritance. As for Alexander and Ann, Chilton confirmed that they should be regarded as "free persons of color," receive their inheritance, and "never more be taken to a slave State."[12]

As a result of the ruling, the remainder of the enslaved Atwood family was taken to Ohio, arriving at Ripley on May 15, 1853.[13] There, after a decade and a half of separation, they were reunited with Alexander and Ann. Henry Atwood would have been happy to know that the families of his two slave mothers, Candis and Mary, were comfortably living side-by-side, their children attending colleges when they came of age, and, within seven years, thanks to wise investments by the executors, each child having a net worth of $17,750.[14]

A year later, the size of the family increased when Alexander married Priscilla J. Hartsell, formerly from Jonesboro, Tennessee, in nearby Brown County, Ohio, on June 13, 1854. Shortly after their marriage, the couple, along with Alexander's sister, Ann, and her husband, moved to Chatham and started both a family and a successful business, which they regularly advertised as having "a large assortment of groceries of the first quality, which will be sold on the most reasonable terms" in the *Provincial Freeman*, whose office was just down the street.

Atwood's feelings against slavery ran deep, writing to his friend and business partner, Henry Jackson: "If roasting on a bed of coals of fire, would do away with the curse of slavery, I would be willing to be the sacrifice." Demonstrating that his words were not hollow, he left Priscilla and his thirteen-year-old daughter from a former marriage, Sarahfine, and departed to Providence, Rhode Island — as did many others from Canada. He quickly became a model soldier. William H. Chenery, a white officer and historian of the 14th, was effusive with his praise when it came to Atwood, writing:

> He was known throughout the regiment as a modest and conscientious man, and was greatly respected by both officers and me. His patriotism was unquestioned, having journeyed from Canada to enlist in the Union army in the States. At home he was a man of prominence among his people, having acquired considerable property, and it is said was the proprietor of a grocery store, and was doing a thriving business at the time of his enlistment.[15]

Other officers in the regiment concurred with Chenery's assessment. On August 22, 1864, Private Atwood was promoted to corporal, and by the end of the month was made sergeant. He also assisted the captain with record-keeping, copying information on muster rolls, and performing other duties as the company's clerk. Interestingly, Alexander and three of his brothers became referred to as "the fighting Atwoods," as all left comfortable positions to serve in the army: twenty-eight-year-old Julius, a graduate of Iberia College, Ohio, who had lived in Chatham with Alexander at the beginning of the war, enlisted into the 100th USCI in Cincinnati, later appointed as quarter master–sergeant; twenty-two-year-old Daniel, also a graduate of Iberia College, enrolled in the 100th USCI in Columbus, Ohio, and later appointed quarter master–sergeant-major.[16] Twenty-five-year-old brother John enrolled in Cincinnati in the U.S. Navy and served aboard the USS *Grossbeak*.[17] Younger half-brother Kinchin, who had a black father, pulled himself erect to his full height — which was variously given as five foot two inches and five foot four inches — while having his medical examination, and stretched his age by a couple of years when he joined the 5th USCI in Cincinnati. In the 1840s and 1850s, their brother William was active in the Underground Railroad at the critical spot of Ripley, across from the slave state of Kentucky, on the shore of the Ohio River, metaphorically known as "the River Jordan." According to William's obituary, he helped many slaves make their way through Ohio enroute to Canada.[18] In the earliest days of the Civil War, William organized a volunteer company of coloured troops in Ohio and offered their services to the Union army, an offer that was refused.[19]

Of course, every soldier had their own history that is worthy of being remembered. Some, like Atwood's, were covered in the national press. Richard M. Johnson, who enlisted in Michigan's 102nd USCI, was originally a slave from Bath County, Virginia, who made a daring and eventful escape to Ohio, and was a part of one of the watershed national stories related to slavery, commonly referred to as "the Lemmon slave case." Those persons were brothers, sister, and family members of Richard Johnson. Jonathon Lemmon and his wife, Juliet, decided to move with their eight slaves from Virginia to Texas. They made the mistake of going to the free city of New York to catch the ship. Once there, the slaves were advised by other blacks that they were free by virtue of being in the free state of New York. Dramatic and lengthy court cases that lasted for over six years followed, in which the Lemmons' and the State of Virginia's lawyers argued against the validity of a state law vs. federal law. Richard Johnson, who was then working in a Cleveland hotel, learned of the story and escorted these slaves to certain freedom — first to Amherstburg, and then to Buxton — removing any chance that his relatives would be returned to their former owners.[20] In one of the famous Lincoln/Douglass debates for a U.S. Senate seat in 1858, during which Lincoln delivered the famous lines, "A house divided against itself cannot stand," and, "I believe this government cannot endure, permanently half slave and half free," the future president referred to the case, illustrating its national importance.

The story of Benjamin Blackburn, who was in the 102nd USCI along with Johnson, did not make the newspapers, but it survives in his own few words on the pages of abolitionist Benjamin Drew's important work, *A North-Side View of Slavery: The Refugee: or the Narratives of Fugitive Slaves in Canada*:

> I was born in Maysville, Ky. I got here last Tuesday eve-
> ning, and spent the Fourth of July in Canada. I felt as
> big and free as any man could feel, and I worked part of
> the day for my own benefit: I guess my master's time is
> out. Seventeen came away in the same gang that I did.[21]

Touissant L. Delany, an eighteen-year-old student from Chatham, was enlisted into the 54th Massachusetts by his famous father, Martin, who had long been in the national spotlight. He was among the many wounded at Fort Wagner and remained hospitalized at Beaufort, South Carolina for over four months. He returned to duty in December, before being hospitalized again in February, this time at Jacksonville, Florida. After recovering, he was detached from his regiment on recruiting duty, following in his father's foot-steps. He was mustered out at Charleston on August 20, 1865. Despite his service and sacrifice, he was charged ninety cents for having lost his haver-sack and canteen. He had not received any clothing since August 31, 1864, and by the reckoning of army officials, he was due $1.92 for his thriftiness.[22]

John Brown, a sailor from Fort Erie, was also a member of the 54th Massachusetts, Company F. Brown, who had experienced the carnage of war, must have been in for a different shock of a lifetime when he peeked inside one of the regiment's stables. He was called as a witness to testify at the court martial of a lonesome fellow soldier, James Riley. The charge was "Bestiality" with the specific details:

> In this that Private James Riley, Cp A. 54th Mass Vols., did on the 5th day of November 1864 between the hours of 8 and 9 o'clock P.M. proceed to the stables of the horses belonging to the Field and Staff of the 54th Mass Vols. and did then and there hold sexual connection with a mare.[23]

Brown gave explicit details of what he had witnessed. The doctor, who was called in immediately to examine both the horse, which he observed "showed unusual irritability," and the man, had his suspicions but was unable to definitively prove the charges. Two other soldiers spoke well of Riley's character. As a result, Riley was found "not guilty." Despite this, the same doctor directed guards to strip, tie, and gag Riley while he circumcised the man. The doctor did not use any anaesthetic, and seared the wound with a hot iron to make it more painful.[24]

It is interesting to note the distance that some Canadian men would travel to enlist. William Hooper of Buxton travelled to Toledo, Ohio to enroll as a substitute on November 15, 1864. Rather than being enrolled in an Ohio regiment, Hooper was placed in one from Tennessee: the 14th USCI. Hooper survived the Union victory at the Battle of Nashville in mid-December 1864, while sixty-five of his regimental comrades were killed, wounded, or missing. The regiment also joined the pursuit of the retreating and battered Confederate army of Tennessee into Alabama. By the following March, Hooper was entrusted with the position of orderly at the First Colored Brigade Headquarter, and by July was appointed a provost guard in Knoxville, a position often reserved for some of the most trusted and capable soldiers. The provost guards served as the military police for the Union army, enforcing military discipline and acting as the security force for the headquarters. Their duties also included guarding Confederate prisoners.

William Hooper of the 14th USCT, who survived the Battle of Nashville, is the author's great, great grandfather. *Courtesy of BNHS&M.*

Henry Cosby was a diminutive five-foot-two, twenty-two-year-old barber from Kingston when he enlisted in the 5th Massachusetts Cavalry on July 23, 1864. For a portion of his enlistment he served as a company clerk. Some of the cavalry's time was spent in Maryland, and his regiment was among those who were sent to Texas near the end of the war. While there, Cosby fell ill and spent most of July and August in the hospital at Brazos. At the time that he was mustered in he received the first one-hundred-dollar instalment of the three-hundred-dollar bounty that was promised. Like all of the others, he was to find that their monthly pay was extremely irregular. When he was mustered out at Clarksville, Texas on October 31, 1865, he had not been paid since December 31, 1864.[25]

Black Canadians continued to enlist even into the war's final days. A twenty-year-old young man with a name that brought a smile to the face, departed from the Chatham area farm of his father and namesake and enlisted into the 102nd as a substitute in March of 1865. It would be the end of the month before Pleasant Kidd was delivered to the Department of the South in South Carolina, and the end of April before he was assigned to a company.

Not everyone signed for noble or pecuniary reasons. In March 1865, forty-three-year-old William Wheeler of Dresden had been committed to prison on charges of raping Emily Wilson. Wheeler was well connected in the area, and through his influence was released on bail and immediately was whisked across the border to Pontiac, Michigan. There, he enlisted in the 102nd USCI, pocketing a $331 bounty. His father-in-law and a friend had agreed to stand surety of two hundred dollars each that Wheeler would appear in court to answer to the charge of attempted rape. The Grand Jury ruled that the more serious charge of rape was appropriate. Wheeler was now beyond the reach of the courts and a Kent County magistrate demanded the bail money from the guarantors. Following the strict letter of the law, Judges of the Queen's Bench ruled that bail had been set on the condition that Wheeler attend court to face the lesser charge, but not the more serious charge. Therefore, his sureties were under no obligation to come up with the money.[26]

There were a few black men in Canada who in fact joined white regiments. George H. Dunn and his younger brother Charles were two such examples. Their family's story was quite unique. Their father, George Braxton Dunn, had been born a slave in Virginia, but was raised in Frankfort, Kentucky by a Baptist minister. Dunn considered his owner to be more tolerant than many and felt that having been beaten only once made his lot relatively painless.

Dunn's recollection of the past, which was mildly dismissive about observing or experiencing cruelty, is common with that of a great many former slaves. When asked by a member of the Freedmen's Inquiry Commission about his treatment as a slave, he replied "our folks weren't treated so awful bad. We couldn't do more work than are boss wanted us to do, of course, but then, we weren't worked and drive so bad as some people were."[27] As to what he had witnessed, his answer was, "I never saw any particular cases of cruelty; but at the time I was a boy, they used to be very cruel with their slaves round about Louisville, whipping selling and driving them, and all such as that."[28] He also mentioned a slave trader named Moffit, who lived near him in Frankfort, who would drive hundreds of handcuffed slaves at a time.

Number 11 is George Dunn Jr., a mixed-race Canadian in the white 27th Michigan, posing with his comrades in this Grand Army of the Republic's Col. Wm. Fenton Post No. 24 photo taken in Fenton, Michigan on July 4, 1892. Dunn opened a barber shop in Fenton after the war, returned to Canada in the 1890s, and spent his final years in Kansas until his death in 1921. *Courtesy of Fenton Historical Society with special thanks to Cheryl Hill Canty.*

Despite his comparative contentment, Dunn, who "bought my time, & paid $500 for it" was philosophical and expressed, "but slavery as a general thing is a hard system, and as soon as I could get out of it, I thought I would."[29]

When that opportunity arose, Dunn moved to Cleveland in the free state of Ohio, and on August 26, 1838 the bachelor, who was in his late thirties, married Mary Ann Jackson, a Creole woman twenty years his junior.[30] The couple quickly began their family, having two children in Ohio, before having eight more after moving to St. Thomas, Canada West in 1851, and later to nearby London. Dunn's barbering business prospered in the new country, where he occasionally cleared the princely sum of fifty dollars a month. However, in the Civil War years, times became more difficult, and by 1863 his monthly income fell to less than five dollars. Perhaps to help supplement the family's income, in February of that year his sons George Henry and Charles decided to travel due west to Port Huron across the St. Clair River, which separated the United States from that portion of British North America, to enlist in a Michigan regiment.

These sons participated in some of the major engagements during the war, including the Battle of the Crater, where George H. was wounded in the knee.

Numerous white Canadians served as officers in the coloured regiments. Among them was Thomas Kennedy, who had been born in Montreal. He had worked as a blacksmith before enlisting as a drummer in the 117th Illinois at Camp Butler, Illinois on August 12, 1862. When the opportunity arose for a higher rank, prestige, and pay, the nineteen-year-old was accepted as an orderly-sergeant in the 1st Tennessee Heavy Artillery, African Descent, later renamed the 3rd United States Colored Heavy Artillery, which spent much of the war defending Memphis. A scant four weeks after his twentieth birthday, Kennedy applied for the position of 2nd Lieutenant, a position he received after a detailed examination of his qualifications and abilities by a military board.[31]

Private Louis Labrush, also from Montreal, followed a similar path, transferring from the 45th Illinois Volunteer Infantry to become First Sergeant of the 2nd Battery Louisiana Colored Light Artillery, which he was mustered into at Black River Bridge, Mississippi.[32] Joseph Fitzgerald and Alonzo Wolverton, both of Wolverton in Oxford County, Canada West, were officers in the 9th U.S. Colored Heavy Artillery.[33]

Like Thomas Kennedy, Alonzo Wolverton was also promoted as a very young man, as he revealed in his letter of acceptance:

20th Battery O V A Nashville Tenn.
Dec 17th 64

I have the honor to acknowledge the receipt of an appointment as 2nd Lieut. in 9th U S C Art and accept same.

I am (21) years of age, was born in the town of
Blenheim Canada West and my present residence is
20th Battery O V A
I am very respectfully

Your Obt. Servt.
Alonzo Wolverton Corp.
20th Battery O V A

Wolverton was one of four brothers who fought in the Union army. He
had been forced to mature very quickly, having previously fought in the
white 20th Battery Ohio Volunteer Artillery, and having become a prisoner of war following the Union surrender at Dalton, Georgia. He and
the other white men who were captured were more fortunate than the
black soldiers who surrendered with them, the men of the 44th USCI.
Following the surrender, soldiers were separated by race, and the blacks
were stripped of their shoes and uniforms and placed into slavery.[34]
Wolverton and the other white soldiers were compelled to sign a document on October 15, 1864 that included the words "I A. Wolverton
being a prisoner of war in the hands of the CSA do solemnly swear that
I will not bear arms against the Confederate States or aid or assist any
one so doing until regularly exchanged."[35] Wolverton was soon paroled,
and perhaps it was that experience that helped to motivate him to soon
become an officer in a black regiment.

Sergeant Edward J. Wheeler of the 4th USCI was a freeborn black with
Native American ancestry on his mother's side. As a few other soldiers
felt compelled to do, Wheeler wrote to *The Christian Recorder* to keep
the interested public informed of life at the front. In one letter written
from their base near Yorktown, Virginia, he shared that he had a hand
in recruiting his regiment. A deeply religious man, Wheeler's letters were
full of optimism, spiritual references, and praise to God. He was at peace
with himself and whatever might lie ahead, vowing "that I will fight as
long as a star can be seen, and if such should be my lot to be cut down
in battle, I do believe, from clear experience, that my soul will be forever
at rest."[36] In another letter, Wheeler spoke of living in Quebec before the
war, where he learned that the soldiers of Queen Victoria's dominion all

received the same pay, regardless of race; he lamented that they had not received any money, leaving their families in desperate straits.[37]

A final glimpse at a man with a Canadian connection brings us to Horace Lee, the slave of John W. Lee of Fayette County, Kentucky. Although a slave state, Kentucky remained in the Union during the war, and therefore the slaves were not freed by the terms of the Emancipation Proclamation. Kentuckians were still eligible for the draft, and when John W. Lee's name was called, he elected to have his slave go in his place. It is interesting to note that the official form that Horace signed with an "X" listed his occupation as "laborer," and the form itself was titled "Substitute Volunteer Enlistment." Perhaps the enlistment was voluntary because the slave would be granted his freedom by being mustered in.

John Lee completed the "Claim for Compensation for Enlisted Slave" by making oath about his loyalty to the Government of the United States in accordance to the general orders of the Department of War and signed the Oath of Allegiance. Further, John Lee provided proof of ownership of the slave by having two white men swear that they were positive that John was the rightful owner of Horace, and that John had faithfully remained loyal to the Union. These men also had to swear the Oath of Allegiance. These documents that were part of the claim "for compensation for service of a slave," which allowed up to three hundred dollars for the lost services of the slave, were not signed until January 7, 1867, nearly three years after Horace had enlisted, and more than a year and a half after the war was over.

Just eighteen years old, Horace was described as having black hair and eyes with a copper complexion. The five-foot eight-inch man was mustered in at Lexington on May 8, 1864. He was promoted to corporal of Company C on August 19, 1864. The regiment spent much of their tour of duty in defense of Nashville and the Northwestern Railroad.

Horace was wounded at the Battle of Nashville on December 15, 1864. His wound must have been relatively minor as he returned to duty in January, and remained so for the rest of the war. After being mustered on the day after Christmas, 1865, Horace made his way to the Raleigh Plains in Kent County, Canada West, where his parents were already living. Finding that they had changed their surname from Lee to Black,

Horace Lee adopted the surname "Black" after joining his family in Canada after the war. *Courtesy of BNHS&M.*

Horace followed suit and did so as well. He spent the remainder of his life on the Plains, becoming a wealthy landowner with hired men to care for the farm. He became the father of six children, and, after the death of his first wife, remarried and had nine more. Both Horace Black, and later his widow, Julia, received pensions from the U.S. government for his service during the war.

CHAPTER 5

"They Also Serve ...": Doctors, Nurses, and Chaplains

It became a struggle between beautiful right and ugly wrong — it determined whether civilization or barbarism should rule, whether freedom or slavery should prevail upon this continent.

— Dr. Anderson Ruffin Abbott[1]

D octors played an important role in the conflict by examining black recruits as soon as they were allowed to enlist. Occasionally, they slipped up on the job. Eighteen-year-old Albert J. Ratliff from Gosfield Township, Essex County eagerly travelled to Ypsilanti and enlisted in the 102nd on November 18, 1863. For most of the following months, he was a patient in the barracks hospital in Detroit. On August 20, 1864, it was noted that he had been unfit for duty for sixty days within the past two months, suffering from a disease of the lungs. On September 1, 1864, his disgusted military commander gave Ratliff a Certificate of Discharge, noting that the soldier's ...

Phythisis Pulmonalis disease evidently existed prior to enlistment. This soldier should not have been passed by

the examining Surgeon, as there must have been sufficient evidence at that time of a sowfulous diathesis. He
is totally unfit for the service.

During Ratliff's brief stint in the army, one of the only military duties
that he could relate to his family was that he had been on light duty and
had served as a guard at the kitchen in February of 1864. By March of
1866, Ratliff died and was buried in Detroit's Elmwood Cemetery.[2]

Two black doctors from Toronto, Alexander Thomas Augusta and
Anderson Abbott, as well as John Rapier, who received part of his education in Canada and was a friend and former classmate of Abbott's,
served as surgeons during the Civil War. The relationships between these
three men hint at the interconnectedness of Canada West's black community across the province, despite the distance that may have separated
the individuals. Indeed, there were close relationships from individuals on both sides of the international border, many which were further
strengthened or established because of the war.

Alexander T. Augusta and Anderson Abbott's father, Wilson Ruffin
Abbott, were both originally from Virginia, and although Augusta was
twenty-four years younger, both established themselves as leading figures in
Toronto's black community. As such, they had many opportunities to meet
a great number of important anti-slavery activists included in this book,
including Delany, H. Ford Douglas, and the Shadds. Augusta was a friend
of the Shadd family and had boarded at the patriarch's Raleigh Township
farm for some time in 1858.[3] Augusta regularly advertised his Toronto
Drug Store in the *Provincial Freeman*, informing the public that he not only
filled prescriptions, applied leeches, performed bleedings, and pulled teeth,
but also sold other chemical products such as perfume and dyes.

Augusta was freeborn in Norfolk, Virginia. When he attempted to
attend the University of Pennsylvania's medical school, he faced the same
racial barriers as Martin Delany and numerous other blacks. Augusta
shared some of that background in a January 7, 1863 letter, written from
Toronto directly to President Lincoln and Secretary of War Stanton, in
which he requested that he be granted the position of surgeon for one of
the coloured regiments that were going to be formed, or as a physician

Major Alexander T. Augusta. *Courtesy of Sharon Knecht, Archivist, Oblate Sisters of Providence Archives.*

for one of the depots where freedmen gathered. He explained that he had been forced to leave the country of his nativity because prejudice would not allow him to attend a medical school in the United States. Since then, he had received his degree at "one of the principal educational institutions [Trinity College] of this Province," had practiced for six years, and could provide references by some of the most distinguished members of the profession as to his character and qualifications.[4] Within two weeks Augusta received a reply from the Assistant Secretary of War, directing him to arrange an examination with the U.S. Surgeon General.

The examination was set for March 25, 1863 in Washington. However, two days before the examination was to take place, the Surgeon General wrote to the Secretary of War, stating, "I believe there has been a mistake in this case, and I respectfully ask the within invitation be recalled." The issues raised were not only that he was a "person of color," but also that he was a British subject, and it would be against the Queen's neutrality for him to be hired. However, the colour issue seemed to be the foremost obstacle.

The *New York Times* of March 30, 1863 reported that the medical department had received an application from a Canadian (Augusta) who wished to be examined by the examining board in Washington. It was necessary for the applicant to receive a permit endorsed by a senior doctor before being examined. This doctor readily signed the permit, which was handed to him by "a respectable looking colored man, whom he supposed was the would-be Doctor's servant, never dreaming that the colored gentleman was himself the candidate."[5] Upon discovering that this was indeed the case, the astonished examiners refused to proceed and instead contacted Edwin Stanton, Secretary of War, to ask that the permission be revoked.

In response to this, Augusta wrote to the presidents and to the members of the army's medical board, protesting that he had made it clear in his previous correspondence that he was a black man and complaining that after an expensive trip of nearly one thousand miles, he had not been treated fairly in his examination. Despite whatever his instincts told him, things were happening behind the scenes and on April 1, the medical board recommended that Augusta be appointed as surgeon for one of the black regiments.

Augusta would continue to face challenges that were particularly unworthy of his military status. On May 1, 1863, while riding on public transportation in Baltimore, dressed in full uniform with the shoulder straps indicting that he was a major in the United States Army, the black officer attracted a great deal of attention. Sensing the disgust of the onlookers from the slave state of Maryland and from the city that historically was the base for several slave pens, a police officer advised Augusta to take a less prominent seat and hide his rank. When the latter refused, a group of men attacked him and cut off his straps. As the crowd worked themselves into a frenzy, it was feared that Augusta would be killed. Were it not for the nearby presence and rescue by a group of soldiers who were guarding the train depot, the murder would have been accomplished. Instead, the guards rushed Augusta to the offices of Colonel William S. Fish, provost marshal of Baltimore, while a mob of several hundred people followed. After hiding Augusta away for hours, he was taken to the depot under the protection of an army officer and several detectives. Despite this guard, Augusta was physically attacked by a citizen, whose punch to the face caused a gush of blood to flow from the wound. Fearing death, Augusta ran to a nearby house, all the while pursued by a crowd that was yelling "kill him," but the woman who was observing the scene slammed the door and refused to allow him to enter. The officers who were charged with guarding Augusta finally had to threaten the rioters with their revolvers before they could safely deliver Augusta to the train station, which carried him to relative safety further north.[6]

One of Augusta's first duties was to examine would-be recruits to determine if they were physically capable of withstanding the rigours of army life and of war. While so employed, several white soldiers from two white Pennsylvania regiments attacked and wounded some of the coloured volunteers with stones. The blacks did not respond, knowing that later that day some of them would be a part of a parade of a black battalion that would have the morale-boosting experience of marching on Capitol Hill, past the Capitol building.[7]

Days later, on May 23, the Surgeon General, acting under the direction of the Secretary of War, ordered Augusta to take charge of the Contraband Camp near Alexandria, Virginia — a position that he physically assumed four days later. One of his first overwhelming challenges was dealing with a smallpox epidemic that was then raging, according to *The Christian Recorder* of October 3, 1863, "at the rate sixty and a hundred a month." Augusta served at the camp for just over four months, after which he was transferred to join his regiment, the 7th United States Colored Troops, at Baltimore. That assignment was very brief, as new orders were issued on October 28, 1863 directing him to report to Colonel William Birney of the 2nd USCI for duty as an examining surgeon for new recruits. By the last day of the year he was transferred once again, this time to Camp Stanton in Benedict, Maryland, before moving to Birney Barracks in Baltimore where Augusta continued in the same role.

In a letter to his superior, Augusta listed the tools of the trade that he possessed, conjuring up grisly images of the bloody realities of treating wounded soldiers. These tools that he carried in a mahogany case included two amputating knives; dissection forceps; five scalpels; one hernia knife; one sharp, pointed, and curved fistouring knife; one artery needle; bone forceps; two pair of bullet forceps; catheters; one tourniquet screw; twelve surgeon's needles; and a variety of saws that he described as "one Capital, one Chain, one Metacarpal & one Hey's saw." In what he described as his "pocket case," Augusta carried a smaller and more portable combination of a select number of instruments.[8]

While Augusta was on detached duty, rumblings were stirring at his regiment as the challenges of racism that had dogged him throughout his personal and professional life again arose, this time by one of his subordinates who had specifically requested and received a posting with a coloured regiment. On May 14, 1864, assistant surgeon Joel Morse wrote a lengthy letter from the 7th USCI's posting in Jacksonville, Florida to Ohio Senator John Sherman, complaining of "a wrong to which I, with others have been subjected" — that is, "to my surprise and indignation" working under a commissioned officer who was "a colored man!" Morse had immediately written to the Surgeon General, "remonstrating against being placed in such a relationship and asking a transfer to some Regiment where my Superior Officer should be a white man." That request was forwarded to the Secretary of War who pointedly refused it. Before an outraged Morse had a chance to tender his resignation, Augusta was placed on detached service away from his regiment, thereby also away from Morse. Even in the absence of his commanding officer, Morse sent yet another letter to the Department of War to remedy this "grave, unjust, and humiliating" situation. Receiving no reply, Morse turned to his senator to use his political influence. In an unconvincing attempt to justify his position, Morse included his personal feelings, which were not uncommon among many other Northerners:

> I claim to be behind no one in a desire for the elevation and improvement of the colored race, and am willing to Sacrifice much in So grand a cause or noble a work; but I cannot willingly compromise what I consider a proper self-respect, and if Surgeon Augusta were to return to the regiment today, I should resign immediately; not from any personal feeling against him, but from principle.

Continuing with his letter, Morse posed additional arguments that would resonate throughout the war and for generations to come:

If a sufficient number of intelligent and educated colored men can be found to officer a regiment, complete from Colonel down to Second Lieutenant, I say well and good, appoint them, and have a colored regiment complete in officers as well as men. Either make the officers all white or all black. I for one do not care which; but this thing of amalgamation or miscegenation in the appointment of officers I do not believe in. Perhaps when I shall have attained to perfect manhood with full sense of the word, I shall just as cheerfully assent to having my most intimate associate or Superior officer a colored man, as a white one; but I am free to confess that I do not expect to attain that State of perfection in this life.

Morse did not have to follow through on his threat to immediately resign, as Augusta remained away from his regiment for the rest of the war; he was stationed at Birney Barracks until May of 1865, when he was reassigned to the recruiting service at the Department of the South in Beaufort, South Carolina — a posting that lasted through the end of the war. In those final months, Augusta had the distinction of being promoted to the rank of lieutenant-colonel of volunteers.

Being the son of parents who were actively involved in social justice activities, Anderson Abbott, born in Toronto on April 7, 1837, grew up instilled with anti-slavery sentiments. One of his parent's most courageous acts, which occurred during their son's childhood, was the sheltering in their home of Solomon Moseby, a runaway slave from Kentucky who had been captured in what was then Upper Canada. Moseby was found guilty of stealing his master's horse during his escape, but an angry crowd rescued the shackled prisoner as he was about to be extradited back to the United States under an armed escort. Two people were killed and another was wounded in the violent rescue, as Moseby slipped out of his handcuffs and was whisked away to the Abbott home, where he was secreted safely away from a massive manhunt before he could be sent to a safer haven in England.[9]

Abbott spent much of his pre-war life in Toronto, with the exception of a few years in the early 1850s, when his family moved to Buxton for the benefit of educating the children, and where his father was an important figure in the Elgin Association, which helped found the settlement. After returning to Toronto, Abbott eventually attended Knox College, where he was one of three black students. After graduating, he attended Oberlin College in Ohio for two years, before returning to Toronto, where he studied medicine at Trinity College at the University of Toronto under the care of Dr. Alexander T. Augusta, graduating at age twenty-three.

On February 6, 1863, Abbott sent his first letter to Secretary of War Edwin Stanton, applying for a position as an assistant surgeon in one of the coloured regiments that were soon to be formed. He provided his educational background and informed Stanton that he would receive the degree of Doctor of Medicine in the spring.

Apparently receiving no response, but inspired by Augusta, who had recently received his own commission, Abbott again wrote to Stanton on April 30, 1863, requesting an appointment as a medical cadet in one of the coloured regiments. Informing the Secretary that he was also black, Abbott referred Stanton to Augusta, who could give all necessary particulars about his character and ability.[10]

Surgeon Anderson Abbott. *Courtesy of BNHS&M.*

128

This time Abbott was successful, and on June 26, 1863 in Washington, he signed his first "Contract with a Private Physician." Terms were that he would be paid eighty dollars per month, as long as he performed the duties of a medical officer. The contract was good for "at least three months, unless sooner determined by the commanding officer." On July 26, 1863, Abbott was given his first commission and placed under the direction of Alexander Augusta at the Contraband Camp and hospital in Washington. The facility had eight hundred beds and was specifically designated to treat black soldiers and freedmen. Abbott described the hospital as being about three miles from Washington, and having "a competent staff of nurses, laundry women, cooks, stewards, clerks, &c."[11] Jill Newmark, a present-day historian, described the camp as being constructed of a single-story frame building along with more temporary tented structures. There were separate facilities for men and women, as well as a separate area for patients suffering with smallpox. A morgue was a necessity, as well as stables for the horses, and all of the rooms necessary for daily life — kitchens, laundry areas, living quarters, supply areas, etc. Conditions were extremely crowded, with as many as fourteen people in a single tent. There were shortages of food, clean water, and basic supplies. The ground underfoot was damp and swampy, which easily contributed to sickness and disease.[12]

Many of Abbott's experiences in the war resembled that of Alexander Augusta. In July 1863, Abbott actually accompanied Augusta's wife, Mary, from Canada to Washington, where she would join her husband. While waiting in the New York City depot for a connecting train, a man who was pretending to be drunk fell against Mrs. Augusta. Abbott came to her defense, pushing the man away. The aggressor soon returned with "a big Irishman," who profanely threatened to kill Augusta and Abbott. The frightened pair sought the help of a nearby watchman, but he ignored them. It was not until several white soldiers who knew the assailants came into the room and distracted them that Mrs. Augusta and Abbott took flight, running to a well-lit area on a busy street, where they took shelter in an oyster saloon. This event took place on a Friday night, two days before the New York riots commenced. From that time, Abbott was convinced that he and Mrs. Augusta had been singled out as the first victims of the planned riot.[13]

Abbott continued to follow in Alexander Augusta's footsteps. Shortly after Augusta was transferred, Abbott replaced him as Surgeon in Charge of the Contraband Camp and Freedman's Hospital. He remained in that position until August 21, 1865, shortly after the end of the war.

On September 2, 1863, Abbott was required to sign an oath that he had never borne arms against the United States or had never given aid of any kind to any entity that was hostile to that government. On February 26 of the next year, Abbott signed a new "Contract with a Private Physician," in which he "promises and agrees to perform the duties of a Medical Officer, agreeably to Army Regulations, at Washington or elsewhere." As had been asked of Dr. Augusta, Abbott also had to agree to provide necessary medical tools. His pay was significantly higher than before, and, like that of other doctors, was to be $100 per month plus $113 per month transportation expenses if he performed services in the field.[14]

One of Abbott's most memorable experiences occurred on January 1, 1864, when he, along with Dr. Augusta, both dressed in full military uniform, attended a "levee" at the White House. The elite of Washington were in attendance that night, all elegantly dressed and arriving in splendid carriages. The atmosphere was electric — "ushers, lackeys, waiters, messengers were scurrying here and there and attending to guests" — all while the Marine band played in the background. Augusta and Abbott were respectfully escorted by a commissioner of the Treasury Department to be introduced to the President. Upon seeing them, President Lincoln eagerly approached them and shook Augusta by the hand. The President's son, Robert, who until that time had been standing beside his mother elsewhere in the room, was taken aback and hastily went to his father to ask if the affront to propriety was going to be allowed with the presence of two black men. Lincoln's reply was "why not?" With that subtle chastisement, Robert retreated and returned to his mother's side.

In his turn, Abbott was also warmly greeted by Lincoln. After exchanging a few words with the President, Augusta and Abbott were introduced to his wife, Mary Todd Lincoln, who incidentally had been born in Kentucky into a wealthy slave-holding family, many of whom now supported the Confederacy. In Abbott's own account of the experience, he made no mention of the latter introduction being uncomfortable for either party.

He did, however, paint a vivid picture of the rest of the evening:

> We then passed out into a room on the opposite side
> from where we entered called the East Room and there
> we were destined to undergo an ordeal in comparison
> with which what we had experienced thus far was on
> a dream. The moment we entered the room which was
> crowded and brilliantly lit up we became the cyno-
> sure of all eyes. I never experienced such a sensation
> before as I did when I entered that room. We could not
> have been more surprised ourselves or created more
> surprise if we had been dropped down upon them
> through a sky-light. I suppose it was because it was first
> time in the history of the U.S. when a colored man had
> appeared at one of these Levees. What made us more
> conspicuous of course was our uniforms. Colored men
> in the uniforms of U.S. military officers of high rank
> had never been seen before. I felt as though I should
> have liked to crawl into a hole. But as we had decided
> to break the record we held our ground. I bit my lips,
> took Augusta's arm and sauntered around the room
> endeavoring or pretending to view the very fine pic-
> tures which adorned the walls. I tried also to become
> interested in the beautiful music discoursed by the
> Marine band but it was the first time that music had
> failed to absorb my attention. Wherever we went a
> space was cleared for us and we became the center
> of a new circle of interest. Some stared [at] us merely
> from curiosity — others with an expression of friendly
> interest, while others again scowled at us in such a sig-
> nificant way that left no [doubt] as to what views they
> held on the Negro question. We remained in the room
> and faced monocles, lorgnettes, stares and fascinating
> eyes levelled at us for about half of an hour or so and
> then we passed out of the room.

A reporter from Washington's *Chronicle* was waiting for the two black officers when they departed, eager for an interview. The resulting article, which noted that "years ago had any colored man presented himself at the White House at the President's levee, seeking an introduction to the chief magistrate of the nation, he would, in all probability have been roughly handled for his impudence." The reporter referred to the interviewees as being of "genteel exteriors and with the manners of gentlemen;" his sentiments were reprinted in newspapers across the country.[15]

Abbott took a tremendous pride in his race during the war years. He praised their military bearing, and took special pleasure in watching black troops parade through Washington, past throngs of cheering people who crowded the sidewalks. According to Abbott, President Lincoln, Secretary Stanton, and other cabinet ministers watching from a balcony were likewise impressed.

Abbott made the most of his time in the service. Despite the demands of his work, he found time to indulge in social activities. He belonged to Washington's "Reunion Literary Club."[16] He also found time to socialize with his friend from youthful days in Canada, a fellow literary club member and now his fellow doctor at the Contraband Camp, John Rapier.

On one particular special occasion, the two friends perhaps found another way to unwind apart from the literary club. In the fall of 1864, Abbott and Rapier were charged with supplying whiskey for a celebration held in Washington's 15th Street Presbyterian Church for the ratification of a new constitution by the Maryland Legislative Assembly, which prohibited slavery in that state. The allegation was that the two young men, as members of the planning committee (in which Rapier served as one of the vice-presidents and Abbott as a secretary),[17] had purchased the alcohol and charged it under the heading "Coal Oil," presumably to disguise the expenditure from inquiring eyes. The pair was also accused of "indulging in the use of intoxicating drinks in the Matron's room." Rapier vehemently denied the truth of that rumour, stating, "I am not addicted to the use of alcoholic drinks, and have yet to learn the peculiar sensations of drunkenness." In a weakly worded defence of his friend, he wrote that he would leave "Dr. Abbott to protest himself," but added that in the fourteen years that he had known him he did not regard him as a "drunk or a habitual tippler."[18]

Surgeon John Rapier, ca. 1864.
Archives and Research Collection, Western University, Annie Straith Jamieson fonds, Box B4192.

Rapier was ever the inquisitive one: popular and intelligent, handsome and articulate, motivated and opinionated. He had acquired his hunger for knowledge while he and younger brother James had lived with their grandmother in Nashville, Tennessee, following the death of their mother. While there, he was taken under the wing of a distinguished lawyer who allowed him access to his books. When the lawyer's library caught fire, he gave the damaged books to Rapier, which the latter eagerly devoured.[19]

After his grandmother's death, Rapier returned to his father's home in Alabama, but in 1853 it was decided that he would be sent to Buxton to attend the mission school, where he rapidly progressed in his studies, including the subjects of Latin and Greek. For eighteen months he boarded with the family of his uncle, Henry K. Thomas, who long ago was a runaway slave before returning to the United States. Although struggling themselves, and already having many mouths to feed, they asked the very small amount of six shillings per week.[20]

Rapier's thirst for knowledge and experiences was insatiable. He returned to the U.S. for a period of time, but became exceedingly unhappy there and declared that he could not live there. Nevertheless, the lure for adventure was too great to pull John back to Canada, even though he had purchased a farm there. His letters revealed that he lived in New Orleans, Alton, Illinois, and Chicago, then New York, before moving to Granada in Central America. At one point it was reported that he joined in a political revolution in South America, was arrested and sentenced to death, but managed to escape. In February of 1861 he was living in Port-au-Prince, Hayti.[21] By March of 1862 he was in Jamaica, recovering from "a touch of yellow fever aggravated by the bite of a scorpion."[22] From there, he moved to Minnesota for a short time, where he wrote for newspapers before enrolling in a medical college in Iowa.[23] By April of the next year he was leaving his studies, and by July was in Fort Wayne, Indiana, looking for work and bemoaning the fact that he was short of money, which he needed for getting "some clothes washed, Tobacco to smoke and occasionally some beer to make me Stoical in troublesome times."[24]

In the troublesome time of civil war, shortly after black recruitment began, Rapier wrote in a letter to his uncle: "I suppose that you have long before this concluded that I had either enlisted in the 54th Mass and left for the sunny South or found a more tropical climate than even existed in Dixie and often mentioned by divine and profane men."[25]

But he was neither in the army nor in the underworld. During the early days of the war, Rapier remained aloof from the larger cause of fighting. He had even felt that the end of slavery would be a disaster because the blacks that he had witnessed in the West Indies had no ambition and could not be trusted.[26] Surely he came to regret the harshness of his words, being the first generation of his family who had been born free. He finally came around and found a cause to attach himself to. In April of 1864, while still a medical student in Iowa, he wrote to the U.S. Surgeon General asking how he could apply to the medical service of the army following his graduation in June. On June 23, 1864, he wrote again, this time from St. Louis, Missouri, to formally apply for a position as an assistant surgeon for the Union army, declaring that he was an undergraduate from the University of Michigan and a graduate from the University of Iowa. He was quickly accepted and within a week he was in the divided nation's capital at Washington D.C., signing a contract as a medical officer in the U.S. army. Anderson Abbott was the ranking doctor and authorized the formal agreement. The two friends both put their names to the document.[27]

While stationed at the Contraband Camp, where he worked on the grounds rather than inside the hospital, Rapier seemed to have quite a transformation as he spent so much time in close proximity with those suffering. He also found it astounding that white soldiers saluted him because surgeons were assigned an officer's rank. Encouraged that the tide was turning, Rapier and Abbott joined 183 others to sign a petition to the Secretary of War, stating that blacks had demonstrated their abilities while serving under white officers during the war, and that the time had arrived for all black regiments to be commanded by worthy men of their own colour.[28]

Throughout the 1850s, Doctor Amos Aray had set up a medical practice at Dresden, and later in Chatham. When he began his Chatham practice in the spring of 1856, the eloquent and progressive physician made it clear that, unlike many others, he was "directly opposed to the use of certain agents, such as Mercury, Arsenic, Antimony, &c."[29] At the Convention of Coloured People held in Chatham on August 30, 1858, in which delegates, including Martin Delany, George W. Brodie, James Henry Harris, and Abraham Shadd were in attendance, Aray was commissioned as surgeon to accompany Delany and others as a member of the Niger Valley Exploring Party; this party was to travel to Africa to choose a location for an industrial colony where North American blacks could settle and produce staples, such as cotton, that would directly compete with and undermine the Southern economy, which depended on slave labour.[30] Aray closed his practice in preparation of going, but some obstacle prevented him from making the trip. However, he maintained a close relationship with Delany. In September 1863, the thirty-year-old Aray travelled to Camden, Rhode Island and signed a volunteer enlistment form to serve as a soldier. Although his Compiled Military Service Record contains the enlistment document, there is nothing further to indicate that he was mustered into Rhode Island's 14th Colored Heavy Artillery, nor into any other regiment, but he did examine recruits for Martin Delany.[31]

Doctor Thomas Joiner White was a colleague of Amos Aray and Martin Delany. Like them, he too planned on returning south to lend his skills to the Union cause. Born to free parents in Petersburg, Virginia, White later received his medical degree at Bowdoin College in Maine in 1849, and was apparently the third African American in the United

States to receive the degree. The intention was that he was to go to the black colony in Liberia, Africa, which had been established for American blacks by the American Colonization Society.[32] Instead, he practiced first in New York City, and in the latter half of the 1850s he moved to Hamilton; by 1859 he was living in Chatham, where he set up an office. In July 1863, as White was making preparations to return to the U.S., he was stricken with disease. His friends and family believed that he was only slightly ill and would recover. However, the doctor knew better, and, fearing the worse, penned the following letter:

> A few days ago I seemed to be in the full enjoyment of health and life — but, alas, how changed now, for Saturday last I was attacked with "Cholera Morbus," and just as I supposed I was about well of that erysipelas of the face, claims me as a victim. This last disease will most likely terminate my earthly career. O Lord if thou hast ordered it so to be, Thy will be done — One favor I would ask and that is, that you, my little child, may always enjoy Thy especial care; early may she learn to love Thee and always walk in Thy paths. Lord bless my dear Mother, my Wife and my beloved Father. Oh, God! bless the cause of human liberty — may colored men prove themselves worthy of the trust committed to their hands, viz: the emancipation of their race from slavery — Strike the oppressor wherever you find him. Freedom now or never. I was just endeavoring to consummate arrangements with the Secretary of War whereby I should have returned to my native land and joined some of the "colored troops of the U.S." But my Lord and Master, it seems, intends taking me to himself — glory be to His holy name.
>
> — Thomas Joiner White
> Chatham, July 10th, A.D. 1863.
> I should like to be buried in Greenwood Cemetery, Brooklyn.
>
> — T.J.W.

White died within days. The crumpled letter was later found in his coat pocket.[33]

One Canadian who left a most profound mark on the human history of the era was Laura Haviland, nee Smith. Born December 20, 1808 to Quaker parents in Leeds County, Canada West, Laura devoted much of her life to humanitarian works. In 1815, she and her family moved to New York State, where Laura became consumed with reading about the cruelties of the slave trade and the horrors of the middle passage, including the sharks that were known to follow ships to devour the bodies of the thousands who died and were thrown overboard. Always a compassionate soul, she was profoundly saddened by the abuse she witnessed being thrown with impunity at black members who lived in her community.

After marrying Charles Haviland Jr. in 1829, the couple moved to Raisin Township, Lenawee County, Michigan, where Laura co-founded the state's first antislavery society.[34] In 1839, Laura and Charles opened a school for orphaned and indigent children on their farm. Within a couple of years, this evolved into a manual labour school christened "The River Raisin Institute," which was opened to all races and both sexes. As an almost natural progression of events, the Havilands became "conductors" on the Underground Railroad.

Laura Haviland holding instruments of horror that were used on slaves. *http://commons.wikimedia.orgwiki-File%3ALaura_Haviland_holding_slave_irons_ca._1864.jpg.*

Following the series of tragedies that beset Laura in 1845 — the death of her husband, her youngest child, both parents, and a sister, Laura committed her energies to working with the enslaved and the Underground Railroad, travelling extensively through the United States and into Canada. In 1852, she moved to a planned settlement for blacks in Essex County, Canada West, near Windsor, known as The Refugee Home Society. There she taught school for a year, gave religious instruction, assisted with business issues, and helped new arrivals get established. Having made arrangements with sympathetic whites in the South prior to their own escape, illiterate members of the settlement came to her to write letters to relatives that had been left behind. Laura even helped with reuniting some of them in their new country. As a result of her clandestine activities, one incensed owner of runaways sought revenge on her for over a decade, both legally and personally, with slave catchers who were inspired by a three-thousand-dollar reward for her capture, dead or alive. The owner's son, Thomas K. Chester, displayed his family's venom in a letter to Haviland:

> ... By your cunning villainies you have deprived us of our just rights, of our own property.... Thanks be to an all wise and provident God that, my father has more of that sable kind of busy fellows, greasy, slick, and fat; and they are not cheated to death out of their hard earnings by villainous and infernal abolitionists, whose philanthropy is interest, and whose only desire is to swindle the slave-holder out of his own property, and convert its labor to their own infernal aggrandizement ... Who do you think would parley with a thief, a robber of man's just rights, recognized by the glorious Constitution of our Union! Such a condescension would damn an honest man, would put modesty to the blush. What! To engage in a contest with you? A rogue, a damnable thief, a Negro thief, an out-breaker, a criminal in the sight of all honest men; ... I would rather be caught with another man's sheep on my back than to engage in such a subject,

and with such an individual as old Laura Haviland, a damned nigger-stealer ... What do you think your portion will be at the great Day of Judgment? I think it will be the inner temple of hell.[35]

The Chesters were never successful in getting their vengeance on Haviland. On one of her trips to the south, Haviland learned that the master, John P. Chester, was shot through the heart by a mulatto man who refused to produce free papers when demanded to do so. The suspected slave was then taken by a mob, hung from a tree, and riddled with bullets. Within months, the master's son, Thomas, who helplessly witnessed his father's death, contracted yellow fever and died an agonizing death. According to a witness, it took six men to hold the sick and hallucinating man down. In further describing the scene, the witness stated: "Thomas K. Chester's death was the most awful I ever witnessed. He cursed and swore to his last breath, saying he saw his father standing by his bed, with damned spirits waiting to take him away to eternal burnings."

During the Civil War, Laura again travelled extensively through the South, visiting hospitals, prison camps, distributing supplies that had been accumulated by a Freedmen's Relief Association from Detroit, arranging for the care of orphans, and providing aid and comfort to ragged and starving blacks and whites. Later in the war, she became an agent for the Michigan Freedmen's Aid Commission. She was also appointed as inspector of hospitals for the newly formed Freedmen's Bureau, and travelled through Washington, D.C.; Virginia; Tennessee; and Kansas. During her travels she also helped establish refugee camps and schools, volunteered as a nurse, and reported on social and living conditions of those who had been decimated by war.

Elizabeth Comstock, one of Laura Haviland's intimate friends and co-workers in the anti-slavery and humanitarian field, also had a Canadian connection. Born into a devout Quaker family in England, Elizabeth emigrated to Belleville, Canada West in 1854, remaining there until 1858, when she moved to Michigan. Comstock had a lifelong love for Canada, and was involved in assisting slaves escape via the Underground Railroad. During the Civil War, she, like Haviland, travelled in and across the Union and Confederate lines, ministering to the physical and spiritual needs of soldiers, prisoners, and newly freed slaves.[36]

No one more deservedly holds her place among the highest ranks of heroes or heroines of the era than does Harriet Tubman, a runaway slave who lived for several years in St. Catharines. She is the most famous of all Underground Railroad conductors, whose story many of us thought we knew — until historian and author Kate Clifford Larson published *Bound for the Promised Land: Harriet Tubman, Portrait of an American Hero* in 2004. In that book, as well as in additional information that she and others have unearthed since, Larson has added immensely to the body of knowledge about Tubman, and has dispelled some of the myths that grew up around her legend.

Among the chapters in Tubman's life that Larson fleshes out, is her time serving in the Civil War as a cook, a nurse, and a spy. Larson tells us that in January 1862, Governor John Andrew of Massachusetts engaged Tubman to go to South Carolina, where she helped distribute food, clothing, and other supplies to slaves that had been left behind as their owners

Harriet Tubman, Civil War nurse, scout and spy. *LC-USZ62-7816. LOC.*

fled the Union's army and navy in and around the state's Sea Islands. In what was known as "The Port Royal Experiment," designed to allow African Americans to establish their own economic and social community, Tubman served as a nurse to those who fell ill from diseases such as "small pox, dysentery, measles, malaria, scarlet fever, typhoid, pneumonia," and yellow fever.[37] Acting with the true altruism that she exhibited throughout her life, she accepted no pay for her work.

Tubman drew from her multiple dramatic and clandestine Underground Railroad experiences, and from the relationships she forged with blacks in the area, to effectively gather information on Confederate activities, which she forwarded to Generals Stevens, Hunter, and Sherman. The trust that she earned due to her personality, her stature, and her determination also served the army well, as she helped with recruiting the Second South Carolina Volunteers. An article written by an admiring interviewer during the war gives a clear description of some of those traits:

> She is well known to many by the various names which her eventful life has given her; Harriet Garrison, Gen. Tubman, &c.; but among the slaves she is universally known by her well-earned title of Moses, — Moses the deliverer. She is a rare instance, in midst of high civilization and intellectual culture, of a being of great native powers, working powerfully, and to beneficent ends, entirely unaided by schools or books.
>
> ... She has a very affectionate nature, and forms the strongest personal attachments. She has great simplicity of character; she states her wants very freely, and believes you are ready to help her; but if you have nothing to give, or have given to another, she is content. She is not sensitive to indignities to her color in her own person; but knows and claims her rights. She will eat at your table if she sees you really desire it; but she goes as willingly to the kitchen. She is very abstemious in her diet, fruit being the only luxury she cares for. Her

personal appearance is very peculiar. She is thoroughly negro, and very plain. She has needed disguise so often that she seems to have command over her face, and can banish all expression from her features, and look so stupid that nobody would suspect her of knowing enough to be dangerous; but her eye flashes with intelligence and power when she is aroused. She has the rich humor and the keen sense of beauty which belong to her race.[38]

Tubman, who was an intimate of many leading figures of the time, including Secretary of State William H. Seward and the martyred John Brown, developed a particularly close relationship with the Colonel of the Second South Carolina (Colored) Volunteers, James Montgomery, who was described as "a perfect dare-devil, a splendid fighter, and one of the most mild gentlemen I ever met." She assisted him in planning and carrying out a raid along the Combahee River in the interior of South Carolina, in which the party uprooted Confederate defenders and caused a detachment of cavalry to retreat. They also destroyed plantations, rice mills, storehouses, and warehouses filled with cotton, and confiscated all that they could carry that could be of use, including horses and livestock. One report stated that despite armed slave-drivers threatening to kill them, 727 "contrabands" (slaves) of all ages fled with the Union troops as they returned to Port Royal after the expedition.[39]

Throughout much of the final three years of the war, Tubman continued to work in the South, cooking, laundering, and treating the sick and wounded, often using herbs and other traditional medicines known to slaves. Unable to read or write, she was also hired by the New England Freedmen's Aid Society as a "practical teacher" in the Hilton Head area of South Carolina.[40] On April 1, 1865, Tubman addressed 24th USCI, which was stationed at Camp William Penn, Pennsylvania. The soldiers, who had heard stories of this legendary Underground Railroad conductor, were delighted to see her in the flesh and to listen to her "very entertaining homespun lecture," which included a thrilling account of her trials in the South, during the past three years, among the contrabands and colored soldiers, and how she had administered to thousands of them, and cared for their numerous necessities.[41] When the Civil War ended, and in its immediate aftermath, Tubman nursed wounded and dying soldiers at Fortress Monroe, Virginia.[42]

Chaplains also played a crucial role in the lives of soldiers. Samuel Lowery, the son of a free Cherokee mother and an enslaved father who had his freedom purchased by his wife, was freeborn in Tennessee. Lowery was a gifted student, and after receiving a good education there, became a schoolteacher at the age of sixteen. After joining the Church of the Disciples three years later, he began preaching. However, a local race riot in 1856, which was sparked by debates on slavery, made life unsafe and sent several free blacks fleeing north. After serving as a pastor in Cincinnati, Lowery moved to Canada in 1858 to continue his ministry, settling on the Raleigh Plains of Kent County, just north of the Elgin Settlement.[43]

By June 22, 1864, Lowery had returned to Cincinnati. Once there, a committee of the American Christian Missionary Society wrote to Assistant Adjutant General Captain C.H. Potter, stationed in that city, requesting a pass for Lowery, which would allow him to travel unmolested through Kentucky and on to Nashville, where he could serve as a missionary to freedmen.[44]

In April 1865, Lowery was appointed chaplain for the 9th U.S. Colored Heavy Artillery, which had been organized in Tennessee. However, he was troubled that he had not received the proper paperwork confirming his appointment. In the letter that he wrote to the Tennessee Adjutant requesting that certificate, he also pleaded for books so that he might be able to teach the illiterate soldiers to read. Lowery hinted to his superior officer that since the enlisted men had not yet received any pay, they might be somewhat appeased by receiving the gift of schooling.[45] After Union forces occupied Nashville, Lowery also became a teacher for the 2nd U.S. Colored Light Artillery.[46]

Rev. William H. Jones was a Methodist minister in Chatham, and was involved in starting BME connection in 1856. During the Civil War, he contributed to the war effort in an imaginative way, returning to the U.S. with a panorama of slave and war scenes in order to raise money for American sanitary aid societies.[47]

Reverend Augustus R. Green of Windsor had not only served as a recruiter for the coloured regiments, but continued to devote himself to the war effort. Answering charges that a minister should take no part in the war, he responded:

> ... any man that won't do all he can to forward the cause of God in the emancipation of millions of human beings, is not worth of the name of a Christian, much less a minister. If Jehovah is Captain of this war, I don't believe it is anything wrong for his minister to push the battle to the gate, — "and let the oppressed go free, and that ye break every yoke."[48]

To that end, Reverend Green travelled to the south and helped keep Northern and Canadian blacks informed of what was happening at the frontlines. Writing from the army barracks at St. Louis, Missouri, he shared his unbridled optimism, declaring:

> ... what a glorious age we live in! It is indescribably fraught with interest in every step to the long oppressed race; and, indeed there are but few, I find of our people, that are prepared to realize the true magnitude of the present era. The effulgent brightness of the rising sun of freedom, after so dark a night, and the transition so great, that it blinds the eyes of those merging from the darkness of oppression, and causes them to wonder if it is not a fond dream![49]

Green celebrated the breaking down of racial animosity among the troops; blacks and whites were living in harmony in the same barracks. Crystallizing his point further, he relayed the story of eleven white soldiers refusing to ride on a streetcar because their black comrade was denied a seat. Green also travelled to Washington in 1864, where he devoted himself to giving medical care to the "contrabands" — those recently liberated blacks who were homeless, impoverished, and, as a result, often sick.[50]

Green's friend and fellow recruiter, Garland H. White, to whom we were introduced to in a previous chapter, remained active throughout the war, long after his initial recruiting duties were done. He himself enlisted in an

Indiana regiment that he had helped recruit: the 28th USCI. On December 14, 1863, he signed his volunteer enlistment form in Indianapolis, and two weeks later was mustered in to Company D as a private. However, his true ambition was not to be a soldier in arms, but rather a chaplain. As he had done previously when offering to the Secretary of War the services of himself and other blacks in Canada, White again tried to use his association with Secretary of State William Seward to further his cause.

In this case, White wrote to Seward on May 18, 1864, from Camp Casey, Washington, where the 28th was stationed, with a penmanship that had remarkably improved over the past two years. White apologized for imposing upon the busy Secretary, informing him that he had "recruited colored men for every colored regiment raised in the north ... canvassed the intire north & went urging my people to inlist & have succeeded in every instant." White mentioned that he had been promised the chaplaincy of a coloured regiment at various times. He continued that he had recruited nearly half of the men in the 28th USCI and that Indiana's Governor Morton had promised him the chaplaincy, but now that the regiment was under the jurisdiction of the U.S. bureau and not the state, the governor's promise could not be binding. Should there be any doubt as to White's claims, he referred Seward to Governors Andrew of Massachusetts, Morton of Indiana, Seymore of New York, and Spridge of Rhode Island. Before closing the letter with blessings for Seward's family, White shared his intention to do his duty — "I also joined the reg't as a private to be with my boys & should I fail to get my commission I shall willingly serve my time out, but I know you can get me my commission if any other gentleman in the world can."[51]

Seward quickly sent his personal recommendation to the Secretary of War, writing "I knew the writer of this letter when he was a slave of Robert Toombs in Washington and I knew him after becoming a fugitive in Canada." (Seward had met Garland White in September 1860, shortly after his escape, when White boarded a train carrying Seward that stopped in Chatham on route through Canada West from New York State to Michigan.[52])

Seward's letter of May 19, 1864 was forwarded to the Department of War, but the reply of the Assistant Adjutant General, dated May 26, 1864, stated that the chaplaincy was not filled , and that, at any rate, the position could not be filled until there was a full regiment with ten companies. Three days later, the 28th's lieutenant-colonel wrote to headquarters of the Provisional Brigade in Washington on White's behalf, informing his superiors that "it is the wish of most of the officers that Garland H. White should receive the appointment of Chaplain, he having been very useful as a rec'tg officer for the regt."[53] It was not until October 25, 1864 that official orders were finally issued to discharge White from his service as a private so he could accept the position of chaplain.

As the minister to his troops, White was called upon to perform painful duties. The most painful was initiated one April morning when White was awoken by an orderly who handed him an official order from Brigadier-General Russell and his assistant adjutant general, which directed White "to call upon Samuel Mapps, private in company D, now under sentence of death, and confined in the bull pen, to prepare him to meet his savior"

Chaplain White penned a hasty reply, stating: "I will comply promptly, and do all in my power to point him to the Lamb of God that taketh away the sins of the world." In one of his many letters to *The Christian Recorder*, White laid out in vivid detail what transpired next:

> (At the prison) "Well, my friend, how stands your case?"
>
> He began to plead innocence, and commenced to enter into a lengthy discussion of all that was connected with his trial.
>
> To this I said in reply, "I came to see you, not to discuss a point of law as to the nature of your trial and decision, for that is all useless; and my friend, I must tell you that to-day at 12 o'clock, you will be executed — yes, you will be shot. Now, let you and myself kneel down and address a throne of grace, where you may obtain mercy and help in time of need." He complied, and prayed fervently, after which I read several passages of Scripture, and sang a hymn = "Jesus, Lover of My Soul," &c, at the conclusion of which we bowed again in prayer to God … I then spent some time in reasoning upon what he thought about religion. He replied, "It is very good, and

I wish I had it." I then cited in plain terms the case of the dying thief: — that seemed to give him hope. We prayed again, and he appeared somewhat relieved; but at this moment the wagon and a squad of guards appeared at the door. He did not see them; I did. He continued to pray fervently, and an officer came in and announced that the time to repair to the place of execution had come. I told him to stand up, and walk with me. I took his arm, and went out to the gate, where thousands of persons had assembled to see him. He entered the wagon, and sat on his coffin. I then got in with him, took a seat by his side, and commenced talking and praying all the way to a large, open field, about a mile out of the village, where, it appeared to me, all the people in the place had congregated. (At the grave.) The officer went through all the necessary arrangements, and then made a sign for me to proceed to pray for the last time, with the poor man who would soon be in eternity.

I asked him for the last time, "Do you feel that Jesus will be with you?" "Yes," he replied.

"Do you put all your trust in him?"

"I do," was the answer. "Do you believe that you will be saved?"

"I do; for though they may destroy the body, they cannot hurt the soul." "Let us pray" I replied. "Eternal God, the Master of all the living, and the Judge of all the dead, we commit this our dying comrade into thy hands, from whence he came. Now, O my Lord and my God, for thy Son's sake, receive his soul unto thyself in glory. Forgive him — forgive … Save him Lord, — save him … Amen. Good-by, my brother, good by." The order was now given. Ready! Aim! Fire! About as long as it would take me to speak a word was the interval. I approached the corpse, and found all of life was gone. Five or six bullets had pierced his heart. It was the saddest spectacle I ever witnessed, and I hope never to witness another the longest day I live. He was the first colored man shot in this army, to my knowledge, during the war, and [I] hope it may be a warning to others.[54]

Garland White had another occasion to contact Seward on July 29, 1864, echoing the same offer that he had made from London to Secretary Stanton; in this request he outlined that he would be most valuable if he were sent to Georgia, where he intimately knew the plantations, the geography, and the roads, so could act as a guide and could also be valuable as a recruiter, as he knew many of the slaves there. White also offered strategic military advice, which included hinting at raiding and liberating the thousands of Union prisoners of war who were housed in the Civil War's most infamous camp, Andersonville prison, where forty-five thousand men were held during the war, nearly thirteen thousand of whom died of disease, malnutrition, exposure, and overcrowding.[55]

Andersonville prison for Union soldiers was the most notorious prison of the war. *LC-DIG-ppmsca-33768. LOC.*

White composed the letter from near Petersburg, Virginia, while stationed with the Army of the Potomac. In a cryptic conclusion to the letter, White wrote, "there are many things connected with the tenor of my letter which I have not time upon the immediate Battlefield to mention."[56] The next day, at the Battle of the Crater, the tenor vaguely referred to would be crystallized beyond even Garland White's imagination, as the acting chaplain was asked by many of the men who knew that they would die that day to write to their mothers and fathers to tell them that they faced death with bravery. Those who had families of their own requested that their wives receive the back-pay that was due to them, and that their children be raised in a Christian home.

CHAPTER 6

Battles

It was not a war for white men or black men, for yellow
men or red men, it was a war for humanity.

— Dr. Anderson Ruffin Abbott[1]

Canadian blacks fought in many skirmishes and major battles
from 1863 to 1865. The 54th Massachusetts was the first regiment in which numbers of them were engaged on the battlefield. Records indicate that there were approximately fifty British
North American men in that regiment, four from Nova Scotia, two
from New Brunswick, one from Canada East, and the remainder from
Canada West. The regiment departed from Camp Meigs in Readville,
Massachusetts on May 28, 1863, after having been reviewed by
Governor Andrew; they boarded the transport ship *De Molay*, bound
for Hilton Head and then Beaufort, on the coast of South Carolina.
Portions of the first weeks were spent on manoeuvres in and around
the coastal islands. During that time they suffered one of their earliest
casualties, when twenty-year-old Abraham Brown from Toronto, while
cleaning his pistol, accidentally shot and killed himself at James Island,
South Carolina on July 12, 1863.[2]

Abraham Brown from Toronto was among the Canadians who fought with the 54th Massachusetts. *Courtesy of Massachusetts Historical Society, #72.3.*

Their first ordeal by fire came four days later when they were attacked by a Confederate force near Secessionville on James Island. The 54th suffered thirty-five casualties: fourteen killed, eighteen wounded, including William Henderson from Woodstock, and three missing. When some of the remains of dead soldiers were found, it was initially believed that the enemy had mutilated them, but upon closer inspection it was found that fiddler crabs had attacked them.[3]

The battle that would mark their place in history took place two days later on July 18, 1863 at Fort Wagner, also referred to as "Battery Wagner," on Morris Island, South Carolina. The black regiment, the 54th Massachusetts, led the assault force. One of the lieutenants who survived the ordeal reported that the men were exhausted and hungry, having

Death of Colonel Shaw of 54th Massachusetts, mural at the Recorder of Deeds, D.C. *LC-DIG-highsm- 09903. LOC.*

been moving for three days and nights and not having eaten for twenty-four hours before they arrived on Morris Island. After a brief rest, they made the four-mile march to within a thousand yards of the foot of Fort Wagner. After laying there for half an hour until dusk, the men were ordered to charge, which they began with a rousing shout and an advance at double time. As they came within close range of the fort, the Confederates opened fire, with the individual projectiles of grape and canister shot from cannons and the balls from thousands of muskets mowing the advancing men down.[4] There was a moat surrounding the fort, then half-full because of low tide, that the men had to descend into before climbing the ramparts. In the darkness and confusion, it was difficult to distinguish who was Union and who was Confederate, so some of the 54th were gunned down by "friendly fire." One soldier was convinced that the 3rd New Hampshire, which arrived as re-enforcements, were particularly guilty, as "they, to a man, emptied their rifles into us.

The Shaw Memorial, which also pays tribute to the soldiers of the 54th Massa-schusetts, was sculpted by Augustus Saint-Gaudens over a period of fourteen years, and was completed in 1897. *LC-D4-90156. LOC.*

Thus we lost nearly as many men by the bullets of our presumed friends as by those of our known enemies."[5] The same soldier believed that after the order to retreat was given, some members of the rear guard, who had been drinking whiskey, fired on and killed some of the wounded men as they attempted to retreat to safety and have their medical needs tended to. Tragically, other wounded men who were physically unable to escape were drowned when the high tide returned.

Colonel Shaw, who had long since left his reluctance to be associated with black men behind, led the attack and died a hero's death at the top of the parapet. His body was buried in a mass grave along with forty-five of his soldiers. Among the casualties were George Albert, a forty-two-year-old farmer from Fredericton, New Brunswick, killed; Silas Garrison, twenty, a painter from Chatham, wounded and missing and supposed killed; Corporal Franklin Willis, thirty-three, Chatham farmer; John Weeks, nineteen, cook from Chatham, missing and supposed killed; Benjamin Grinnidge, eighteen, Canada West farmer, died at Morris Island, South Carolina, November 16, 1863 of wounds received at Fort Wagner; Elias S. Rouse, twenty-two, Chatham labourer, wounded in the wrist; William Homans, twenty-four, from Malden, wounded; Thomas P. Riggs, twenty-three, upholsterer from Georgetown, killed.[6]

Some of the missing and wounded were shot or bayoneted on the spot, while some were taken as prisoners of war. Those men faced particularly uncertain fates. Many were held at Charleston in a jail with an enclosed brick wall — placed there in hopes of discouraging Union bombardment of the city. One of the four hundred of both races who were taken there recalled that there was no shelter from the elements, only one privy that was never cleaned and always a shortage of rations. No clothing was provided, and some were left naked. Yellow fever ran rampant in the crowded conditions. Death was a frequent visitor and a gallows in the yard helped serve as another constant reminder of the precariousness of their position. Many suffered mental breakdowns; some lost any will to live. The dozens of colored prisoners were singled out for punishment and neglect.

Those that survived on scant pieces of cornbread were forced to clean all of the filth left by the other prisoners. They were allowed water only once per day. First lady Mary Todd Lincoln's brother and Confederate surgeon at the prison, George Rogers Clark Todd, was identified as being particularly cruel to the inmates, kicking and abusing them without cause. On one occasion, a black man warned a Southern deserter who was also imprisoned there not to remove a washbasin because Dr. Todd forbade it. Both deserter and Dr. Todd took exception to the man's insolence at speaking to a white man in such a manner, and Todd ordered the offender to be given forty lashes. In spite of everything, the men would spend the evenings singing to entertain themselves and the white Union officers who were held with them.[7]

Conditions were as bad or worse when prisoners were later moved to Florence, South Carolina, as one newspaper correspondent observed:

> The camp we found full of what were once human beings, but who would scarcely now be recognized as such. In an open field, with no inclosure but the living wall of sentinels who guard them day and night, are several thousand filthy, diseased, famished men, with no hope of release but death. A few dirty rags stretched on poles give them a poor protection from the hot sun and heavy dews. All were in rags, and barefooted, and crawling with vermin ... A few tents, covered with pine tops, were crowded with the dying and the dead in every stage of corruption. Some lay in prostrate helplessness; some had crowded under the shelter of the bushes; some were rubbing their skeleton limbs. Twenty or thirty of them died daily, — most of them, I am informed, of the scurvy. The corpses lay by the roadside waiting for the dead-cart, their glassy eyes turned to heaven, the flies swarming in their mouths, their big toes tied together with a cotton string, and their skeleton arms folded on their breasts.[8]

Many of the 54th's wounded that were not taken prisoner suffered greatly in the aftermath. Those who were slightly wounded were treated at the camp and the severely wounded were taken to a hospital in Beaufort. According to a report written by a visitor to the hospital days after the battle, many had

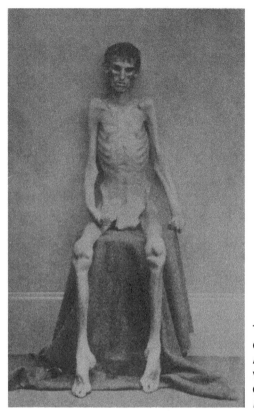

The photo of this emaciated skeleton of a man from Andersonville prison, Georgia vividly depicts the horrific conditions that prisoners faced. *LC-DIG-ppmsca-33758. LOC.*

still not had their wounds dressed and the patients were suffering greatly. Describing the scene, the writer noted that "some lay with shattered legs, or arms, or both; others with limbs amputated. Rebel bullets, grape, shell, bayonets have made sad havoc." When asked if they had been prepared for what had happened, the replies were philosophical acceptance: "Oh, yes, indeed, we expected to take all that comes," said some. Others said, "Thank God, we went in either to live or die." If out of it and home, how many would enlist again? With brightened faces and some raising of even wounded arms or hands, all said, "Oh yes, yes." Some sang out, "Oh, never give it up till the last rebel be dead," or "the last brother breaks his chains," or, "if all our people get their freedom, we can afford to die."[9]

The 54th remained a part of the siege of Fort Wagner on duty in the trenches and on "fatigue duty," which included doing the necessary daily chores at an encampment, such as construction, sanitary tasks, security,

Blacks unloading ships at Union headquarters for the Petersburg Campaign at City Point, Virginia. *LC-DIG-cwpb-01754. LOC.*

and other common labourer jobs; fatigue duty was a common practice with many of the colored regiments and was often resented throughout the war because it was considered to be more than their fair share of assignments, suggesting that they were believed to be inferior to white troops. When the enemy troops finally evacuated Fort Wagner on September 7, 1863, the 54th was the first regiment to enter it.

Their next major engagement took place on February 20, 1864 in Florida at the Battle of Olustee — or Ocean Pond, as named by the Confederates. It was one of the bloodier battles of the Civil War, in which there would be nearly three thousand casualties. The Northern manoeuvre had the objective of cutting off Confederate supply lines and finding slave recruits for the black Union forces. Many blacks from Canada fought at Olustee. In addition to those of the 54th Massachusetts were the members of the 3rd USCI, who had previously joined the 54th at the siege of Fort Wagner, and the 8th USCI, both of which had been raised

Camp William Penn in Pennsylvania was established specifically as a training ground for the Colored Troops. It was the official introduction to the war for dozens of Canadians who enlisted in one of the eleven USCT regiments, including the 3rd, 6th, 8th, 41st, 45th, and 127th. *LC-DIG-ppmsca-10898. LOC.*

in Pennsylvania. The 8th had only been out of Camp William Penn for a month, where it had been organized and drilled before this engagement. Those soldiers entered the fray ill-equipped and inadequately trained.

At noon on February 15, the 3rd and 8th attempted to set up camp. Hampered in trying to find a dry place in the marshy surroundings, they had to raise the bottom of the tents two feet off the ground and place boards under them. For the next four days, the men were on picket duty, building stockades and rifle-pits. On the nineteenth they marched eleven miles, set up overnight camp on a large plantation, and by 6:00 a.m. the next morning were on the move again. The total Union force — consisting of artillery, infantry, and cavalry, including the coloured troops, and, among the white regiments, the 7th New Hampshire — was around five thousand.

In mid-afternoon, the firing of guns was heard in the distance as Union advance troops began to fight their way through the enemy pickets. The 8th USCI were ordered to immediately rush to the scene without time taken to remove the knapsacks that they carried, nor the sergeants to remove the sashes that they wore to demonstrate their rank — a fateful decision for the latter, as they were easily distinguishable and therefore particular targets to be focused on by the enemy. Many of the men of the 8th were lacking ammunition, as meeting the enemy had not yet been expected. With some of their officers wounded or killed, and with ammunition sparse, the 8th was ordered to the rear of the 54th Massachusetts, who were then in the thick of the fight, having been summoned from three miles in the rear — a distance they ran before unflinchingly withstanding heavy fire, despite their comrades falling around them. The battle continued until darkness fell and the beaten Union commanding general ordered retreat.

When the numbers were added, the official report registered 1,861 Union casualties — the Confederates with just over half that amount. The 8th suffered most heavily, with 49 killed, 188 wounded, and 73 missing. The war-tested 54th Massachusetts had 13 killed, 65 wounded, and 8 missing.[10] Their sister regiment, the 55th, whose nucleus had been formed by the overflow of recruits for the 54th, and which had 15 Canadians, as well as William Herbert from Yarmouth, Nova Scotia, left Olustee unscathed. Their single Canadian casualty to that point was Silas Robison from St. Catharines, who had died of disease back at Readville, Massachusetts on July 16, 1863 — the same day that the 54th was fighting at James Island.

Following this Confederate victory, an observer wrote that the casualties of coloured troops were so severe as to be called a slaughter. Their white Canadian comrades also suffered greatly in the fight. One participant wrote that many of the soldiers in the 7th New Hampshire Regiment could not speak any English, having recently come from "the Canada French settlements" and from Germany. To further complicate matters, they were new recruits who had received little training and had never before been under fire. Instead of carrying the more advanced Spencer rifles, they were given older guns, many of which were damaged so as to be unable to fire. Previously, the bayonets had been discarded under the misguided notion that they would be cumbersome and useless, thereby denying the men any chance in hand-to-hand combat. Helplessness, hopelessness, and defeat naturally followed.[11]

Observers admired many of the wounded blacks as they returned to camp still clutching their rifles and equipment so they could "defend themselves till the death."[12] Special praise was given to Dr. Alex. P. Heickhald, surgeon of the 8th, who, although tending to white soldiers, made treating the coloured wounded and getting them safely away a priority, believing "I know what will become of the white troops who fall into the enemy's possession, but I am not certain as to the fate of the colored troops."[13] The doctor's suspicions were well founded. When rebel commanders provided a list of wounded soldiers that they held as prisoners, the Union officers were surprised at the scant number of blacks, knowing that there were large numbers of them who had been left on the battlefield. Brigadier-General John Porter Hatch discovered that they had been murdered on the field.[14]

Among the wounded who were born in Canada were the 54th's John Henderson, twenty-three, who had been a cook before enlistment; William Henry, nineteen, from Fort Erie, hostler; and the 8th's William Chandler, thirty-one, a London farmer. Henry recovered from his wound and was mustered out with the rest of his regiment after the war. Henderson's wound shows the variety of dangers involved in battle when cannon fire screams overhead. He was injured when a large limb from a tree fell on his back, causing two severe scrotal hernias, and was discharged because of disability on December 5, 1864. Chandler had his left arm amputated, and after months spent in the Beaufort hospital, he was discharged for disability "at his own request" three weeks after Henderson. "Lion," an old white dog that was the mascot for the 8th USCI, and who had been with them since the regiment's mustering in at Camp William Penn, was also wounded, shot in the foreleg. Although he had not recovered two months later, his two-legged companions had no doubt that he would be ready to march with the regiment as soon as called upon to do so.[15]

The Battle of the Crater, which took place near Petersburg, Virginia on July 30, 1864, was another of the bloodiest clashes, in which many black Canadian troops participated as members of New York's 31st, Indiana's 28th, and Illinois's 29th USCI. The Union objective was to break through the Confederate lines that protected Petersburg, which protected a rail line that supplied the Southern capital of Richmond. Rather than make a frontal assault, the Union corps commander, General Ambrose Burnside, decided to lay siege and to employ a tactic that had been used in medieval Europe when an attacking army sought to capture a well-fortified castle. In late June and early July, the 48th Pennsylvania Infantry, some of whose men were experienced at mining coal before the war, began digging a tunnel that they determined would end beneath the enemy fortifications. The tunnel was completed by the end of July and eight thousand pounds of gunpowder were packed at its end.

The fuse was lit shortly before daylight, and the mammoth explosion that resulted created a crater in the earth that was almost two hundred feet long, sixty feet wide, and thirty feet deep. Chaplain Garland White of the 28th described the scene as the troops prepared to charge the earthworks:

> Just at this juncture the earth began to shake, as though the hand of God intended a reversal of the laws of nature. This grand convulsion sent both soil and souls to inhabit the air for a while, and then return to be commingled forever with each other, as the work of God commands, "From dust thou art, and unto dust thou shalt return."[16]

The Union army charged. The original plan had been for the coloured troops to lead the assault, and they had taken two weeks of specialized tactical training on avoiding the crater, but General George Meade, the commander of the Army of the Potomac, reversed the plan, fearing the angry repercussions stirred by abolitionists who would accuse him of purposely sending them to the slaughter. Therefore, the initial assault was led by untrained white divisions, soon to be followed by two brigades of coloured infantry, some summoning up motivation by yelling their battle-cries of "No Quarter" and "Remember Fort Pillow," a massacre that had taken place earlier that spring in which three hundred African Americans in Tennessee had been killed after they had surrendered. The enemy at the crater, incensed that blacks would take up arms against them, agreed that no quarter would be shown by them either.

In the attacks and counter-attacks that took place well into the afternoon, the Confederates, who had regrouped after the early morning's explosion, gained the upper hand and the rout was on. In the panic and confusion, many of the Union soldiers who had run into or had been driven back into the crater became trapped and could not escape as bullets rained down upon them. Much of the fighting was hand-to-hand.

One of the soldiers from the 12th Virginia wrote of the coloured soldiers:

> They fought like bulldogs and died like soldiers. Southern bayonets dripped with blood and after a brief struggle the works were ours. The only sounds which now broke the stillness was some poor wounded wretch begging for water and quieted by a bayonet thrust which said unmistakenly "Bois ton sang. Tu n'aurais plus de soif" translated from the French as Drink your blood. You will have no more thirst.[17]

Perhaps most chilling of all was a report that some of the white Union soldiers were so terrified that some began to bayonet their black Union compatriots in the hope that the enemy would then show mercy to them. George L. Kilmer of the 14th New York Heavy Artillery stated:

> Some colored men came into the crater and there they found a fate worse than death in the charge. It was believed among the whites that the enemy would give no quarter to Negroes, or to the whites taken with them so to be shut up with blacks in the crater was equal to a doom of death … It has been positively asserted that white men bayoneted blacks in the crater. This was to preserve the whites from Confederate vengeance.[18]

Historian Bryce A. Suderow's thorough examination of "The Battle of the Crater: the Civil War's worst massacre" that appeared in the September 1997 issue of *Civil War History* relates many first-hand accounts of the carnage — from both Union and Confederate soldiers. They contain vivid and grisly recollections of the atrocities: skulls cracked by the butt end of muskets; blacks being killed so numerously as they attempted to retreat that their enemies could not keep up; the floor of the crater so filled with black bodies, sometimes stacked three or four deep, that it was difficult to walk; bayonets being plunged into those who had surrendered; and Georgian soldiers being told to load their guns and take their bayonets and roam among the defeated men and finish them off, but "not to kill quite all of them."[19]

Suderow also did an analysis of the Compiled Military Service Records and Civil War pension records, and concluded that blacks suffered 1,269 casualties: 423 killed, 13 mortally wounded, 744 wounded, 3 mortally wounded and captured, 13 wounded and captured, and 73 captured.

Nearly seventy men from Canada were at different times in the 31st US Colored Infantry, which suffered heavy losses as it led the assault to the left flank of North and South Carolinian defenders. Many of these men enlisted after the Battle of the Crater to fill the depleted ranks. Considering the carnage that took place that day, the Canadian men were extremely fortunate to survive, with few exceptions. The strain on the medical staff that treated the wounded, including the 31st's surgeon, William S. Tremaine from Prince Edward Island, must have been enormous. Among those killed was George Hall. William Harris, a twenty-year-old from Windsor, was wounded.

John Hedgeman from Hamilton was also in the 31st USCI, and was without doubt shaken at the experience. He briefly deserted his regiment the next month, but soon returned and remained for the rest of the war. Sergeant John Tinsley of Canada saw action that day and months later deserted. He was apprehended and reduced to the ranks on February 18, 1865.

Charles Henry Griffin was among those survivors whose lives were forever changed at the Crater. Born in Cleveland, Ohio, before moving with his parents and siblings to Chatham Township, in Kent County, seventeen-year-old Charles, whose occupation was "trunkmaker," travelled to Chicago, thwarted the legal enlistment age, and signed with the 29th USCI on January 3, 1864. Although young and of slender build at five feet five inches, he was determined to be a part of the war, but the Crater was his undoing. Although not wounded, he had to be hospitalized at Philadelphia after the battle, "for fatigues, nerves and everything unstrung."[20]

Many white Canadians also fought at the Crater. Robert F. Dodd of Galt, who joined Company E, 27th Michigan Infantry, received the U.S. Medal of Honor for voluntarily assisting in carrying wounded from in front of the crater, all the while exposed to heavy fire.[21] Another Canadian, Oliver Arpetargezhik of the Ojibwa tribe (spelled "Ojibway" at the time) from Walpole Island in Canada West, was also there. He was wounded there while serving with the 1st Michigan Sharpshooters and died of his wounds on July 9, 1864. He has the distinction of being buried among the honoured dead at Arlington National Cemetery.[22]

More than forty-eight Canadians belonged to the 6th USCI, which had been organized in the summer of 1863 at Camp William Penn near Philadelphia, and whose regiment was an integral part of the Battle of New Market Heights, Virginia on September 29, 1864. While most of the Canadian men joined the 6th after this date when the ranks needed to be replenished, nine of them had enlisted previously. The action that day was part of a much larger offensive to push to Petersburg and Richmond, which included preventing Southern units from reinforcing Fort Harrison, a key Confederate stronghold that would be attacked simultaneously. Confederate General Robert E. Lee's Army of Northern Virginia was among those that waited in defense of these two critical Southern cities. Major General Benjamin F. Butler commanded the Union's Army of the James, which included a large contingent of coloured troops, including the 6th.

Before sunrise on the foggy morning on September 29, the men of the 6th who had been on the move throughout the previous night completed a two-mile march to New Market Heights and formed a line to the left of their fellow regiment, the 4th USCI, which had been organized in Maryland. These two regiments began their advance through the haze across an open field that was split by the Four Mile Creek and a marshy area. As the men became visible as they emerged from the mist, the Southerners on picket duty shouted the alarm, were quickly reinforced, and opened fire as the coloured troops attempted to make their way through the defensive works of embedded trees with sharpened branches, which had been fashioned into stakes. The black men were ordered not to take the time to fire, as it would slow the momentum of their charge. The 4th was decimated by enemy artillery and musket fire and the 6th took over the lead, bringing much the same result, with 210 casualties of the 367 men from the regiment that made the charge.[23] Although they were forced to fall back, the surviving members of the

6th played a critical role in what soon became a Union victory, with the largest number of coloured troops to fight in a single engagement during the war joining with white troops to carry the day.

Years later, when Surgeon Anderson Abbott recorded incidents of the war, he made special mention of the Battle of New Market Heights, making reference to General Butler's praise for black troops, which he used as ammunition to encourage Congress to pass a civil rights bill. Butler mentioned that three thousand coloured troops advanced on the Confederate position at the top of a hill that was defended by two rows of Abatis which advance soldiers armed with axes had to hack openings in so the columns could move forward. Butler recalled that the men proceeded as "a very fire of hell is pouring upon them. The head of the column seems literally to melt away under the fire of shot and shell."[24]

In a moving and melancholy tribute to his men, Butler recalled the scene later that day:

> It became my painful duty, sir, to follow in the track of that charging column and there in a space not wider than the clerk's desk and 300 yds. long lay the dead bodies of 543 of my colored comrades slain in defence of their country, who had laid down their lives to uphold its flag and its honor as a willing sacrifice and as I rode along among them guiding my horse this way and that way lest he should profane with his hoofs what seemed to me the sacred dead. And as I looked on their bronzed faces upturned in the shining sun as if in mute appeal against the wrongs of the country for which they had given their lives and whose flag had only been to them a flag of stripes upon which no star of glory had even shown for them. Feeling I had wronged them in the past and believing what was the future of my country to them, among my dead comrades I swore to myself a solemn oath. May my right hand forget its cunning and my tongue cleave to the roof of my mouth if I ever fail to defend the rights of those men who had given their

blood for me and my country this day and for their race forever and God helping me I will keep that oath.[25]

Despite having proved themselves time after time by facing death on the battlefield, the nagging question of unequal pay and the ineligibility for officer's positions for black troops who were dying or willing to die was brought forward. The Massachusetts State Legislature passed a supplemental pay act on November 16, 1863, in hopes of righting the wrong that had been done to its soldiers. However, when delegates arrived at Folly Island on December 11 at the camp of the 54th and 55th Massachusetts, they declined to accept it, feeling that the entire Union should recognize their worth.[26] As one soldier wrote in a letter composed from deep within a Southern battle zone: "Give us our rights, and we will die under the stars and stripes for the glorious old Union."[27]

Word finally arrived in South Carolina in August 1864 that all coloured troops were to receive equal pay from January 1 of that year. Under section 2 of an act adopted on June 15, 1864, no bounty was to be paid to coloured soldiers from that date to July 19, 1864 unless they were free as of April 19, 1861. Those who had been free prior to that date would get equal pay retroactively from the time of their enlistment; those who had been enslaved would not. All men claiming to have been free were required to swear an oath to that effect. Most of the men, humiliated and angry, some with tears in their eyes, begrudgingly submitted.

On Monday, October 10, 1864 at Folly Island, South Carolina, the 54th and 55th Massachusetts held a celebration after finally being paid after one year of refusing to accept lower pay — a long battle finally won. After the speeches were completed, the skilled regimental band "played a number of popular airs." A soldier who recorded the event wrote:

> There could be nothing finer than their performance … We all love our band. "Music hath charms" of a very superior kind in a place like this, and in a business like this. It seems to link us with home, recalling to the mind its pleasant associations, thereby going far towards ennobling and refining the character of the soldier.

Bombproof quarters for the Colored Troops on the lines in front of Petersburg, Virginia in August, 1864 offered some protection to sleeping soldiers. *ppmsca 32443u LOC.*

John Gooseberry of St. Catharines was a musician in the 54th Massachusetts. *Courtesy of Massachusetts Historical Society #72.5.*

Presumably, Canadian-born John Gooseberry, who was recorded as having once been a sailor from St. Catharines and was then a musician in Company E of the 54th, was among the band members that day. The writer described the celebration:

> It was a most impressive scene — a regiment of brave men celebrating, in the midst of war, one of the triumphs of peace, without arms, in the presence of their officers — a band of veteran warriors doing honor, by solemn ceremonies, to the recognition by Government of their citizenship and equality.

There were speeches, an elegant supper, toasts, songs, and cheers. "Gentlemen sang that night who were never known to sing before."[28] These gestures toward equality did much to spur enlistment, and many black men from the U.S. and Canada were inspired to enlist throughout the duration of the war.

Grieving widows and orphans were also given some small consolation by a recent act. Section 14 of an act approved July 4, 1864 stated that widows and children of coloured soldiers who had been or would be killed or who had died of wounds or disease while in the army would now receive pensions as provided by law. The proof needed would be affidavits from credible witnesses that the couple had lived together for at least two years immediately previous to enlistment. If those couples lived in a state where their marriage was legally performed, proof must be provided. Also, to qualify for a widow or orphan's pension, the widow and children must be free persons.

This same act provided that a bounty of one hundred dollars be paid for enlistees who signed up for one year, two hundred dollars for two years, three hundred dollars for three years: one third to be paid on mustering in, one third after half of the term, and the remaining third upon expiration of term. If the soldier died during service, this money would be paid to his widow; if there was no widow, then to his children; if there was neither widow nor children, then the bounty would be paid to his mother if she was a widow.

Scenes such as this dead Confederate soldier at Petersburg were captured in the early days of photography and brought the grim realities of war to the public. *LC-DIG-cwpb-02568. LOC.*

Of course, during times of war, any sort of jubilation would be short-lived. A month after the 54th and 55th held their celebration, Union forces in South Carolina attempted to cut the Charleston & Savannah Railroad. A force of 5,500 men boarded federal gunships and eventually made their way to a small ridge known as Honey Hill, where 1,400 Confederates had dug in. Although they had vastly greater numbers, the Union forces could not defeat their entrenched foes, and nearly eight hundred of their number were either killed or wounded in the attempt. Involved in the battle were Canadian troops in 32nd USCI (Pennsylvania), 54th and 55th Massachusetts, and the 102nd from Michigan.

John Saunders, twenty-two, from Chatham, of the 54th Massachussetts, was wounded at Honey Hill, as was William Henderson, also twenty-two, who had already survived being wounded at James Island on July 16, 1863. This wound was more serious and he had to finally be discharged for disability seven months later. Like many of his comrades in the 54th, Samuel

Duncan, a twenty-two-year-old sailor from London, had been at the skirmish on James Island, at the assault on Fort Wagner, and at the Battle of Olustee. His luck finally ran out when he was wounded at Honey Hill and was forcibly discharged from service on June 3, 1865 at St. Andrews Parish, South Carolina for physical disability caused by wounds received in action. The 55th Massachusetts also suffered their heaviest casualties in the war, with 33 men killed and 109 wounded, none of whom were from Canada.

Canadian-born Joseph Marshall fought in the battle with his regiment, the 102nd. He was severely wounded and lingered on for three weeks before dying at the Beaufort hospital on December 22. His regiment had been raised in Michigan following a July 25, 1863 order from the Department of War to Governor Austin Blair to raise a regiment of coloured men. It was initially known as "The 1st Regiment Michigan Colored Volunteers," before being officially re-designated the 102nd, in keeping with federal policy.[29] This regiment had by far the greatest number of men who lived or had lived in Canada — approximately 200.

Burial duty, such as this one on the battlefield at Cold Harbor, was a melancholy task for surviving soldiers. *LC-DIG-ppmsca-12615. LOC.*

A story that tugs at the emotions, related to the Battle of Nashville in the late autumn of 1864, is that of William Fields, who had found freedom and a farm and homestead within the Buxton Settlement, and his daughter, Mary, who remained enslaved in Tennessee. Foreseeing his own death, William recorded his will, which began:

I William Fields of the Township of Raleigh in the County of Kent and province of Canada Yeoman of the age of forty two years and being of sound mind and memory do make publish and declare this my last will and Testament in manner following

To wit my will is that my funeral charges and just debts shall be paid by my Executrix hereinafter named the residue of my estate and property which shall not be required for the payments of my just debts funeral charges and the expenses attending the execution of this my will and the administration of my estate I give devise and dispose therof as follows

That is to say

First I give and bequeath to my wife Hardinia Fields the entire and exclusive and undivided use of my dwellinghouse and property on which I now live being the north half of the north half of the South half of lot number Nine in the Ninth Concession in the Township of Raleigh in the County and Province aforesaid containing twenty five acres more or less to have and to hold the same for and during her natural life then

Second At the death of my wife I give and bequeath to my daughter Mary Fields now in bondage should she come to this country, the whole of my property as above described

Thirdly. Should my daughter already named not come to this country at the death of my wife I give and devise all the rest residue and remainder of my real estate in the Township of Raleigh and County aforesaid as described above for the purpose of educating poor colored Students for the Presbyterian Church of Canada.

Mary was still enslaved in 1859, when her father died without the comfort of knowing his daughter's future or how his estate would be distributed. For several years there was little optimism that Mary would be able to receive her inheritance — that is, until the Civil War changed everything. On November 29, 1864, Mary, who was then living in Nashville, indeed visited Canada to see and take possession of the land that her father had bequeathed to her.[30] The timing of her visit raises some interesting questions. Nashville had fallen to the Union army on February 25, 1862, therefore eventually making slaves in that city free — including Mary, if she was living there at the time — following the Emancipation Proclamation of January 1, 1863. However, the Confederate army marched back on Nashville in November, 1864, reaching the city on December 2. A large and bloody battle with 6,602 casualties took place December 14 and 15, before the Confederates were repulsed and forced to retreat. We are left to wonder if the fear of the upcoming battle, and her possible return to slavery if the Confederates won, caused Mary Fields to flee to the safety of Canada at that particular time.

CHAPTER 7

The War at Home

God bless Canada and her illustrious future. As she carried her flag westward and still westward, it would be her glory, above every nation that dwelt on this hemisphere, to carry a flag that in her hands had never been held over the head of a slave, and she would become the free nation of the North, and the mother of freedom.

— Rev. Henry Beecher[1]

The Underground Railroad continued to be active leading up to and after the opening shots on Fort Sumter, which ignited the Civil War. The *Providence Evening Post* of April 9, 1861 reported that three hundred blacks had recently crossed at Detroit into Canada. The next day, Washington's *Daily National Intelligencer* reported that 106 fugitive slaves had left Chicago for Canada in the days previous, as a result of five fugitives being arrested by a marshal who had been appointed by the Lincoln administration to return them to slavery in Missouri. The *Vermont Journal* of July 6, 1861 claimed that there was no attempt being made to capture hundreds of slaves from Virginia who were fleeing to Canada. The mountains of Virginia were full of runaways, it reported, and they had learned that scores of them were passing through Pennsylvania,

Ohio, and Michigan to cross at Detroit. A resident of Battle Creek, Michigan observed that there continued to be a constant flow of runaway slaves passing through that town on route to Canada in 1861.

Some had fled because of Southern rumours that slaves would be placed in the front lines of battles to take the Union fire. Others were fearful of the ill treatment that they had received from invading Northern armies. The editor of New York State's *Jamestown Journal* of August 16, 1861, had little sympathy for the refugees and none for their angry owners, writing:

> Let the thunder fall upon the rebels, and if the negroes hear the crash and wish to run, let them run — it is their godsend. Let them scamper to Canada, the north star, or wherever they can get shelter. Why should the army, the staff or the Camp, be hindered in the great work of crushing the nest of treason, with nice adjustments of the whither-from and whereabouts of these ebony runners, and whether they are from rebel or loyal masters.

Some curious stories related to flight also surfaced during the Civil War. According to the diary of Reverend William King of Buxton:

> ... there were a few fugitives that came into the settlement but there were quite a few of their masters came to escape the draft of the Southern army and hastened to Canada and some of them found asylum in the Elgin [also known as Buxton] settlement.

A similar story surfaced in St. Catharines. While on a trip through that city in 1861, William Wells Brown wrote a letter that was published in the Haytian Emigration Bureau's newspaper *Pine and Palm*, stating:

> Not long since, a slave run away from Virginia, came here, and settled down; a few months after, his master "broke down," cheated his creditors, escaped to Canada, came

and settled by the side of his former chattel. Their families borrow and lend now, upon terms of perfect equality.[2]

Other curious stories also made their way onto the pages of Canada's
newspapers. One such story concerned a runaway slave named Stuart
Kirke and appeared in the *Canadian Gleaner* from Huntington County,
Canada East. In the article it was reported that Kirke had been impressed
into the Confederate army and had fought in several engagements in
nearly one year's time. During one of these battles he was wounded in his
knee, and, unable to keep up with his retreating regiment, was captured
by the Union forces. They treated his wounds, and after he recuperated
he was signed on to do garrison duty in Philadelphia. Still living in fear
that he might be captured and returned to slavery, Kirke requested a two-
hour leave, and, along with a boy who was also a runaway, fled to a bush
where they hid until nightfall. In the darkness, they found some members
of the Society of Friends (Quakers) who provided changes of clothing
and gave him five dollars for his rifle. After this fortuitous meeting, the
pair of refugees hopped a freight train to Ogdensburg, New York. There,
they crossed the St. Lawrence River into Canada West to the port of
Prescott. They then walked three-hundred kilometres to Oshawa, where
they were pitied by some people who witnessed the weary pair's condition and bought train tickets for them to Toronto. Revealing the incredible lines of communication that existed by those who were enslaved or
involved in the Underground Railroad, Kirke knew that he had a cousin
who lived comfortably in Chatham, whom he hoped to connect with.
With tears in his eyes he commented that his only regret was that he had
a sister who was still in slavery.[3]

Harrison Webb, who fled to Hamilton, had a dramatic story where-
upon he took advantage of his master becoming a Confederate soldier:

> Kentucky was my home. I belonged to George D. Dicken,
> a planter … but old master I never cared so much about.
> I had heard tell of this hear underground railroad, whar
> it ended in Canada, and I says, say I, can't I git thar?
> Somethin' says "I kin." I was powerfully feared he would

ketch me, for he was mighty cunnin' about runaways. One day, 'pears as if he just kinder "suspected somethin'," when old marster he says, say he: "if one of my slaves should run away, I would follow him to hell, and if I saw him in thar I would just jump in and get him." Then old marster he went to jine the Confederates, and I started for Canada. I travelled at night. In the day I would hide in the woods. I lived on raw potatoes; turnips and anything I could get. I went to the stable of preacher Mason in Madison and two nights later he had a man start with me and two others for a pint thirty miles north. It took us two nights to make it. Then we was in an old cave for more 'an a week. A man comes one night when we was nearly starved and give us some apples and says the officers were watching for us. I was most scart to death. Then another man comes, and he say, say he "hit will take a lot of money to git you out of here, has you got inny?" I says $25. I had more but You see I was a hoss-trader for my marster and mighty cunnin' and cute. "Gimme that $25, says that man, and I will git you away 'To Detroit.'" I knowed that was right across the river from Canada but the Kaintuckians used to tell us that the river between Detroit and Canada was a thousand miles wide. So I gin him $25. We walked two nights, sleeping all day in a hollow tree.... Then he brought another man with lots of other runaways, and he loaded us all in a big covered wagon and we started agin. In the day he covered us with bedclothes, and sometimes I heard him talking with fellers who said they was lookin' for runaways. But they didn't git us. In 'bout a week we comes to a big town and a big river, and the man tells us to git out. It was night, and a man on a long boat with big paddles told us to git in quick, and he fetched us across and says, say he; "This is Canada and you is free." I jist hollered. I wanted to see my old marster thar, jist to laugh at him, for they couldn't get us in Canada.[4]

A twist to the story of slaves fleeing their Confederate masters appeared in a letter dated from Chatham, December 7, 1862, when Isaac Shadd informed George Whipple, secretary of the American Missionary Association, that the school that he and his family were associated with had that very morning "admitted a young man, a native of Alabama who was captured by the federals. He exhibits every appearance of being Alabama's best blood. The prejudice to the Negro race, will not at all interfere with him." Shadd added that within the past few days he had accepted applications from several students who were "contrabands from Kentucky, all well grown."[5]

Samuel Green had quite a unique story about his journey to Canada. A former Maryland slave, who had purchased his own freedom but remained in that state, had made what turned out to be the mistake of visiting his son, who had escaped to Salford, Canada West. Upon his return to Maryland, suspicion was raised that Green was involved in helping slaves escape. His home was raided and the constable found a map to Canada, a picture of a hotel at Niagara Falls, and a copy of what was considered in the South to be incendiary abolitionist literature, the

Isaac Shadd, brother of Mary Ann and Abraham W. Shadd. After the war, Isaac and his wife Amelia worked on the Davis Bend plantation, on what had once been Joseph Davis's (the elder brother of Confederate President Jefferson Davis) experiment as a model for transitioning slave labour to free labour by giving slaves the independence and responsibility to run their own affairs. This utopian ideal was restructured and continued during the Reconstruction period.

Sam Green, who was sentenced to ten years in the penitentiary for possessing a copy of *Uncle Tom's Cabin*. Sam Green sketch from William Still's *Underground Railroad. Courtesy of BNHS&M.*

book *Uncle Tom's Cabin*. Green's punishment for those crimes was a sentence to the penitentiary for ten years. After serving seven of those years, Maryland's newly elected governor released Green in 1862 on the condition that he leave the state. Green promised to go to Canada, presumably along with his wife Catharine — who he affectionately called "Kitty" and who he had purchased for one hundred dollars and manumitted twenty years earlier — quickly began their journey to be reunited with their son.[6]

The fleeing refugees could not be certain what would await them upon reaching Canada. In the immediate time leading up to the war, there was an extremely high-profile legal case taking place in Canada West that had international repercussions.

John Anderson (named Jack Burton before coming to Canada), had been born into slavery in Missouri. He was separated from his mother after she was sold to a slave trader as punishment for angering their master. As a young man, Anderson married a slave woman, Maria Tomlin, from a neighbouring plantation. The couple had a child together, but when Anderson was sold in 1853, his new master forbade him from visiting his family. This final assault upon Anderson's emotion motivated him to attempt to escape to the North. During that flight, he was recognized by a white slaveholder, Seneca Diggs, who, in the attempt to capture the resisting runaway, was stabbed and killed by Anderson.

After crossing the Detroit River in November 1853, and assuming the new name that he would become famously known by, Anderson frequently moved about the province and occasionally changed his name. Those additional precautions were prudent, as in 1854 the governor of Missouri made a request to Canadian officials for the extradition of Anderson to stand trial for the murder of Seneca Diggs. Anderson eluded capture for years, until March 1860, when he was arrested after being betrayed by someone that he had trusted and confided in while living in Caledonia. The resulting legal arguments were fought in Canada West and in England, as there was uncertainty as to whether the colony or the mother country had jurisdiction. The influential anti-slavery societies on both sides of the Atlantic were active in Anderson's defense. In the end, the Court of Common Pleas in Toronto ruled that Anderson was innocent of the charge of murder and therefore could not be extradited, and, on February16, 1861, ordered his release.[7]

The Court's ruling gave comfort to the thousands of former slaves who had found or were making their way to Canada. However, although courts could administer justice, they had little power over public opinion and could not assure racism and prejudice would not continue to be part of daily existence, try as they may. Newspapers on both sides of the border occasionally printed articles to illustrate that fact. An article about a court case at the Kent County Assizes informed readers that two white men, Thomas Russell and Surgeon Verrall, refused to serve on the same jury as a black man, stating that a coloured man is not intelligent enough to act. Justice Richards insisted that he was. Two other men were selected. They were both fined and threatened with jail if they did not pay.[8] St. Thomas's *Weekly Dispatch* of January 29, 1863 gave another example, stating that the *Essex Journal* reported that a coloured man was elected school trustee for School Section #1 of Anderdon Township the previous week, but as a result two white men who were also elected declined to serve.

Another issue that seemed at odds with Canada's reputation as a desired haven was that of colonization — an emotional issue that had deeply divided both the black and the broader anti-slavery community.

When the first rumours of war surfaced, the African Aid Society was preparing to establish a new black colony in Africa that would be settled by "carefully selected Free Coloured people from the United States and Canada." The Society had been formed with the support of Queen Victoria's husband, Prince Albert, after a meeting in London with Britain's Lord Alfred Churchill and three men then living in Canada: Martin Delany, William Howard Day, and Reverend William King. Delany had already done a lot of legwork on his visit to Africa with the Niger Valley Exploring Party, and the partnership was a natural fit. The Society's secretary in London, Ferdinand Fitzgerald, wrote to inform then-President-Elect Lincoln of the plan, and to ask him to consider it.[9]

But the outbreak of hostilities in the United States occurred before the plan could be implemented, as related by Reverend King:

> In the spring of 1861 I had several young men prepared to go as pioneers of the colonies. While I was corresponding with the Society in London about sending the young men out, the southern states seceded and war was declared. I then wrote to the Society in London that the sword had been drawn from the scabbard and would not be returned until liberty was proclaimed for the captives. The market for slaves as far as the U.S. was concerned would come to an end with the war. The young men who intended to go out to Africa to colonize the West Coast were prepared to go south to fight for liberty as soon as the opportunity would be given them to enter the northern army.[10]

During that same time, there was a more active colonization plan afoot, designed to send blacks from both Canada and the U.S. to Hayti. Free passage from the ports of New York, Boston, or Philadelphia aboard vessels that would take passengers on the two to three week voyage to Hayti, as well as free land grants, would be provided by the Haytian government to those who would commit to staying for a minimum of three years.[11] The official invitation of the island's president, Geffrard, which appeared in newspapers and was designed to appeal to black pride, stated in part:

Listen, then, all ye negroes and mulattoes who, in the vast Continent of America, suffer from the prejudices of caste. The Republic calls you; she invites you to bring to her your arms and your minds. The regenerating work that she undertakes interests all colored people and their descendants, no matter what their origin or where their place of birth.[12]

James Redpath, a white American journalist and anti-slavery activist, became the leading advocate and the director of the Haytian Bureau of Emigration, with the official title "General Agent of Emigration to Hayti from the United States and the Canadas." Redpath came with impressive credentials, having been a friend and biographer of John Brown and the author of the 1859 publication, *The Roving Editor: or, Talks with Slaves in the Southern States*, which included interviews that Redpath had conducted. Initially, Redpath was cautious about the Haytian scheme, in 1859 warning those who were considering leaving that they had "better turn your faces to the snow-drifts of Canada than the sunny mornes of Hayti."[13] However, after a second visit that same year and a third trip in 1860, he was convinced that the black-governed island was an ideal home for African Americans and Canadians who wished to escape prejudice and oppression.

Redpath hired agents to travel and lecture in an effort to encourage the emigration. Among them were John Brown Jr.; prominent black abolitionist and former slave William Wells Brown; and William J. Watkins, who was Frederick Douglass's assistant newspaper editor — all of whom travelled in Canada West. H. Ford Douglas was one of those commissioned to recruit in the United States.[14] By the beginning of 1861, John Brown Jr. was in the Windsor/Sandwich area of Essex County promoting the Haytian Colonization Society.[15] He soon got results, as he shared in a letter printed in the June 27, 1861 *Chatham Planet* that forty-nine blacks had left Windsor and Amherstburg for Hayti on June 10, 1861.

Rumours attributed to returnees soon began to reach North America that Hayti was not the paradise that had been promised. In a letter from Dresden, dated August 15, 1861, Parker T. Smith felt compelled to write to *The Christian Recorder* that Reverend William P. Newman, who once

John Brown Jr. maintained a close relationship with Canadian blacks through-out this era. In a letter to his wife, dated from Windsor, Canada West, Friday Eve, March 22, 1861, he wrote:

> It will really afford me a resting spell to get once more to a land where prejudice against Color assumes a milder type than it does in Canada. Indeed, if I were myself as black as ebony should not receive more undisguised coldness from the white inhabitants here than I now do, and this simply because I treat the colored man as an equal socially. In all of Canada West, a man would be read out of what they call "Good Society" who should ask a Colored man or woman to eat at the same table with him. In consequence of my boarding and lodging at their Houses, and in the street and at all places meeting them on terms of social equality, I have scarce been recognized by the white inhabitants here, as belonging to the human family. Every where I have met the cold shoulder. It is perhaps well. I am thereby enabled to sympathise with these people in their experience of a new form of Slavery, at least to me. "Man's inhumanity to me makes countless thousands mourn."

Transcription of original letter in John Brown Jr. Papers, held in the Manu-scripts Collections of the Rutherford B. Hayes Presidential Center. *Image from John Brown, 1800–1859 by Oswald Garrison Villard, (Boston and New York: Houghton Mifflin Company, 1910). 166a.*

lived at Dresden, had returned from Jamaica where he was then living and spoke to an assembled crowd, warning them that Mr. Redpath and John Brown Jr. only told the good things about Hayti, but Newman brought to light the many bad things.[16]

Brown was also hearing more than rumours, and immediately changed his mind after receiving several letters from the emigrants warning any people who were considering the move to remain in Canada, stating that if they had the means they would return. As a final warning of caution, one of them wrote:

> And now my friends you see that we have not come in sight of the promised land yet; we have to choose between two evils, to endure the prejudice of the Canadians, or hasten on the untimely graves of Hayti. Let the Canadians tread upon as they have, but for the just laws of good old England, we must prove ever loyal to Her Majesty — our Gracious Queen — and fight for her in Canada if needed.[17]

But others from different parts of Canada West were not yet convinced. In the autumn of 1861, Reverend David Hotchkiss, missionary of a black settlement in Essex County, informed George Whipple of the American Missionary Association that he was convinced that the residents of the Refugee Home Society would be better off moving to Hayti. Crop yields were poor due to extremes in the weather, with periods of rain that caused flooding, followed by extended periods of drought. Black landowners were also shackled with binding clauses in their deeds, which prohibited the sale of their land to anyone other than other American fugitive slaves, who were without any means to make payment.[18] Apparently many residents acted upon their desire to move. Referring to the Little River Settlement, Hotchkiss wrote on May 5, 1862, that "most have gone to Hayti." Later in the same letter he wrote "… others have thought they could better their condition by going to Hayti and have gone there. They have our best wishes both for Time and Eternity."[19]

Reverend Thomas Hughes, the Anglican priest who served as missionary to the black settlement at Dawn Mills on behalf of England's Colonial Church and School Society, recorded in his diary the melancholy story of a visit to one of his parishioners, Dennis Hill, who would not be able to make his planned-for trip:

> Found him very sick indeed — do not believe he can live for many days. Poor man, he has actually agreed to sell his farm and made arrangements to emigrate with his family to Hayti, and told me he thought when he got on the sea he would soon be better. I spoke to him of another land of promise and besought him to think of another voyage.[20]

Warnings and horror stories about Hayti began to become more prevalent. Such is the one outlined in a letter, dated February 15, 1862 and signed by George and Emeline Wells and Benjamin Baker:

> This is to certify that Hayti is a place not fit for any person to live in who has been accustomed to a residence in the North ... The spiders are as large as a medium-sized cat — walking wonders in fact. One vessel called the Truxilla sailed from New York, with one hundred persons on board, and at the present time there is not one of them living. Another vessel called the Flight also went from New York with twenty-five emigrants on board, and only three survive.[21]

The June 4, 1862 edition of *Chatham Weekly Planet* carried the news that, "of 14 people who left Buxton for Hayti last fall, 9 are now dead."

However, many emigrants then living there disputed such claims in a letter dated April 15, 1862, which appeared in *Douglass' Monthly* in July 1862. The writer, on behalf of the large group, proudly proclaimed that they had not been deceived and were perfectly capable of being able to judge whether or not their decision to move had been a wise one. Many of them had visited the island before committing to settle there, and had experienced for themselves the resources that the country offered, including a beautiful climate and rich soil for farming. They were pleased that the promises of land and building supplies that lured them there had been fulfilled, and many had been supported until their first crop had been harvested. Doctors had been provided, as had land for churches and schools.

While admitting that there had been some adversity, such as sickness and death, they felt that "no reasonable man expected anything less." The letter concluded:

In fine, friends in America, whatever may be said to the contrary by those whose characters we have no need to expose, we believe that no people ever rose sooner from the inferior positions accorded to us a few months ago in the States and the Canadas, to the respected position which we, thanks to a beneficent Government, occupy to-day in Hayti.

The thirty-two signators of the letter included sixteen Canadians: Dr. William Brazier, Reverend George Jacobs, Henry Rann, Peter Simmons, Perry Haughey, all from Buxton; Charles Harrison, Alfred Smith, and Pleasant Cross from Chatham; George W. Morgan of Rondeau; and those who simply stated that they were from Canada West — David Cooper, William James, Henry Moore, Samuel Parker, Wm. G. Jones, Richard Jones, and Eliza Harris.

Others also adapted to their situation, at least for a while. George and Delilah Morgan, from Harwich Township in Kent County, took their family to Hayti in 1861. Their twenty-one-year-old son, Zachariah, joined the Haytian army and served as first lieutenant. While there, Zachariah also had the pleasure of marrying Mary Nevitt, who had come to Hayti with her parents, James and Aramentha, from Sandwich East Township in Essex County. The Morgan family survived Hayti for seven years before leaving.[22]

Zachariah and Mary Morgan surrounded by their family in 1888. The Morgans settled in an unbroken forest in Michigan after leaving Haiti, and eventually established a prosperous farm and brickyard. The hardy Mary Morgan lived to be 106, a beloved figure in Boyne City, which she and her husband helped found. *Courtesy of Charlevoix County historian Bob Morgridge, with thanks to Jim Baumann, Executive Director of Boyne Area (Michigan) Chamber of Commerce.*

Reverend George Jacobs, who had long since distinguished himself in Canada, serving as a sergeant in Captain Nelson's company of coloured militia in the Rebellion of 1837, and later as a minister of the Anti-Slavery Baptist churches in Gosfield Township and in Buxton, was one of those who never left Hayti. Arriving there in 1862, he survived for two years before passing away shortly after his wife, leaving no will, thereby complicating the distribution of his estate for his children who had remained in Canada, and for a son who was in Hayti and required the assistance of the British Consul there.[23]

Margaret Rebecca Neal, originally from St. John's, New Brunswick, had nightmares for the remainder of her life when she recalled her childhood experiences in Hayti. According to late historian Arlie Robbins, Neal was taken to Hayti by her parents, along with her brother, an aunt, Mary Morgan, and other relatives. The family was forced to work in the sugar cane fields, where cruel overseers drove them, as did those in the American south. Armed guards prevented them from escaping. Both of Neal's parents succumbed to the harsh working conditions in the swampy fields. The determined Aunt Mary devised a plan to get herself and her nephew and niece away from that hell. On one occasion, while working as a washerwoman for the ships that docked at the nearby port, Mary covered the children with laundry, and with the help of sympathetic sailors, secreted them away, eventually reaching Canada West.[24]

As time passed, it was becoming more widely apparent that the horror stories of Hayti were too prevalent to be untrue. An open letter dated April 25, 1863 from Port Au Prince claimed that people had been seduced by lies to go, and once there, their lives developed into a tragic story:

Now let me ask them a question, where are two thirds of those people who emigrated to Hayti? Can you tell? When the friends and relations inquire for their welfare, can you answer? I presume not. You dare answer, but let me answer for you; let me tell them the truth; they are gone, they are dead. Then let me ask another question, did they die a natural death? No, they died with hunger, thirst, and for the want of proper medical treatment when they had the fever. Then let me ask you another question, did not the government hear and see the cries of the people, and did they not promise to support them until they could get along? Yes, they heard but they would not listen, they saw but they would not see. For their promises they are like crust, they are made but to be broken. Were these people located in a beautiful meadow where the water streams from the mountains and waters their gardens and corn fields? No, but they were located by the government, upon the highest mountains and in burning plains, where they were compelled to go five or six miles before they could get one glass of water to quench their thirst. Their cries did reach the government, but they were unheeded ...[25]

There were occasionally horror stories that occurred much closer to home. On March 14, 1863, the "negro shanty-town" in Oil Springs, Canada West, was destroyed and burned by a mob. Newspaper reports from both sides of the border carried the story and placed the blame on some of the American draft dodgers who had brought their racial hatred north with them.

According to the *Douglass' Monthly* on April 1863:

> A riot of serious character occurred here on Saturday night, owing to a grudge against the colored people. The rioters to the number of 80 or 100, assembled at the east end of the town, chose a captain, and then marched to the dwellings of the negroes. On arriving at their destination, they ordered the negroes to leave town; and, before they had time to obey the order, the mob commenced their work of destruction by destroying the furniture belonging to the negroes, and then fired the houses, of which four were destroyed, and beating any negro they could catch. Detective McKain swore in a number of constables, and succeeded in capturing three of the rioters. It was reported that one negro was killed, but it is now denied. One is badly hurt. The others ran to the woods and escaped. Great excitement still prevails here.

The *Montreal Commercial Advertiser* reported:

> Oil Springs has been indulging in an eruption of negrophobia; and this odiferous neighborhood yesterday disgraced itself by an emute directed against the colored inhabitants, whose houses were destroyed and themselves driven to the woods. As those who have sustained losses have their legal remedy against the municipality, it will find this kind of amusement more expensive than profitable. We trust the Government will take care that the aggressors are brought to exemplary punishment.[26]

The *Chatham Planet* of March 16 stated that:

> the rioters were principally skedaddlers from the United
> States, cowardly scamps who had accepted Uncle Sam's
> bounty and a suit of army clothes — men who had vio-
> lated their oaths, and stand recorded as perjured desert-
> ers. The *Planet* learns that some forty of the rioters have
> been arrested, and it warns those who ran away from their
> native land and come to Canada, that they will be taught
> that Canadian law is for the vindication of even-handed
> justice to all, and not to protect the rascally and the lawless.

The *Daily Cleveland Herald* of March 25, 1863 reported that the
negroes were peaceful and industrious, "and the destruction of their
homes by a gang of 80 or 100 teamsters and wood-choppers, was in keeping with the Detroit mob."

The "Detroit mob" referred to in the article had been active only days
before the Oil Springs outrage, and there too was a Canadian component
to the story. On March 6, 1863, a race riot broke out on the streets of
Detroit after a court case where a man who was rumoured — probably
inaccurately — to be black, was sentenced to the penitentiary for assault-
ing a ten-year-old white girl.[27] As the outraged group tried to seize the
imprisoned black man to levy their own brand of justice, they were fired
upon by the provost guard, killing one and wounding several others. This
naturally fuelled the rioters, who were further incensed that one of their
own had been killed by guards who were defending a person who they
felt was unworthy of due process. The crowd then turned their vengeance
onto any blacks in the area. It began by attacking them with bricks,
stones, and clubs. The blacks defended themselves with bullets fired from
windows. The scene quickly deteriorated as the mob set fire to one of
the dwellings and waited with pistols drawn and axes, clubs, and spades
in hand as the terrified victims fled from the flames. The carnage was
bloody and unrelenting, with no mercy shown to the elderly, women, or
children. As large neighbourhoods were put to the torch, the conflagra-
tion could clearly be seen from the Canadian side of the border, which

soon became a haven for many fleeing blacks.[28] Joshua Boyd, a young mechanic who had been struck in the head with an axe, severely burned half-an-inch deep on his leg and buttock, and then severely beaten while still unconscious, was carried to Canada that Friday night. There was no hope for his survival, despite being returned to St. Mary's Hospital in Detroit a day later to receive medical treatment. It took until Tuesday night for death to mercifully end his suffering. Boyd was a runaway slave from Virginia who had recently taken advantage of the chaos of civil war to escape to Michigan.[29] At the time of his death, he had almost raised enough money to purchase his wife and children, who were still enslaved. All of his savings were consumed in the fire.[30]

William Jones, a fifty-nine-year-old Methodist minister from Windsor, was among those unfortunate Canadians who found themselves on the wrong side of the border that day. While innocently visiting a black family who lived in a home that was attached to a cooper shop, "a shower of clubs and stones came through the window."[31] After the mob set fire to the building, Jones's attempt to escape from the flames was hindered by the crowd, which included United States soldiers. Jones finally rushed into the crowd, was knocked to his knees several times, and was stabbed in the neck. Despite these injuries, he broke free and ran to the shop of a white couple who hid him away in the upper story of their home.

Canadian connections with the city of Detroit continued to be troubling at other times during the war. According to a report in the November 12, 1864 *The Christian Recorder*, on October 30, the border city was alarmed by the ringing of church bells and the calling out of soldiers. Word quickly spread that the mayor had received a dispatch from the U.S. consular agent in Toronto that warned that a group of one hundred heavily armed Southerners had left the city with the intention of invading either Buffalo or Detroit. Blacks in those cities were warned to seek shelter. When the notice was read in their churches, the panic-stricken parishioners jumped up and ran down the aisles to the exits, some jumping over the pews. As rumours circulated that four boatloads of men were coming down the river from the port at Sarnia, officers on horseback galloped through the streets, attempting to give orders to the thousands of people who were milling about. More than two thousand people applied to the authorities for permission to be armed to meet the raiders. The scene only exacerbated racial tensions, already fuelled by recent attacks on city blacks. Fortunately, the story of the expected raid turned out to be groundless.

A bloodier riot — the same one that Anderson Abbott believed he and Mary Augusta had been the first victims of — erupted in New York City on July 13, 1863, after names began to be drawn for involuntary conscription into the Union army. Many poorer people resented that wealthier people could pay a substitute to go in their place, and many opposed the war in principle, having no interest in risking their lives so that slaves could be freed. The riots began as growing mobs — which included many working-class Irish — who looted, destroyed, and burned property, including that of known, prominent Republicans; the wealthy; and charitable Protestant establishments. They then turned on the blacks — beating them, burning their homes, lynching a man and setting him on fire as he was going through his death throes, and burning the Colored Orphan Asylum that housed over two hundred children, ages four to twelve. A mob of around four hundred people first stole furnishings and anything of value before burning the building. The children were thankfully rushed out of the back door by the matron and the superintendent and taken to safety at the police station from Monday until Thursday. The final death toll was uncertain, but many placed it as over one hundred.

An executive committee was appointed to help those who had lost property during the riots, and to provide for widows, orphans, and other dependents of those who had been killed. A donation total of $40,779 was raised. Blacks had scattered to hiding places within and outside of the city. The committee members visited these people, or had local black pastors discover those who were in need. It is interesting to note that in the report submitted by Secretary Vincent Colyer, he had special praise for blacks from British colonies that applied for aid:

> Several applications for relief and claims for damages, were made by those who had previously resided in Canada and the British West Indies, and I have observed with some interest, that all such persons have had a more clear,

straightforward, unembarrassed, yet equally respectful way of presenting their claims. Whether this comes from habits formed, by living in a country where the black man is more respected than with us, I am unable to say.[32]

Cross-border life and travel continued as usual for many blacks during the war years. Curiously, some of that travel involved going into the slave states. Thomas Arthur Brown, originally a slave in Maryland, had purchased his freedom from his own relatives and then married and lived in Pittsburgh for several years, where his home was an Underground Railroad station. He moved to Canada West around 1860 along with his wife, Frances, and their five children. After spending a year in Chatham, the family moved to a more rural setting on the 9th Concession, a few miles out of the city. However, Thomas Brown maintained his job as a steward on a Mississippi steamboat that travelled between St. Louis and New Orleans. On one occasion, during the Civil War, when the steamboat was docked in St. Louis in early autumn, Thomas was approached by two men who asked him to take care of their two large carpetbags while they did some shopping. The porter graciously agreed. The two men left the boat and did not return when it departed to claim their bags. When the boat docked in Memphis, Tennessee, officers boarded to check for any contraband goods. When they examined the carpetbags, they discovered percussion caps that were destined for the Confederate army. Thomas Brown was unable to persuade the officers that he had been duped into being the courier, and was put into chains, returned to St. Louis, and imprisoned. He remained there until late spring the following year, when he was finally released and allowed to return to his family in Canada.

In the absence of their husband and father, Frances and the children — as did their neighbours whose loved ones had joined the Union army — struggled to get by during the severe winter months. There was meat to cure in the smokehouse, fruit and vegetables to can, firewood to cut, wool to card and spin, livestock to feed and care for. But all was not drudgery and sacrifice. There were gatherings with song around the fireplace, books to read, quilting bees, and moonlit sleigh rides with wagons mounted on bobsleds.[33] Life went on.

Thomas Arthur Brown left the security of his Canadian home and worked on a Mississippi River boat during the war. *Ohio History Connection, Hallie Q. Brown Collection NAM_MSS5_B08F08_B.*

Frances Jane Scroggins Brown remained in Canada to raise her family during the war, while her husband returned to the U.S. for employment. *Ohio History Connection, Hallie Q. Brown Collection. NAM_MSS5_ B08F08-A.*

Reverend Thomas Hughes recorded many details about day-to-day life in his diary. On August 1, 1861, he wrote:

> This day the Anniversary of the Emancipation of Slavery in British West Indies is quite a red letter day with the colored population of Canada. There was quite a large gathering at Windsor, to which a considerable number have gone from this neighbourhood. The people here have had a sort of picnic in the bush which has been well attended.

The next day, he reflected on a strange talk that one of the speakers had made at that anniversary the day before, which he had been asked about:

> Was asked a very strange question today, which I must confess completely posed me. It appears that at the picnic yesterday, some addresses were delivered, and one individual undertook to explain to the people how it came about that a portion of the human family became white. According to his account, original color of all was black, but that on a certain occasion the ancestor of the white race told one of God's prophets a lie, and immediately became white, which color the prophet told him should, as a mark of God's displeasure for his wickedness, cling to him and his seed forever.

Hughes, who was born in England, displayed his conservative beliefs that were at odds with the character of many blacks in his August 25, 1861 entry:

> A large colored camp meeting a few miles on the other side of Chatham is being held now, and to which a large portion of the colored people of this district had gone. The distance is great (between 20 and 30 miles). Numbers went yesterday and not a few started in the middle of the night in order to be there in time. I understand that the

194

Methodists closed their church so that their members and preachers might go. I was thankful to find that those who profess to have attached themselves to my congregation had resisted the excitement.

Hughes was described by a black man who knew him as "an untiring advocate of the equality of man, and knows no complexional distinctions." Hughes stood in sharp contrast to his fellow Anglican clergyman, Reverend John Gunn, who made insensitive remarks to a black audience at a picnic that occurred on Reverend Hughes's farm. At the conclusion of a pleasant afternoon, during which students proudly demonstrated what they had learned in school, both adults and children sang "God Save the Queen" around the British flag, and adult speakers praised Hughes for helping to tear down prejudice, Reverend Gunn spoiled the occasion by trying to justify the prejudice around Dresden, telling the crowd that it was natural for English people to look down on fugitives since it was the English disposition to rule, and blacks had arrived in Canada as runaway slaves and were inferior. In an apparent reference to the John Anderson extradition case, he said: "It would be wrong to kill your masters in attempting to escape, for the word of God teaches me, Servants, obey your masters." Gunn also suggested that, like the biblical children of Israel had done, blacks should wait until God sent them a deliverer. One of the angered audience members could not help but be reminded of the first verse, second chapter of Job which stated: "And Satan came also among them to present himself before the Lord."[34]

On May 21, 1862, Reverend Hughes made a diary entry in which, though the central event was heartbreaking, there was nevertheless the opportunity for optimism:

Buried the girl Cross this afternoon at Dawn Mills, and was pleased to find a number of white people at the funeral.... It is pleasing also to record that the corpse was borne to the grave by both colored and white young men, a circumstance that I have never witnessed before. Dawn Mills is notorious for its inveterate prejudice against the colored people, but Cross has lived a long time amongst them and appears to have gained even their goodwill.

Of course, many other examples existed of walls that divided the races being slowly pulled down, and of Canadian sentiment shifting to support the North. When New Orleans-born Louis Moreau Gottschalk, the son of a Jewish father and Creole mother, who was recognized as the greatest piano virtuoso on the continent, performed in Montreal, loud calls erupted from the audience shouting "Dixie!" Bewildered at first, Gottschalk gradually realized the pro-South meaning of the chant and responded by vigorously playing "Hail Columbia," the "Star Spangled Banner," and "Yankee Doodle," thereby shaming and quieting the crowd and earning their genuine applause.[35]

More and more Canadians also expressed their support for Lincoln and his policies, as witnessed by a letter to the President, dated November 8, 1864, and signed by one hundred people from Hamilton:

We can assure your Excellency that the best and most intelligent people of Canada are this day earnestly praying that success in this Electoral struggle may attend the efforts of yourself and your friends. We believe that their prayers will be favourably answered — and on your re-election that you will unwaveringly pursue the course you have already adopted by means of which American freedom — freedom in the true sense of the word — shall be permanently secured not only to the white man but to every enslaved child of Africa.[36]

The war was also an ever-present topic from the pulpit and in the sanctuary. Although the delegates at the BME General Conference, which was held in Chatham in 1864, still had to deal with the business and doctrines of the church — such as attempting to reach a consensus on issues such as divorce and remarriage — everyone in attendance had an eye to the South as they expressed a desire to help the newly freed people and sent their love and prayers to relatives and friends they had left behind in slavery, as well as to their sons who were in the Union army. Incidentally, many white families of Chatham also attended the meeting, and the daughter of the ex-mayor of Chatham donated a dollar to be sent to Virginia to help with the cause.[37]

To show that there could still be some levity during challenging times, Reverend John M. Brown reported that Methodist preachers were particularly great eaters, and "they may differ about predestination, election, ordination, reprobation, church government, and a thousand other things, but when a good dinner is to be discussed, there is a great unity of action as well as sentiment."[38] Not only was Reverend Brown's humour appreciated, but even more so were the letters that he brought with him from slaves in Virginia, which were to be distributed to friends who had previously made their way to Canada via the Underground Railroad. The acting postal-carrying minister could not resist quipping that the Underground Railroad "has gone entirely out of use, except for our 'Southern brethren' who don't like the near approach of Generals Grant, Sherman and Butler. It is astonishing with what facility white men learn to do just what colored men do."[39]

In the winter of 1864–65, the black churches of Buxton, Chatham, Windsor, Amherstburg, St. Catharines, and Vancouver were all hosting revival services, partially fuelled by concern about the war. A newspaper correspondent who was familiar with them used appropriate language when he trumpeted that:

> The work of the Lord is still going on. Last evening the anxious seat was crowded with mourners, crying for mercy, and still there is room for more, and by the help of the Lord we intend to push the battle to the gate. The Lord is on the giving hand, and sinners are falling and crying for mercy. They are flocking to the anxious seat as doves to their windows… The battle is getting hotter every day, and sinners can't stand the fire.[40]

There was another heated battle going on through the courts, newspapers, on the streets, and in the sanctuaries by the British Methodist Episcopal ministers throughout the war years. There had been a schism in the church after the Canadian churches decided to become distinct from the African Methodist Episcopal (AME) church, renaming themselves in honour of the country that had given them freedom. Reverend Willis Nazrey, who was a bishop of the AME church of the United States and Canada, and stationed in Canada, was elected the first bishop of the BME conference. After a controversy arose about the propriety of Reverend Nazrey being a bishop in both countries, he offered his resignation from the Canadian position. The resignation was not accepted, and Nazrey continued in that role. Several ministers of the BME took issue with Nazrey's holding on this senior role and sought to re-establish the conference under new leadership. At an 1861 convention held in Windsor, Reverend Augustus R. Green was appointed bishop, and a few other ministers, including Charles H. Pierce, joined with him, thereby igniting the firestorm with their previous friends.

Two of the unfortunate victims of this ongoing fight were the young lovers John Perry and Amy Simpson, from Colchester Township in Essex County, who were joined in marriage in July 1862 by Reverend Charles H. Pierce. Lawyers soon entered the fray when the old established BME ministers laid charges for "unlawful marrying," on the grounds that Pierce did not belong to a recognized denomination in Canada. Pierce was found guilty by a jury at the County Court. However, there were still some points of law that needed to be ruled upon at the Provincial Court of Common Pleas in Toronto in February 1862. The judges there confirmed the ruling of the lower court and turned the case back to it for sentencing. At the spring assizes at Sandwich, a nervous Reverend Pierce, who had been free on bail, awaited the penalty, which by the Consolidated Statutes of Upper Canada, allowed for up to a two-year imprisonment at the provincial penitentiary as well as a fine. Although by the exact letter of the law, it was recognized that Pierce had previously been an ordained minister with the original BME conference and that body's counsel made it clear that his clients only wanted a judicial ruling on the legitimacy of the splinter group. To that point, a relieved Pierce was fined one dollar. A smug minister who aligned himself with the established church and who had a personal vendetta against Pierce, gleefully wrote that if this ruling did not once and for all quash the splinter group, "then the North has gained no victory over the South, in the present war."[41]

However, the jubilation of the victors was short-lived. Bishop Green was himself asked to perform the marriage of two of his parishioners, James W. Thompson and Mary Maden. Feeling duty-bound, and not a little bit defiant, Green performed the ceremony at 7:30 p.m. on April 16, 1863. A constable with a summons for Green to appear in court for "pretend[ing] to solemnize, matrimony" was there by 8:00 p.m., just as the newlyweds and their guests were about to enjoy a wedding feast. Learning from the mistakes in Reverend Pierce's case, Green pleaded not guilty, and, after the fumbling statements of some witnesses for the prosecution, the prisoner was found not guilty. In a hasty move to remove the tarnish from Reverend Pierce, the same judge accepted the one dollar and legally restored him to the ministry.[42] Newlywed couples John and Amy Perry and James and Mary Thompson would naturally share in the relief that their marriages had been legal.

The death of two of the most prominent figures of the anti-slavery movement occurred in Canada during the Civil War years. Anthony Burns was the subject of international attention in 1854, when, as a runaway slave, he was arrested in Boston, famously escorted to the wharf by armed marines before thousands of irate and screaming Bostonians, returned to slavery, later redeemed, and eventually travelled to Canada; Burns died of consumption in St. Catharines on July 27, 1862 after a four-month illness that he contracted from the exposure and overexertion he suffered while trying to raise money to clear the debt owing on the Zion Baptist church that he pastored. Burns's friend and fellow minister, Reverend Hiram Wilson, attended the funeral and wrote a moving and reflective letter:

The concourse around his peaceful grave were mostly colored — the adults of whom, like himself, had fled from bondage; and yet there was quite a number of white people of various churches and different nationalities. While there consigning his mortal remains to the silent dust, I thought of the awful excitement a few years ago in Boston, attendant on his arrest, and rendition to the hands of bloody men, who are now in open rebellion against the government, and against God and humanity. I seemed to have a sort of panoramic vision of the pro-slavery treachery — the arrest, the court proceedings, the mass meetings, the vast array of marshals and of the military, and the countless throngs of people blocking up the streets of Boston — his dark and awful doom as a victim of the fugitive slave law, and the hellish exultations of the slave power on the one hand — while lamentations spread all over the coasts of New England and rolled back to the Rocky Mountains. I thought of that iniquitous system as having culminated to the awful crisis now hanging over the American people. The name of Anthony Burns fills an important place in the history of events which led to the great conflict now pending between the marshalled hosts of freedom and the fiendish friends and minions of slavery, and will be pronounced with honor when the fetter shall have fallen from the limbs of millions of his suffering brethren.[43]

This image of Anthony Burns is surrounded by dramatic scenes from his life, including his sale at auction, his escape from Richmond, his arrest in Boston, and his escort back to slavery by federal marshals and troops. *LC-DIG-pga-04268. LOC.*

Hiram Wilson would also not live to see the war's end and the freedom of the race that he devoted most of his life to. He died in his St.
Catharines home on April 16, 1864 at the age of sixty.[44] Wilson was an
active abolitionist as a young man attending college in Ohio, and had
moved to Toronto in 1836, where he became an agent of the American
Anti-Slavery Society. He travelled the province of Canada West for years
— often on foot — establishing schools and ministering to fugitives. In
1842 he, along with James Canning Fuller and Josiah Henson, established
the British American Institute at what became the Dawn Settlement,
remaining there until 1850, when he moved to St. Catharines. He was
an active conductor of the Underground Railroad, provided food and
shelter for new arrivals, and periodically travelled to the eastern U.S., as
well as to Britain, to raise funds for Canadian refugees.

Blacks in Canada shared many stories of longing for home. In his
letters to a friend in Philadelphia, Parker T. Smith shared the everyday
details of his life at Dresden — he wrote of people in the community
building a house for "old father Henson," that they would soon build an
Odd Fellows Hall, and that there were community social events, such
as debates held by "The Dresden Mutual Improvement Association."
On a more personal level, he wrote that his "children are as sprightly as
Larks, and have their health better than when in the city. There is splendid sleighing here now." He had a smokehouse filled with both beef and
pork; plenty of wheat, which could be ground into flour; peas that could
be made into coffee; and lots of firewood to comfort his family during the
winter. Further to that, he trumpeted: "I can only say as I did before, and
that is that I never have lived in a place where I felt so free." Despite all of
that, Smith wrote: "I make money and could soon accumulate property,
but a contented mind is a continual feast you know, and unless a person
is satisfied there is no use of talking about staying in a place."[45] In short,
he was lonesome and intensely missed old friends, and his mind was
made up that he would return to them.

Most poignant of all the personal stories, both from before and after
the war, were those of loved ones who mourned for friends and family
who had been sold away from them. Eliza Beck, who had been enslaved
in Plattsburgh, Missouri, but had gained her freedom during the war and

moved to Leavenworth, Kansas, desperately tried to find her son, John Terry, who had been separated from her when he was sold south. It had been three years since she had heard from him after he had escaped and made his way to Chicago on route to Canada. Through the columns of *The Christian Recorder*, she beseeched anyone with information on him to contact her.[46]

On a broader scale, while the war was going on, and perhaps because of it, talks began in Charlottetown, Prince Edward Island about the union of the British North American maritime provinces of Nova Scotia, New Brunswick, and Prince Edward Island.[47] Officials from Canada East and Canada West were invited as observers, also suggesting that there be a larger union stretching from the Atlantic Ocean to the Rocky Mountains.[48]

CHAPTER 8

Freedmen's Inquiry Commission

But surely, history will record their blameless life as a people; their patient endurance of suffering and of wrong; and their sublime return of good for evil to the race of their oppressors.

— Samuel Gridley Howe[1]

In March 1863, Secretary of War Edwin Stanton created a commission to inquire, "as to the measures which may best contribute to the protection and improvement of the recently emancipated freedmen of the United States, and to their self-defense and self-support." Another question that they felt needed to be answered was whether or not it was necessary to establish a system of guardianship — be it "provisional or permanent," and if so needed, what details it might entail. Even more important to the issue that was dividing the country and sparking the war, was whether or not freedom could endure if emancipation was not universal for the entire union, including the Confederate States. Further, how could the recently emancipated be used in helping to put down the rebellion? And, of course, the concern of whether the two races could live harmoniously together, and whether blacks could acquire the opportunity to prosper, needed to be addressed.

Three capable men, Robert Dale Owen, James McKaye, and Samuel Gridley Howe, were entrusted to investigate and report their findings. James Yerrington acted as corresponding secretary. Owen, a two-time congressman from Indiana, chaired the commission. James McKaye was a New York abolitionist. Howe was a prominent anti-slavery activist from Boston and was involved in several high-profile and celebrated fugitive slave rescues. He was also one of the "secret six" supporters of John Brown, who spearheaded the bloody insurrection at Harper's Ferry, after which he was forced to flee to Canada for a short period to avoid prosecution from U.S. authorities. Howe was the husband of Julia Ward Howe, who gained her own fame for writing "The Battle Hymn of the Republic."

When considering what approach to take, the commissioners thought it critical to delve into the historical realities of race relations in the Western hemisphere — what had happened, what was happening, and what might come to be. They then looked northward, to one of the obvious places that could provide valuable insight — Canada West. In the report to Stanton, the commissioners justified their plan:

> The fact that many thousands of blacks and mulattoes, who have fled from slavery, or from social oppression in this country, are living in Upper Canada as free men, with all the rights and privileges of British subjects, is too important to be overlooked by a Commission of Inquiry into the condition and capacity of the colored population of the United States, just set free.[2]

With his background and connections in the anti-slavery movement, Howe was the obvious choice to go to Canada. Seeking advice on whom he should contact, Howe turned to George L. Stearns, his old friend and fellow "secret six" supporter of John Brown, who had more recently been in touch with Canadians as he recruited for the coloured troops:

Chicago, August 2nd, 1863
Dr. S.G. Howe

Dear Sir

Your favour of 24th ult. To Major G. L. Stearns asking information of refugees in Canada I rec'd from him yesterday with request to answer the same Which I cheerfully do by referring you to Mrs. Mary Ann Cary of Chatham C.W. who of all that I met in Canada is best advised and who would I know be pleased to correspond or meet you. Rev. Mr. Anderson who married a Mrs. Shad [sic] is a man of intelligence and experience in Canada and who lives some five miles from Chatham. Rev. Mr. Simpson of Chatham is another. At Windsor C.W. is Rev. William Troy who I should place next to Mrs. Cary and who would I know be glad to either write or meet you. If I have not sufficiently answered your request please write me or if I can otherwise serve you command me

While I remain, Yours truly,

J.W. Spooner[3]

Samuel Gridley Howe made two trips to Canada West to interview former slaves on behalf of the U.S. Freedmen's Inquiry Commission. *Image from Portraits of American Abolitionists. Photo. 81.345. Courtesy of Massachusetts Historical Society.*

In addition to George Stearns, the commissioners also turned to Frederick Douglass, who was well connected with and informed about the black Canadian experience. Douglass recommended Reverend Hiram Wilson, then in St. Catharines, and Reverend William King in Buxton as important contacts.[4] In the fading days of summer 1863, Howe and Yerrington began their travels, which would take them across the province of Canada West to most of the areas that had sizeable black communities — including Toronto, the Niagara Peninsula, Hamilton, London, Galt, Queen's Bush, Kent, and Essex Counties.

HAMILTON

On September 3, 1863, Yerrington recorded Howe's first interview, with Reverend Philip Broadwater, a retired Baptist minister from Hamilton who had been born in Upper Canada fifty years before. Broadwater answered the questions put to him. The first question, no doubt nearest to the reverend's heart, was about religion. He mentioned two Methodist and one Baptist church in the city, and he seemed pleased that his people were very religious. He was also happy that race relations were good and that whites would generously donate to a coloured person who was sick. However, this was rarely needed, as blacks were independent and many were too proud to accept charity. Black and white children attended the same schools in Hamilton, unlike in Chatham and St. Catharines, where there were separate schools — something that Broadwater believed was a mistake. He admitted that racial slurs were bandied about, but subsided if they were ignored. If there was freedom in the United States, Broadwater believed that very few blacks would remain in Canada. The eternal question about the harsh Canadian climate was asked, but the reverend dismissed the stereotype, stating that "there is not a whit's difference between this climate and in the Northern States; the winter is a little longer, that is all."[5] In reply to the question about differences in procreation among the two races, Broadwater could see none. Neither could he believe that blacks were any more prone to disease; in fact, he thought there was less illness in Canada than in the U.S. Blacks married in Hamilton churches the same as did whites, owned property, and voted at elections if they were landowners or paid taxes.

Such were the nature of the questions that would be asked at the forthcoming interviews, all designed to address some of the preconceived notions that many people had at the time.

The next interviewee, William Howard, reported that he believed there were five or six hundred coloured people in Hamilton, most of which were mulattoes, and about four out of five were fugitive slaves. Howard agreed with Broadwater that race relations were good, with a few minor exceptions, and that blacks had employment and many owned property. They were allowed to ride the public conveyances and to enter any public buildings. Blacks were welcomed at the Anglican Church, which many attended, although many others preferred to go to the black churches. Howard stated that there was no vagrancy among his people, as was the case with the Irish, and little petty crime. He made special mention of one former slave who had ran away fifteen years previously and now owned a prosperous hotel worth eight or ten thousand dollars. Howard felt that blacks had as many children as whites (with the exception of the Irish), and that they were healthier. Howard differed with Broadwater on the question of whether blacks would return to the U.S. if slavery were abolished, because, as the recent New York and other riots demonstrated, prejudice was still rampant. He declared that the coloured people had a stronger feeling of loyalty, and, although they believed that Lincoln was one of the greatest of men, they "almost go crazy when the name of the Queen is called."[6]

Howe also made a point of interviewing prominent whites in the various locations, to get their perspective. Dr. Henry T. Ridley of Hamilton gave his medical opinion after eleven years of experience that blacks were more liable to suffer from consumption, small pox, and diseases of the bowels, glands, and brain. They were equally fertile; however, mortality rates were higher for those under twenty-five. He believed that venereal disease was more common with them. It was his opinion that there were a sufficient number of blacks in Hamilton at that time and no more need come as there were a limited number of jobs they could occupy. He also did not want any of them living beside him, as he unconvincingly said, "not on account of their color, particularly, but they have a peculiar odor about them which is disagreeable to me."[7]

Anglican minister J.G. Geddes of Hamilton, who welcomed blacks to his church, noted that wherever there were large numbers of blacks in the province, there was more prejudice. He mentioned Chatham in particular. In one case there, parents withdrew their daughters from school because they had heard that coloured people had been admitted. Geddes, who seemed to be very progressive in his feelings, believed that integration was the best way for all to prosper. However, he also felt that the lighter the skin a person had, the greater their intelligence.[8]

Reverend Thomas Kinnard, a former slave from Delaware and BME minister of a new brick chapel in Hamilton during the Civil War years, was asked with which country his loyalty laid. He hesitated in replying, and asked Howe for a pledge of secrecy, reasoning, "because we are between the hawk and the eagle, and God only knows which will devour us. Certainly, we are loyal, but we are more loyal to freedom than to any other parties. I am more loyal to human freedom than I am to Britain or the United States."[9]

Reverend Thomas Kinnard. *Courtesy of Schomburg Center for Research in Black Culture/Manuscripts, Archives and Rare Books Division. New York Public Library, Astor, Lenox and Tilden Foundations. Catalog Call Number: Sc Rare 287-H. Digital ID: 1245673. Record ID: 212506.*

Kinnard had attended the John Brown convention in Chatham and was therefore likely at ease with Howe in speaking his thoughts. He believed that "if freedom is established in the United States, there will be one great black streak, reaching from here to the uttermost parts of the South." As for the question of the black children who had been born in Canada, Kinnard believed that the results would be the same, stating, "the children may be attached here, but you generally see the chickens follow the old hen. If the chickens are hatched in the barn, and the old hen makes for the house for the crumbs, the chickens follow her."[10]

Kinnard made it clear that Canada was not home and that everyone would always be glad to return "home" when the opportunity arose. That sentiment was severely tested the following year when Kinnard attended the annual general conference of the mother organization, AME, held in Philadelphia. While in the United States, he decided to visit his birthplace in nearby Camden, Delaware. Once in that city, he was arrested under one of those punitive laws, which prohibited blacks from entering the state. Kinnard was fined fifty dollars plus legal costs. Unable to pay that amount, the prisoner was put up for sale and ironically purchased by the brother of the man who had owned and emancipated him several years before. This brother then had to post another fifty dollars' security that Kinnard would leave Delaware within five days. Armed with transcriptions of the legal proceedings and other relevant documents, as well as letters to the congressmen from Delaware, an incensed Reverend Kinnard made haste to the nation's capital at Washington to seek redress for the outrage on the grounds that, living in Canada, he was now a British subject. Lord Lyons, the special envoy of Great Britain, took up the fight.[11]

Josiah Cochrane, a black barber, agreed with the prevailing thought that racial toleration was good in Hamilton. His two children attended the integrated school and were well treated. There were no separate burial grounds, and coloured people belonged to all of the churches – Anglican, Catholic, Presbyterian, as well as their own Baptist and Methodist. As for the question of whether he would return to the U.S., he was ambivalent in his reply: "I would not pull straws between the two countries. I would just as lief live here as there, or there as here."[12]

Archibald McCallum (misspelled as McCullum in interview notes), the principal of the Central School, was well pleased with the students and noticed no differences in abilities. However, black students left school at an earlier age to go to work. He noticed that little children never made any distinction because of colour — only older people were capable of instilling that in them. He believed that, "they are quieter, better citizens, for they endure more aggravation than any other class of people" because they were not considered equals. He dismissed the thought that negroes were a distinct species.

McCallum also shed more light on the Oil Springs riot. According to him, the white people that worked in the oil fields there charged six shillings to saw a cord of wood. Black people from Chatham who had less opportunity for work came and charged less, fifty cents a cord. Angered whites organized a plan to have some of them talk to the blacks outside of their shanties, while others crept to the rear and poured oil onto the shelters and lit them on fire. Two of the arsonists were later sentenced to seven years in the penitentiary, and the rioters had to leave Oil Springs, so they gained nothing.[13]

The "honorable" Member of Parliament Isaac Buchanan's brief interview appears a bit indifferent. As a politician, he felt he was not up on all of the facts, and didn't really want to express an opinion; he supposed there were some good blacks and some bad ones, as might be expected, but he thought they might commit more crimes. Unable to waffle on his true feelings any longer, Buchanan did "suppose, if the question was put to vote, the people of Canada would vote against having the niggers remain here."[14]

TORONTO

After two days in Hamilton, Howe and Yerrington travelled to Toronto where their first interview was with another member of parliament, George Brown. Brown was a founding member of the Anti-Slavery Society of Canada and regularly defended their rights through his newspaper, *The Globe*. Brown had grown to be an opponent of separate settlements like Buxton, believing that integrated communities were preferable. Any vices that blacks had, Brown believed, had their roots in slavery. Brown shared a story that when he ran for parliament, 150 people signed a petition pledging their vote for him if he would attempt to pass a law prohibiting black children from the common schools, and to put a tax on any new ones arriving in the county. If he did not agree, they would vote en masse for his opponent.[15]

Brown's brother-in-law, Thomas Henning, who was the secretary of the Anti-Slavery Society and a school board trustee, was convinced that prejudice did not exist in Toronto schools, rather black children were considered as "pets," and if they won a prize for their scholarship they were more highly praised than the other children. Those that attended college were also favourites.[16]

Alfred Butler, who owned a "Periodical depot, Fancy Goods & Circulating Library," believed that at that time, the coloured population was about eight hundred people. They had prospered before a downturn in the economy in 1857, but were now starting to do well again, mostly as labourers and small business owners. He felt that a great many people had an interest in their welfare and would patronize their businesses, and that the law provided recourse to them if they were abused. In his own case, he had a predominantly white clientele. Although the churches were integrated, many blacks preferred to attend their own churches because they had become accustomed to that while in the U.S. Blacks also had their own charitable and social organizations, including a masonic lodge, "Odd Fellows Society," and the St. John's Society, which helped to care for sick or disadvantaged members and to see that the dead were decently buried.

Butler was also sure to mention two of Toronto's sources of pride, doctors Augusta and Abbott, who were then serving as surgeons in the Civil War. New arrivals had difficulty getting a job until they became known, unlike in the States where they might be hired immediately. Butler believed that the Canadian climate did have an adverse effect on the body, particularly on the children, and that most people would sell their homes and businesses and return to the warmer south should freedom come. He felt that British loyalty was waning, especially since the Emancipation Proclamation had returned the focus and allegiance to the United States. President Lincoln was admired for his honesty and willingness to do what was right.

His own history was interesting. Born into slavery in Tennessee, his parents bought a book and his mother taught him to read "on the sly" before he was six. He was sold from an auction block at age eight. Butler did not disclose how he got away from slavery, but did say that he lived in Buffalo for a time, where he seized the opportunity to learn German and French, which served him well as a businessman.[17]

Thomas Smallwood had lived in Canada for twenty years at the time of his interview. He had previously lived in Washington, D.C., but came to Canada to get away from slavery and to educate his children. His intention, however, was still to return to his homeland. He said that he had both made and lost a lot of money during his time in Canada, much of the latter when investing in a failed newspaper. Smallwood appeared to be very politically astute, noting that although blacks had the right to sit on a jury, it depended upon which government was in power as to whether or not they would be selected. Blacks had traditionally supported the Conservatives, who were considered to be truer to British ideals than the Reform party, which they suspected of favouring annexation with the U.S., therefore dooming the future of blacks across the continent. This was widely felt, despite the fact that George Brown, the leader of the Reforms, had proven himself to be a staunch anti-slavery supporter and that the Conservative government had been willing to return fugitive slaves Solomon Moseby and Nelson Hackett to slavery. In yet another fugitive slave case, that of Isaac Brown (who changed his name to Samuel Russell after his escape), was given no support by the Conservative Attorney General for Canada West, who was willing to have Brown extradited back to the U.S. where he would be re-enslaved. If not for the intervention of the Attorney General for Canada East, Smallwood felt that Brown would have been returned. Since the war had begun, the Conservative party was again proving themselves to be the blacks' "worst enemy" by not defending the fugitive slave, John Anderson, who had killed a man who attempted to prevent his escape, which ultimately ended in Canada.[18]

Dr. Joseph Workman, the administrator of the Provincial Lunatic Asylum, had no love for blacks, as he made clear in his interview. But, he conceded that, "we owe a certain duty to them. They are our fellow beings." The doctor felt that although blacks in Canada were afforded certain rights that were denied them in the U.S., popular sentiment against them was the same. He accused them of being lazy and lacking initiative, accepting only easy work. In response to the question of miscegenation, Workman believed that mulattoes were not as strong as pure negroes, stating: "It seems as if Nature has set a certain ban upon the mingling of the blood."[19]

Dr. Egerton Ryerson, Chief Superintendent of Education, differed in his overall opinion, stating that blacks were capable and industrious. Ryerson had been responsible for admitting them to Toronto's public schools. He explained that in cities and towns, boards of trustees had the power to make distinctions between the races, but in the country the coloured people had the right to have separate schools. There were places in the country where blacks were denied entry and parents had approached him to intercede. Ryerson advised them to take the matter to court, which, in his opinion, had always ruled in their favour. He admitted that friction was hottest in the western area, particularly in Chatham, where trustees justified their stance on having a separate school because blacks lived together in one ward of the town, did not want white ministers, and wanted to manage their own affairs. Therefore, the trustees deemed it proper that they go to their own school as well. Ryerson also believed that there were places where blacks brought trouble upon themselves when, "they assert their rights in an ostentatious and offensive manner, pushing themselves forward in a way that even those who are friendly to them cannot justify." As to the young people's ability to learn, Ryerson believed that they did well until they got into the higher branches of learning, which they were unable to master.[20]

George Barber, Secretary of the Board of School Trustees, agreed with Ryerson that blacks were temperate and self-sufficient and were industrious, but only by their own lower standards. However, he believed that Ryerson was mistaken in stating that trustees had the power to establish separate schools. That right belonged to the parents to request it.[21]

John J. Cary had lived in Ohio for fourteen years before coming to Toronto. He left the free state because of oppressive laws that made it no better than living in a slave state. In Ohio, blacks were not allowed to testify in court if the case involved a white person; bonds and securities of five hundred dollars had to be put up by blacks to ensure their good behaviour; and they were forced to pay taxes for schools that their children could not attend. He was well pleased in Toronto where he had lived for just over a decade and where he worked as a barber. Cary was pleased at the equality under the law, and although there was some prejudice, it was generally only a minor annoyance.[22]

F.G. Simpson, a shoemaker by trade, left New York State for Canada eight years previously. He believed that it was more difficult to make money in Canada, and, with a few exceptions, blacks were only eking out a living. Many returned to the U.S. for periods of time to earn money as waiters or cooks, but returned to spend their money in Canada. He gave the example of free people who came from either slave or free cities such as Philadelphia, Richmond, Charleston, or Cincinnati, to escape prejudice. He observed that black children attended the public schools and a group was established to furnish books and clothing to the poorer ones, but that service was only needed on one or two occasions. Since the war had begun, many more blacks had come to Toronto. Simpson offered some unique comments on areas of Canada West that were not often written about. He observed a large black population in Kingston that were struggling financially, while twenty or thirty families in Port Hope, Coburg, and Belleville prospered, which Simpson attributed to the fact that their numbers were small and therefore competition was less for jobs that people would allow them to have. He also commented on the disastrous Haytian emigration scheme that had taken and ruined many lives of people that he knew. Simpson had been involved with the Anti-Slavery Society and had assisted some fugitives when they arrived, including Alfred Butler, who had been interviewed previously. One of Simpson's great regrets was that he had lost a book filled with recordings of conversations that he had with fugitives after they arrived. As for his own allegiance to Canada, Simpson made it clear that although he had taken up citizenship papers, he considered himself to be an exile, and this was not his home.[23]

Dr. James H. Richardson, an examiner for the North American British Life Assurance Company, repeated some of the stereotypical observations made by others: that "mixed breeds" were more subject to tubercular disease and rheumatism. In his business he would "be inclined to look less favorably, I think, on the life of a mulatto than on that of a pure white or pure black." Although he had no statistics to back it up, he believed that mulattoes were more prolific, but that their children did not live as long. Delivering a string of back-handed compliments about pure blacks, Richardson said that he was "favorably impressed with them, as compared with the similar class of lower order whites"; that Toronto "specimens" were "a better class" than those who lived to the west; and that Alfred Butler was "a man of considerable attainments," but it was rumoured that he lived with two women. Showing that he was generous in his castigations, Simpson expressed his bewilderment that "low Irish" women would take up with black men. While on that subject, he shared his thought that blacks committed fewer crimes than the Irish.[24]

Reverend John McCaul, President of the University of Toronto, was effusive with his praise on two black students in particular, Alfred Lafferty and Peter Gallego. Lafferty's scholastic accomplishments surpassed all of the other students — which astonished people from Kentucky, who had come to witness the distribution of prizes at a university public event. McCaul mentioned that doctors Augusta and Abbott had both done very well, but could not compare to Lafferty. Like Dr. Richardson before him, McCaul also commented on his curious observation that many white women married black men, but black women did not marry white men.[25]

George Allen, the governor of the jail, was brief and to the point: "The colored prisoners bear a very favorable comparison with the white."[26]

LONDON

On September 9, 1863, Howe and Yerrington moved on to London. Their first interview was with George Dunn, the father of two sons mentioned in an earlier chapter who fought in a white Michigan regiment in the war. It was the father's belief that if his sons survived, they would move to the south after the war, and he would probably follow.[27]

Francis Evans Cornish, the mayor of London, believed that blacks in his city were different than those in Toronto, inasmuch as they committed more crimes. Cornish contended that they were incapable of governing themselves. Estimating the number of black families at seventy-five,

George Braxton Dunn of London, a former slave, was interviewed twice by the Freedmen's Inquiry Commission. *Courtesy of Dunn descendant Irene Moore Davis.*

he thought that none of them had any considerable wealth or property. The chief of police disputed the mayor on the crime rate, claiming that there was no difference between the races.[28]

Thomas Webb, J.B. Boyle (principal of the Central School), and Miss D. Gurd (teacher), all agreed that there should be separate schools. Webb, who believed that there was no need to have blacks, who he categorized as indolent and lazy except when needed to fill servile positions, contended there was always bickering between the students. Boyle and Gurd's stance was more humane, feeling that the coloured children were being hurt by being snubbed and mistreated in the classroom and the playground. Another teacher, Miss M. Yates, observed that the prejudice was more pronounced with girls than with boys.[29]

Presbyterian minister James Proudfoot believed that blacks were industrious, but needed guidance to direct them as to what to do. He cited the Wilberforce and Buxton settlements as failed examples of independence, and Chatham as an example of the two races unable to co-exist in harmony. Proudfoot blamed ill feeling in London on the many Americans with Southern sympathies who had moved there.[30] William

McBride, Chairman of School Trustees and former mayor, defended the blacks, praising them for their independence and self-reliance.[31]

After a lengthy series of interviews with whites, Howe turned his attention to blacks. Alfred T. Jones, a community leader and prosperous owner of a pharmacy, had run away from slavery in Kentucky, and had settled in London thirty years before. He felt that his people were good workers and they flourished better when they were scattered throughout the population rather than in more segregated groups. He opposed separate churches and schools and had harsh words to say about Thomas Webb, who had previously been interviewed and whom he believed was the instigator in pushing for segregated schools. In Jones's view this would only teach the children to have a hatred for the country of their birth, and one day, after moving to the U.S. as he believed all blacks would do, they might return "with a musket in their hands." Until that time, Jones instructed his children to remain in school until they were physically put out, and then he would deal with it. Jones also prophesized that black soldiers would make the difference in the Civil War.[32]

William Clark shared the feelings of Jones and many others, who contended that it was better to have integrated communities rather than segregated settlements. Using Buxton as an example, he commented that the progress had not been as good as was hoped for, and that the people depended on Reverend King for support too much, which stifled their individual progress. Clark's observations would be of value to the commission that not everyone was drawn to farming as an occupation, and for those who were, wise choices should be made to get productive land.[33]

CHATHAM

The next day, after a full schedule of interviews in London, Howe and Yerrington arrived in Chatham, fresh from hearing repeated stories of racial turmoil in that town. Their first interview put an exclamation mark to those stories, when a hotel clerk named F. Bissell began with, "the niggers are a damned nuisance." Enough said.[34]

Mayor Cross was more conciliatory, stating that of the black population of between four and five hundred people most conducted themselves very well, and the improvements that they made compared favourably to the Irish. He did perceive them as indolent, wanting only light work. However, there were some who prospered and that he admired, mentioning Dr. Martin Delany as a prime example. Cross was also a physician and found no distinction with the races as far as disease was concerned. There was little intermarriage, but Cross could not resist sharing one recent example that caused him an ironic smile, in which after a black man and a white girl ran away together, a coloured man was heard to say, "I always looked upon him as a respectable man. I didn't think he would fall so low as to marry a white girl."[35]

Mr. Payne, the keeper of the jail, found similar crime numbers among the races, and he found black prisoners were generally guilty of petty crimes such as stealing chickens. In a jab at the American interviewer, Payne remarked that the crimes were "thefts that you taught them in the United States." All in all, Payne was very positive, praising them for their ambition and their thirst for knowledge, and eagerness to master reading. Mrs. Payne, who had charge of the female prisoners, proudly shared the story of a girl who could not learn to read while enslaved, but within four months of lessons after work was able to read a chapter in the New Testament.[36]

Schoolteacher Duncan Sinclair was equally impressed with their aptitude and manners. He gave the considered opinion that many of those who came from slavery had little self-respect and possessed no idea what freedom meant or what was their place in society. However, in a few short years they had changed dramatically, were more self-assured, and were a part of a community. Sinclair found it curious that poorer whites held the most prejudice, wanting to hold onto what they considered to be a class above, whereas the more affluent people of Chatham were more likely to be on good terms with blacks. Sinclair opposed miscegenation after watching how white women who married blacks were totally shunned from their former society and considered to be degraded. He also spoke of the nearby township of Orford within Kent County, where blacks were not allowed to live. One man attempted to build a home there and all of the construction work that he would do during the day was destroyed every night.[37]

Watchmaker and court-appointed town constable, John W. Starks, was surprised to find prejudice more rampant in Canada than it was in South Carolina. He heard far more racial epithets hurled about in Toronto than he had ever heard in Ohio, where he had previously lived. He was perplexed that his fellow blacks would not patronize his business, even though he was less expensive than his competitors, but that whites would. Brushing aside the commonly held belief that the climate was adverse, Starks revealed that he had weighed 170 pounds when he arrived, but was now up to a robust 241. He felt that the blacks were doing well economically, but they lacked as much education as their neighbours. Pointing to an example of a superbly skilled craftsman, James Monroe Jones, Starks mentioned that he had made a pair of pistols to be presented to Queen Victoria's son when he travelled through the province, but the presentation committee refused to give it to the prince because they had been made by a black man.[38]

A Mr. Shadd, presumably Mary Ann Shadd Cary's father, Abraham D. Shadd, was brief in his comments, contending that those who suffered from consumption in Canada had contracted it in the U.S. before their arrival here. As for an exodus of blacks to the States, Shadd was uncertain in general, but certain that he would not be one to return.[39] On the contrary, cabinet-maker Henry Jackson thought that many would leave despite the fact that work was plentiful and that it had been his experience that he was well-treated by white labourers that he worked with.[40]

Presbyterian minister and Superintendent of Schools, Angus McColl (misspelled as McCaul in interview notes) referred to James Monroe Jones, Martin Delany, and the Shadd family as being "superior," and that no one in town was the intellectual equal of Jones. The reverend also mentioned that politicians actively sought the black vote, but after the elections abandoned their promises.[41]

BUXTON

On September 12, Buxton's Reverend William King was the next subject. He defended his ideal that separate settlements were the best option for blacks, which was formulated after travelling throughout the province and witnessing their progress elsewhere. He felt that if they were located together on their own land and established their own schools they could become self-reliant and possibilities would be opened up for them. King approached the question of intermarriage, with the observation given elsewhere that white women who married black men were discarded by the society that they were once a part of. It was rare to see these marriages but there were some cases where these couples came to Canada at the woman's urging, in the hopes that she would be better accepted here. King noted the uproar that arose across the country when it was learned that he planned to establish an all-black settlement, and that he had been warned that there would be bloodshed if he continued with his plans. However, he persisted, and after a few years, the prejudice subsided, friendly interracial connections evolved, and the settlement began to flourish. King was adamant in claiming the success of the settlement and in recommending that much of the experience there could be used in rebuilding the South after the war.[42]

Windsor

Howe conducted his first interview in Windsor on September 14, meeting with BME minister Augustus R. Green. Green stated that there were three coloured churches that were well attended, and a separate school that had been requested by the blacks after the recommendation of some abolitionists, who had promised to assist them with the endeavour. He felt that the people were generally healthy and that diseases that runaway slaves did suffer from were from "the effects of getting here, half naked, half-shod and laying out nights." The people of Windsor were independent and had a variety of occupations, including carpenters, plasterers, grocers, hack drivers, and workers at the depots. They had established benevolent societies, including the Samaritan Society, The Lydian Society, and a Union League, whose objective was to help new arrivals. Unlike other parts of the province, Green believed that there was no disparagement placed on an interracial couple within the black community — if the man was respectable and the woman likewise, they would be considered a respectable family. Green agreed with Reverend King that of the rare cases of intermarriage that did exist, most had come from the United States as a couple. In response to the question of a mass return to the United States if freedom was established, Green replied that many of them would go, but they would probably be no better off there than here.[43]

Alex Bartlett, the town clerk, explained the voting qualifications for Windsor. A man would have to have property worth an assessed value of twenty dollars or more to qualify. He claimed that of a coloured population of between seven and eight hundred people, only about twenty qualified. Howe and Yerrington took it upon themselves to examine the town's books and found 152 black and 448 white taxpayers, or, of the total population, one in five blacks paid taxes, while only one in seven and one-quarter whites did. A more complicated formula was used to determine men who were eligible to sit on juries, and by that formula there were only about four blacks who qualified, but Bartlett remarked that they were not wanted anyway.[44]

Alfred Whipper, the teacher at the coloured school, reported that of the 136 students on the rolls, average attendance was about 100. After a liberal use of corporal punishment when he first took charge, Whipper restored order and no longer needed to resort to it. Refugees from the war were still arriving in Windsor and seven children from Missouri had recently enrolled.[45]

Sandwich

Two of the keepers at the Essex County jail were interviewed next. The head jailer, Mr. Leach, estimated that about half of the inmates were black and they were no more trouble than the whites. While Leach listed serious crimes, such as larceny, robbery, and horse stealing, his unidentified assistant said that most were guilty of petty crime, and that there was a great deal of prejudice against all of the black population. The latter also commented that there was a settlement at Sandwich called "The Institution," where half of the married women were white.[46]

Malden

The next destination for the commissioner and his secretary was Amherstburg in Malden Township, where they resumed their task on September 14. Dr. Andrew Fisher, who oversaw the Malden Lunatic Asylum, was their first interviewee. Dr. Fisher remarked that the most successful settlement that he was aware of was at Colchester, where the blacks had gone into the country and built homesteads. He recognized that while very few blacks in Malden had considerable wealth, most were relatively poor but were self-supporting. Fisher believed that the climate quickly encouraged consumption and rheumatism among the blacks, and that most did not live over the age of forty, with about half dying in childhood. Fisher also confirmed that blacks had fled to Malden from Detroit after the riot that had taken place in March of the same year. It was Fisher's feeling that blacks wanted to amalgamate with whites, but were not allowed to. He did mention a rather unique observation that half-a-dozen white men with black wives had arrived that summer, along with half-a-dozen black men with white wives. Fisher did not segregate the patients at the asylum, and had not done so in his previous occupation as a school teacher. He believed that "mulattoes don't have children enough to keep up the breed without assistance from immigration," and that they suffered from disease more than did pure blacks. The doctor made special mention of the growing prejudice that existed, and that grand juries were vigorously pushing judges and legislators to do something to remove them from the county.[47]

The clerk of the asylum, John Meek (misspelled as Meigs in interview notes), was openly critical of blacks, stating that prejudice was on the increase, particularly so after they became so "haughty" after the announcement of the Emancipation Proclamation. An indignant Meek stated that they had the audacity of "looking upon themselves as the equals of the whites." Meek wistfully recalled that Colonel John Prince, a former member of the legislative assembly, had proposed removing all blacks from the county and placing them on the northerly remote Manitoulin Island, surrounded by the chilly waters of Lake Huron and Georgian Bay.[48]

Mr. Park, an Amherstburg merchant, had little new to add, other than to mention that many of the black men worked on boats as deck hands during the navigation season and resided in the county during the winter.[49] A Captain Averill (presumably John W. Averill), who mastered a Great Lakes ship, praised blacks — who he referred to as "darkies" — as making the best deck hands. He told Howe that he never mixed his crew and would have them either all black or all white.[50] Town clerk and bailiff, Thomas Brush, also mentioned that many were employed on ships in season. Brush did not appear to particularly care for the blacks, who he criticized for being uncharitable with their own people, but seemed to place them higher than the local French population, who he called "the worst people in the world."[51]

After taking a comparatively inordinate number of interviews with whites in Amherstburg, Howe turned his attention to the only interview he would do with a black. Levi Foster, the owner of a livery stable business and a hotel, gave one of the longest and most far-reaching interviews. He told Howe that he was born and raised in Ohio, where his people were looked upon as nobodies. One of the differences between Canada and the U.S. that Foster noted was that in the former it was only the "low mean class of people who deny the rights of the colored people," whereas in the latter, it began in the White House and filtered down through all classes of society. He credited prejudice in Canada as having been encouraged by people who had come from slavery, who "rather preferred to be treated like inferiors. They would sooner eat in the kitchens than be guests at the table, and the white people soon found they could treat them in that way." Foster was philosophical about some of the prejudice that former slaves had to endure, suggesting that the social and intellectual disadvantages that they had experienced made them less attractive to be readily accepted. As for Foster himself, he was comfortable addressing people directly, thereby inviting and receiving respect.

Foster was adamant that blacks prospered more quickly in his area than any others. He referred to the "New Canaan" settlement, whose inhabitants came with nothing, worked, and earned some money, and bought land, which they cleared and successfully farmed on swampy land that they had to drain. They built homes, churches, schools, and other buildings, and were living comfortably. In contradiction to the testimony of town clerk Brush, Foster contended that the people helped take care of themselves, citing the example of the "True Band Society," whose members paid dues of one shilling a month to raise a fund to help runaway slaves, who they would board for a time and assist in finding work. Foster believed Canada "to be the greatest place to raise children you ever saw" — but, would still prefer to live in the United States if the war was over, laws were more equitable, and if his debts were all paid.

He also gave his version of how separate schools came to be established. He spoke of having no knowledge of the word "abolitionist" when he came to Canada, and the first one he heard was Hiram Wilson, who, after hearing him give his vision of helping slaves, thought that Wilson had "the noblest vision I ever heard of," which included opening schools for coloured children. However, in retrospect, Foster believed that it would have been better for Wilson to establish schools where all children attended together, which would have the broader effect of having the races remain in frequent contact. Now that there were separate schools that the black children were restricted to attend, they might have to walk miles and past other schools to get to their own. Foster explained his thoughts on separate churches, as the poorer blacks were uncomfortable that they were unable to dress as well as the whites, and that they preferred more "enthusiastic and excitable" services.

Foster gave an interesting analysis of changing Canadian black sentiments towards U.S. politics and the war. During the 1856 presidential election, people had hoped that Republican candidate John C. Fremont would be victorious, because "they like the word 'Free.'" When Lincoln ran in the next election, people favoured him, but he did not ignite the same passion as had Fremont. After the secession of the Confederate States, Foster said that they had "prayed here very hard at first that Jeff Davis would not give out too soon." They later "began to get a little mad when it began to look as if the South was going to whip the North," but when stories reached them that the North was returning runaway slaves to their masters, support for the Union began to dissipate. It evaporated even further when some Northern newspapers carried stories of annexing Canada.[52]

AMHERSTBURG TO COLCHESTER

On September 15, the interviewers began their trip to Colchester, stopping and chatting with numerous people along the way, recording only brief bits of the conversations, and omitting most of their interviewees' names.[53]

ST. CATHARINES

September 17 found Howe and Yerrington in St. Catharines, speaking with Charles P. Camp, the town's clerk and treasurer, who wished all of the blacks would return to the south, calling them "a curse to any country." He accused them of being thieves and of being lazy and that the town had "to support them while they live, and bury them when they die."[54] Although not as venomous in his wording, Camp also had no respect for the Irish, calling them no better than the blacks. Howe and Yerrington had a little fun after they examined Camp's tax assessment records regarding the tax on dogs in St. Catharines. Owners were taxed one dollar for each male dog and two dollars for each bitch. The 1862 tax records showed taxes were paid on 205 dogs but only on one bitch! The writer slyly notes:

> ... these returns furnish vindication of woman's rights with an instance of female wrongs in unjust taxation. Moreover that oppressed canine mother must have marvellous fecundity, or else there are a great many liars among the tax-payers of St. Catharines![55]

John Kinney, barber, acknowledged that there was a great deal of prejudice against his people, but that they were generally well treated. He revealed the hurt that was felt when derisive comments were directed at female companions as they walked down the street. There was some integration in both white and black churches. Kinney fiercely denied all of the allegations made by town clerk Camp, stating "he is a liar, and I will tell him to his face." Kinney said that in St. Catharines there were three organizations established for blacks to care for their own: a female society that provided money to care for the sick and bury the dead, a masonic lodge that cared for their members, and a society whose members put two or three shillings each month into a fund to give to the sick. It was Kinney's intention to return south if freedom was there and that he would not understand if all blacks born outside of Canada did not do the same.[56]

A Mrs. Brown, one of only four women, and the only black woman interviewed by Howe on his initial fact-finding trip to Canada, claimed to have nothing to do with St. Catharines's black community, whose residents "all live just in a heap among themselves, and I never go there." She had come from Albany, New York, where she was born, fifteen years previously. Her husband, who was then eighty years old and still active, was from Maryland and had been an officer's servant in the War of 1812. Their grandson lived with them but they chose not to send him to school, reasoning that they did not intend to stay in the town long, preferring Montreal or somewhere in the States. Seemingly contradicting herself, she pledged that her grandson would receive as good of an education as anyone else, "if it costs the last cent I ever make."

Brown said that the blacks got along quite well, and as had so many before her, testified that they accumulated less property than the Irish, who could survive anywhere and "will live on nothing like a dog. They live like pigs and worse than pigs," subsisting on potatoes and salt and a cup of milk. Even in the winter, she said, women and children will go barefoot except on Sunday, "and that you know, would kill anybody else." Mrs. Brown made no bones about the dislike for Canada that both she and her husband shared, and that he wanted to go "home" to Maryland where he still had children. She found that she suffered far more abuse in Canada than in New York.[57]

William Henry Gibson, a gardener, disagreed with Mrs. Brown, stating that although there was a lot of prejudice, it was not so bad as in the States. He found the climate to be healthy, treatment to be okay, and there were opportunities to make a good living. Gibson did not believe that he would return to the States, he just wanted to be somewhere where he could be free and have equal rights.[58]

Colonel E.W. Stephenson had lived in St. Catharines for thirty-five years, arriving there when there were only about three or four coloured families, mostly runaway slaves. In the intervening years, the black population had increased a great deal, and he felt that they could flourish if their numbers did not continue to grow. Speaking frankly with his opinions, the Colonel said that neither race condoned intermarriage, and that any white woman who would degrade herself to take up with a black man was a "whore." Gibson employed black men as waiters, adding that they were loyal workers, had comfortable little homes, and that their wives took in laundry to help support the family. He found most of them to be very religious (except for a few "vagabonds"), and he encouraged them to attend church meetings in the daytime and in the evening, believing it instilled pride and kept them from "getting a little beside themselves."

Stephenson thought that blacks did not prosper as much as the Irish because the former put a lot of emphasis on dressing well and spent much of their money on appearances. They were always neat, good-natured, and temperate, and he believed that "the country would be worse off if they were all taken away."[59]

Dr. Theophilus Mack agreed with some other physicians that mulattoes would die out because of their weaker constitutions. He claimed to have observed that pure blacks would recover from diseases such as small pox, skin diseases, and yellow fever, whereas those of mixed blood would not.[60]

Elder Perry said that he was the only coloured student to have graduated from Kalamazoo's Theological College and Seminary, and that he had established a private school in St. Catharines for students from age six to eighteen because of the poor quality of education in the public school. He offered classes in English grammar, geography, Latin, and Greek. Despite the cost of fifty cents per month that some of his poorer students struggled to pay, his classes had more students enrolled than he anticipated.[61] James Brown, who taught at the government-funded school for coloured children, had more than twice as many children, and found little difference between their ability to learn than white students. His one complaint was a lack of funds to purchase books, as the children's parents could not afford to purchase them.[62]

Brown's testimony concluded the first round of interviews. Howe and Yerrington returned to Canada and began a second set of interviews on November 5, and heard some familiar stories about prejudice, but also some unique and often heart-wrenching personal experiences. There was a much different approach on this trip: Howe only interviewed blacks — thirty-four who had been slaves and seven of whom were freeborn. This time, the additional subjects of the questions, and the often lengthier responses, had different dimensions to them: treatment while enslaved and incidents of brutality; the desire for freedom; the circumstances of their escape and how they achieved it; the role of religion in slavery; kidnapping of free blacks; separation of families; false stories told about Canada as a deterrence to run; the effect of the war on them; and the desire for education. The interviewees seemed to have much more latitude to share the stories of their lives, thereby giving very powerful and moving insights into the horrors of their existence.

Rather than summarize them all here — because they should be read in their entirety to do them justice — I will list the interviewees:

THE SUSPENSION BRIDGE AT NIAGARA FALLS

Thomas Likers   — runaway slave from Maryland.

ST. CATHARINES

John W. Lindsay — freeborn but kidnapped into slavery and later escaped.

George Ross — runaway slave from Maryland.

Mrs. Joseph Wilkinson — freed by her master in Maryland after her husband ran away.

Joseph Smith — ran away from Maryland.

Mrs. Joseph Smith — ran away from Maryland.

Amy Martin — freeborn daughter of James Ford who had been a slave in Canada, escaped to the U.S., and became an Underground Railroad conductor.

Hannah Henderson Fairfax — 108 years old, ran away from Virginia years before.

Reverend Lewis C. Chambers — purchased his own freedom in Maryland for $1,250.

Henry Stewart — rescued from Maryland by his sister, Harriet Tubman.

C.H. Hall — ran away from Maryland.

Susan Boggs — ran away from Virginia after having been punished for helping her son escape.

John Boggs — ran away from Maryland after having been sold five or six times.

William Cornish — ran away from Maryland.

Thomas O. Casey — freeborn in Virginia.

HAMILTON

George Johnson — ran away from Maryland.

John A. Hill — purchased himself in Virginia.

William H. Howard — freeborn in Maryland.

Willis Reddick — freeborn in Pennsylvania, lived in Virginia and ran to Canada after having trouble with some white men.

J.H. Bland — ran away from Virginia.

LONDON

Dr. A.T. Jones — ran away from Kentucky.

Isaac Throgmorton — ran away from Kentucky.

William C. Bell — freeborn in Ohio.

William Williams — ran away from North Carolina after his white grandfather sold him.

George Williams — ran away from Maryland.

George Dunn — ran away from Kentucky.

John Shipton — freeborn in Missouri after his parents purchased their freedom.

Benjamin Miller — ran away from Missouri.

CHATHAM

Andrew Smith — ran away from North Carolina after being denied the freedom given him by his grandfather's — and master's — will.

James W. Hall — from Rochester, New York.

William Jackson — bought his freedom for $1,005 in Kentucky after saving for twenty years.

Eli Holton — freeborn in Kentucky.

George Ramsey — ran away from Kentucky after his wife and children were carried further south to Arkansas territory.

Washington Thomas — ran away from Kentucky.

Grandison Boyd — ran away from Virginia.

Reverend Horace H. Hawkins — ran away from Kentucky.

John Davis — ran away from Kentucky.

During their trip, Howe and Yerrington also visited Buxton, and although they did not record any interviews, according to newspaper reports, "were highly gratified with what they there saw, and went away greatly strengthened in their faith in the capacity of the free colored man

John W. Lindsay detailed his
warm meeting with John A.
Macdonald (left), who would
later become Canada's first
prime minister. *LC-DIG-cwp-
bh-00412. LOC.*

for self-government and the full enjoyment of the rights of citizenship
and the possession of property."[63] Howe's own account was almost poetic:

> Buxton is certainly a very interesting place. Sixteen
> years ago it was a wilderness. Now, good highways are
> laid out in all directions through the forest, and by their
> side are about two hundred cottages, all looking neat
> and comfortable. Around each one is a cleared space,
> which is well cultivated. There are signs of industry, and
> thrift, and comfort, everywhere: signs of intemperance,
> of idleness, of want, nowhere.
>
> Most interesting of all, are the inhabitants. Twenty
> years ago, most of them were slaves, who owned noth-
> ing, not even their children. Now they own themselves;
> they own their houses and farms; and they have their
> wives and their children about them. They have the
> great essentials for human happiness; something to love,
> something to do, and something to hope for.

After gathering and studying the interviews, Howe was soon ready to present his findings — which, he admitted, were imperfect and contained some speculation — and his recommendations. He published a book containing segments of the interviews that he had conducted, as well as some of those that had been conducted in 1855 by Boston abolitionist Benjamin Drew, and published in 1856 under the title *The Refugee: or the Narratives of Fugitive Slaves in Canada*..

Some of Howe's conclusions reflect the racially biased notions of the time. For example, he agreed that mulattoes were not "robust" or fertile, and that they would die out in a few generations. Also, more crimes that indicated "lax morality" were attributed to them, but overall crime rates were comparable to those of whites. He believed that they were great imitators and in time would imitate "the best features of white civilization, and will improve rapidly. However, for the most part, Howe was complimentary, stating that they were "upon the whole sober, industrious and thrifty," and capable of self-reliance. They made valuable citizens, and their docile nature made them easy to govern. He noted that they were not rooted in Canada, and would dearly love to return "home."[64]

He did not think it wise for blacks to live in segregated communities because it encouraged prejudice by others, and he feared they would "develop a spirit of caste among themselves."[65] More crudely written, he offered:

> The truth of the matter seems to be, that as long as the colored people form a very small proportion of the population, and are dependent, they receive protection and favors, but when they increase, and compete with the laboring class for a living, and especially when they begin to aspire to social equality, they cease to be "interesting negroes," and become "niggers."[66]

Passionate in his beliefs, Howe was adamant that equal rights should be given to blacks and that freedom for them must mean exactly what it did for whites, with no restraints: "free to go or to come; free to accept or reject employment; free to work or to starve." He contended that any restrictions placed in the name of protection because they were "not yet prepared for freedom," would only be "servitude disguised." Drawing on the example of Canada, Howe argued:

> Look at the twenty thousand blacks in Canada! In spite of cold, in spite of prejudice, in spite of utter lack of capital to start upon, they have been, and are, supporting themselves. They clear up the forest, cultivate farms, build houses; they do jobs about cities; they save, and wait, and tend, and keep out of prison and poor-house, as much as any other laboring class.[67]

One of the initial arguments that his commission's findings faced was that they would be of little use because those people he studied, who were referred to as "picked men," who could successfully escape to Canada, were superior to those that remained in slavery. This, so the argument went, was proven by virtue of the ingenuity and courage that they displayed by making that escape. However, Howe rejected that argument, asserting that there were areas in the South where escape was nearly impossible. And, even if some may have lacked the courage or skill to escape, it certainly did not mean that they were not capable of caring for themselves and their families if given the opportunity. There were other reasons to consider as well when contemplating why some chose not to escape: love for their family, attachments to their home, and, in some cases, to their masters and their families. They were taught from the time of their birth that they were to be subservient. Even the scriptures had been used as justification for black enslavement, adding to the difficulty for many slaves and former slaves to overcome what had been implanted in their very being. In an elegantly worded response to the naysayers, Howe concluded:

> No, the refugees in Canada earn a living and gather property; they marry and respect women; they build churches, and send their children to schools; they

improve in manners and morals, — not because they are "picked men," but simply because they are free men. Each of them may say, as millions will soon say, — "When I was a slave, I spake as a slave, I understood as a slave; but when I became a free man, I put away slavish things."[68]

The findings in Canada became an important part of the overall final and supplemental reports written by commission head Robert Dale Owen, and submitted to the Secretary of War. One timely point included an important reference to what both African American and African Canadian men in the war were contributing by virtue of them taking up arms:

The whites have changed, and are still rapidly changing, their opinion of the Negro. And the Negro, in his new condition as a freedman, is himself, to some extent, a changed being. No one circumstance has tended so much to these results as a display of manhood in Negro soldiers. Though there are higher qualities than strength and physical courage, in our present state of civilization there are no qualities which command from the masses more respect.[69]

CHAPTER 9

The War's End

It was a war of the most momentous importance, far reaching and vital, that even stirred the heart of nations and stiffened the fibre of its manhood.

— Anderson Ruffin Abbott[1]

As the war entered its final year, and it was becoming clear that chances of a Southern victory were remote, the inevitable self-analysis and second-guessing of official policies increased. The *Richmond Whig* of January 10, 1865 declared that as soon as the federal government decided to allow blacks into its army, the Confederacy should have done the same. The author specifically complained that Northerners were coming within the lines of their enemy and recruiting blacks from under their very noses. He urged a reversal in policy and the immediate enlisting of those blacks that remained under Southern control into some sort of military service, either as soldiers or as accessories to the army. He flatly dismissed the notion that …

> our negroes should not be parties to the war, because they are not interested in the result. In fact they are interested. The condition of our slave is better, happier,

than that of the northern free negro, to whose condition — even to a worse condition — the Yankee would reduce them; and our slaves are indebted to our people and laws for the difference. Our laws inure to the benefit, to the happiness of our slaves. They protect them and provide for their well-being, in the same way, if not in the same degree, as they provide for white people.[2]

The composer of that editorial was sadly mistaken in his assessment, as the events of the next few months would demonstrate.

Charleston, South Carolina, which, as the "cradle of secession" and whose harbour was the scene of the war's opening shots, was very much the heart of the South, had been under siege for much of the war. During the night of February 17, 1865, the rebel troops evacuated their defenses, leaving burning buildings, vessels, bridges, the railway station, and thousands of bales of cotton that they had torched. Much of the city had already been destroyed by Union bombardment. Most of the more affluent citizens had already fled the city, leaving the starving poor to suffer on their own amidst the devastation.[3]

Ruins of Charleston, South Carolina as viewed through the remains of a church. *LC-DIG-cwpb-03049. LOC.*

Union soldiers marched unopposed into the city and the Northern navy cautiously escorted ships carrying occupation troops and supplies into the heavily mined harbour. The 55th Massachusetts was one of the regiments to enter the city, marching through the streets with the sound of many of the coloured troop's anthem "John Brown's body lies a-mouldering in the grave" ringing.[4] The 54th, as well as Michigan's 102nd, were also there, camping side by side among the tombstones in the Magnolia Cemetery, through which the Confederates had previously established defense lines.[5] The remaining white population of Charleston was outraged at the indignity of having black occupation troops, while those of their own race, many of whom were then suddenly free, benefited from their presence.[6] The regimental record of the 55th described their welcome as they first entered Mount Pleasant, which neighboured Charleston:

> Words would fail to describe the scene which those who witnessed it will never forget, — the welcome given to a regiment of colored troops by their people redeemed from slavery. As shouts, prayers, and blessings resounded on every side, all felt that the hardships and dangers of the siege were fully repaid.[7]

Less than two months later, on Sunday, April 2, word began to spread that the Union army had been rapidly advancing toward Petersburg, that the enemy lines that stretched for miles had been infiltrated, and that fortification after fortification was being captured. Sections of the Southside Railroad, which was vital for receiving supplies, for troop movement, and for communication, were destroyed. The rebel army retreated toward Richmond to defend their capital city, as the noose tightened there and around Petersburg.[8] *The Richmond Examiner* reported:

> We are now in the very crisis and agony of the campaign ... Any hour may decide the fate of Richmond, if that fate be not already determined. It would be weak and idle to deny or blind ourselves to facts which stare

Currier & Ives print of the Fall of Richmond, April 2, 1865. *LC-USZC2-2298. LOC.*

us in the face. We cannot disguise the probability that Richmond may soon be in the hands of the enemy.[9]

By the early morning of April 3, Abraham Lincoln informed the Secretary of War that he had received a telegram from General Grant reporting that Petersburg had been evacuated and that he was confident that Richmond had been also.[10] Grant's confidence was well founded, and on that same day Union soldiers triumphantly entered Richmond.

There has been some dispute as to which regiment was the first to enter the city. Among the first was the 5th Massachusetts Cavalry, which had thirty-four Canadians on its roster during the war. Another was Indiana's 28th, whose chaplain had the most remarkable story to tell, as published in *The Christian Recorder*, April 22, 1865:

City Point, Va., April 12th, 1865.

MR. EDITOR: — I have just returned from the city of Richmond; my regiment was among the first that entered that city. I marched at the head of the column, and soon I found myself called upon by the officers and men of my regiment to make a speech, with which, of course, I readily complied. A vast multitude assembled on Broad street, and I was aroused amid the shouts of ten thousand voices, and proclaimed for the first time in that city freedom to all mankind. After which the doors of all the slave pens were thrown open, and thousands came out shouting and praising God and father or master Abe, as they termed him. In this mighty consternation I became so overcome with tears, that I could not stand up under the pressure of such fulness of joy in my own heart. I retired to gain strength, so I lost many important topics worthy of note.

Among the densely crowded concourse there were parents looking up children who had been sold south of this state in tribes, and husbands came for the same purpose: here and there one was singled out in the ranks, and an effort made to approach the gallant and marching soldiers, who were too obedient to orders to break ranks. We continued our march as far as Camp Lee, at the extreme end of Broad street, running westwards. In camp the multitude followed, and every body could participate in shaking the friendly but hard hands of poor slaves. Among the many broken-hearted mothers looking for their children who had been sold into Georgia and elsewhere, was an aged woman, passing through the vast crowd of colored inquiring for a man by the name of Garland H. White, who had been sold from her when a small boy, and was bought by a lawyer named Robert Toombs, who lived in Georgia. Since the war has been going on she has seen Mr. Toombs in Richmond with troops from his state, and upon her asking him, where his body servant Garland was, he replied: "He ran off from me at Washington and went to Canada. I have since learned that he is living somewhere in the state of

Ohio." Some of the boys knowing that I lived in Ohio, soon found me, and said: "Chaplain, here is a lady that wishes to see you." I quickly turned, following the soldier until coming to a group of colored ladies, I was questioned as follows: "What is your name, sir?" "My name is Garland H. White." "What was your mother's name?" "Nancy." "Where was you born?" "In Hanover County, in this state." "Where was you sold from?" "From this city." "What was the name of the man who bought you?" "Robert Toombs." "Where did he live?" "In the State of Georgia?" "Where did you leave him?" "At Washington." "Where did you then go?" "To Canada." "Where do you now live?" "In Ohio." "This is your mother, Garland, whom you are now talking to; who has spent twenty years of grief about her son." I cannot express the joy I felt, at this happy meeting of my mother and other friends. But suffice it to say, that God is on the side of the righteous, and will in due time reward them. I have witnessed several such scenes among the other colored regiments.

Late in the afternoon, we were honored with his Excellency the President of the United States, Lieutenant General Grant, and other gentlemen of distinction. We made a grand parade through most of the principal streets of the city, beginning at Jeff. Davis' mansion, and it appeared to me that all the colored people in the world had collected in that city for that purpose. I never saw so many colored people in all my life, women and children of all sizes running after father or master Abraham, as they called him. To see the colored people, one would think that they all had gone crazy. The excitement at this period was unabated, the tumbling of walls, the bursting of shells, could be heard in all directions, dead bodies being found, rebel prisoners being brought in, starving women and children begging for greenbacks and hard tack, constituted the general order of the day, the fifth cavalry, colored, were still dashing through the streets, to protect and preserve the peace, and see that no one suffered violence, they having fought so often over the walls of Richmond, driving the enemy at every point. All the boys are well, and send their love to all the kind ones at home. Yours in Christian love, G.H. WHITE, Chaplain 28th U.S.C.T.

As the Union occupation of Richmond began, Major General Godfrey Weitzel issued a public order, assuring all citizens, "that we come to restore to them the blessings of peace, prosperity, and freedom under the flag of the Union." As a precaution, Weitzel also instructed everyone to remain in their own homes and to avoid assembling in groups. Brigadier General G.F. Shepley, who assumed the position of military governor of Richmond, was less conciliatory and more direct. He derided the fleeing army who "could no longer occupy by their arms" for setting ablaze parts of the city, and warned that anyone who plundered or destroyed any property would be "arrested and summarily punished." Going further, Shepley warned that no expressions of insult to the flag or to members of the occupying army would be tolerated.[11]

President Lincoln's triumphant ride through Richmond, April 4, 1865. *LC-USZ62-6931. LOC.*

The end of the war came quickly thereafter. General Grant reported on April 4 that between 1,500 and 1,700 Confederate prisoners had been taken that day. The remnants of the army were scattered and abandoned — "artillery, ammunition, burned or charred wagons, caissons, ambulances, &c" lined the paths of retreat.[12] While many regiments of coloured troops were involved in the siege and taking of Petersburg and Richmond, only seven were with the pursuers of the retreating Army of Northern Virginia. Among those who had Canadian enlistees was the 29th USCI, whose members included Frank Adams, James Adams, and Charles Henry Griffin, as well as Junius Roberts from the U.S., who would later become a BME minister in Canada. The 31st USCI, which had a large contingent of Canadians, also participated.[13]

On April 9, General Lee, on behalf of the Army of Northern Virginia, accepted the terms of surrender as proposed by General Grant. Some of the terms included a pledge that the men would be given parole on the condition that they did not take up arms against the United States unless they were exchanged for Union prisoners. The men were to give up their arms, artillery, and public property, but were allowed to keep their private belongings and their horses. Officers would be allowed to keep their side arms.[14]

As was the case throughout all of British North America, in the early days of April 1865, the blacks in Hamilton rejoiced at the news that Petersburg and Richmond had fallen and that General Lee had surrendered. Metaphorically, even the weather cooperated to usher in a return to spring. A visiting minister recorded:

> ... ice and snow have disappeared, the storms have blown over, the trees are putting forth their buds, and the grass shows verdancy. Truly "the winter is past, and the rain is over and gone, the flowers do now appear on the earth, and the time for the singing of birds is come, and the voice of the turtle is heard in our land."[15]

While still cautiously optimistic that the war was indeed coming to an end, the prevailing sentiment was pride for the Canadian sons who had bravely acquitted themselves on the battlefields and had accomplished an important part in putting down the rebellion. As a reminder to them-selves and to the world, on behalf of the citizens, the reverend continued: "your troubles are ours, your people are our people, your God is our God, and where you are buried, there we want to be buried. So we are one in the great work."[16]

The spring described abruptly came to a tragic end on the evening of April 14, when President Lincoln, while watching an innocent comedy, "My American Cousin," was shot by John Wilkes Booth at Ford's Theatre, Lincoln lingered through the night, but died early the next morning, at 7:22 a.m. The world was stunned.

Anderson Abbott had a particularly personal reaction to the murder of Lincoln, whom he and Alexander Augusta had met at the levee at the White House. Abbott had participated in some of the grand festivities that blossomed after the fall of Richmond and Robert E. Lee's surren-der to General Grant. On the night of the assassination, Abbott and a friend joined in a torch-lit procession that assembled to honour Edwin Stanton. Following the Secretary of War's jubilant address to the crowd, Abbott went to another friend's home to continue the celebrations, when an envoy arrived to share the news that the President had been shot at Ford's Theater, and that Secretary of State Seward's throat had been cut.

For the first time in the nation's capital, Abbott became worried for his safety, imagining that murderers lurked behind every shadow in the streets, which were dimly lit with gas lights. Panicked soldiers patrolling the streets were seizing anyone who appeared remotely suspicious, and terrorized crowds of vigilantes were quickly transforming into a blood-thirsty lynch mob. Abbott and his friend took shelter in their own homes, but were aroused at about 2:00 a.m. by a messenger who had been dispatched by Mary Todd Lincoln to bring Elizabeth Keckley, her black seamstress and confidante, to her.

Being a friend of Keckley's, Abbott agreed to accompany her to the White House. The couple forced their way to their destination through the throngs of people who filled the streets, only to be redirected to a large, three-storey brick house opposite Ford's Theater, where the dying President had been carried. When they reached the building, the two friends parted, as Keckley was admitted into the house and Abbott returned to his home to try to sleep. He and the rest of the city were awakened at 7:20 a.m. by the tolling of church bells, announcing the death of the President.

The city was thrown into a profound mixture of fear and mourning. Abolitionists and blacks were assaulted with threats, one of which was graphically expressed as the index finger of a black person, along with a picture of a coffin superimposed over the image of skull and crossbones, with the word "beware" attached.

Both Abbott and Keckley became intimate witnesses of the grief Mrs. Lincoln and her children suffered inside their private apartments. As the newly widowed woman prepared to leave the White House, she distributed several personal articles that had belonged to the President to people whose friendship he valued. Abbott was given the plaid shawl that Mr. Lincoln had frequently worn on cool evenings when he went to meet with Edwin Stanton at the Department of War. The shawl was very naturally cherished by Abbott and his descendants.[17]

Within hours, the wildfire ignited by the assassination of Abraham Lincoln swept through Canada on its global route. Scores of years later, the aged children of slaves recalled the gloom that enveloped the people of Buxton when they learned of the death of "Ole Massah Lincoln."[18]

President Lincoln's funeral procession on Pennsylvania Avenue, Washington, D.C. LC-DIG-cwpb-00594. LOC.

More immediately, the Canadian press expressed its sympathy and horror. One such article, which appeared under the bold heading PRESIDENT LINCOLN'S FUNERAL IN CANADA, communicated:

It is, we believe, the common belief of all the European residents in the United States, that no country of Europe has ever witnessed anything approaching the exhibition of mourning throughout the United States of the death of President Lincoln. The funeral services in British America are no less remarkable. There is probably no precedent in the world's history of a whole country paying such tribute of honor of the memory of the head of a foreign nation. In almost every town of Canada the places of business were closed on Wednesday from 12 to 2; the churches were thronged for the celebration of the funeral rites. Public buildings and private houses were largely draped in mourning, and all voices united in the manifestation of grief at the loss sustained by the United States and of horror at the work of the assassin. Previously the town councils, with a very credible unanimity, had passed resolutions of sympathy with the family of the murdered President and with the people of the United States. We have had, in the course of this war, to register many acts of unfriendliness towards the United States on the part of a considerable portion of the press and the people of British America. It is gratifying to acknowledge this expression of sympathy on the part of our neighbors in our great national affliction.[19]

The Detroit *Advertiser and Tribune* published a special dispatch, dated April 15, 1865, that had been received from Amherstburg, which simply stated, "We are very sorry to hear the dreadful news. The regret and Indignation is almost universal here. The Southerners here seem to regret it sincerely."[20]

Queen Victoria, the beloved monarch of the British Empire and symbol of free-dom to Canadian blacks, circa 1862. John Jabez Edwin, photographer. In an April 29, 1865 letter of condolence to Mary Todd Lincoln, Queen Victoria wrote:

Dear Madam, — Though a stranger to you, I cannot remain silent when so terrible a calamity has fallen upon you and your country, and must express personally my deep and heartfelt sympathy with you under the shocking circumstances of your present dreadful misfor-tune. No one can better appreciate than I can, who am myself utterly broken-hearted by the loss of my own beloved husband, who was the light of my life, my stay, my all, what your sufferings must be; and I earnestly pray that you may be supported by Him to Whom alone the sorely stricken can look for comfort in this hour of heavy affliction! With the renewed expression of true sympathy, I remain, dear Mad-am, your sincere friend, Victoria R.

Source of quote: *The Letters of Queen Victoria, Vol 1,* edited by George Earle Buckle (Toronto: The Ryerson Press, 1926), 266. Image: *LC-USZ62-14976. LOC.*

These demonstrations of grief appeared to ward off some of the anger that would have been levelled at Canada — a natural result from suspicion that Canada, however unwittingly, may have played a part in the assassination planning. One of Andrew Johnson's first proclamations upon taking over the presidency was to place huge rewards for the capture of Confederate President Jefferson Davis and several of his close associates. In offering the reward, Johnson noted that the Bureau of Military Justice had found evidence that these men "and other rebels and traitors against the government of the United States" had been harboured in Canada.[21]

Some of that evidence surfaced in the trials of those accused of participating in the assassination plans. On July 8, 1865, *The Christian Recorder*, along with most other newspapers, carried the results of the trial:

That as early as October, 1864, the agents in Canada announced their determination to compass the death of Abraham Lincoln; that they began then to discuss this subject in their correspondence with Jefferson Davis; and that about this period they were visited by Booth, and that the contemplated assassination was repeatedly spoken by them in the presence of witnesses who have testified before the Military Commission. That about the 6th or 7th of April, John H. Surratt arrived at Montreal, direct from Richmond, and delivered to Jacob Thompson a dispatch in cipher, from Jeff Davis, which was virtually the death warrant of Abraham Lincoln. That Thompson, about this time, drew from the Bank of Montreal $180,000 in certificates, which could be used any where. It is the theory of the prosecution that Surratt immediately hurried back, with a portion or all of this money to Washington, where he was seen on the fatal 14th of April, and that this reward furnished the last incentive needed to nerve the murderer and his accomplices for their horrid task. That Surratt had, that evening, a short time before the murder, a final interview with his mother, and then hurried back to Canada, where it is supposed, he still remains concealed. That he was dispatched to Richmond in March last, by Booth, for instructions and money; and that his subsequent journey to Montreal was made because it was safer and more convenient to obtain the blood-money in the North, from whence he could return in safety, than at Richmond, as, in travelling back to Washington from that point, he might be detected, when he passed through our lines.

In his youth while attending the Milton Academy in Maryland, John Wilkes Booth had been the "bossom" friend of Thomas Gorsuch. Thomas was the youngest son of Edward Gorsuch, who had been shot and beaten to death in the blood slave resistance in Pennsylvania, which came to be known as The Christiana Riot.[22] Four of the Gorsuch family's slaves had escaped into the free state of Pennsylvania. Two years later, after having been informed of their whereabouts, Edward Gorsuch organized a posse to capture them and return them to slavery. The group was met by an organized resistance in the form of a vigilance committee of blacks who banded together to prevent the capture of slaves. The would-be captors approached the home of the committee's leaders and demanded the return of their slaves, who they suspected had been sheltered there. As the argument became more and more heated, Alexander Pinckney, a resident of the home, who would later become a distinguished soldier of the 54th Massachusetts, initially prevented Gorsuch from being shot. However, as the situation intensified, a determined Gorsuch was eventually killed, igniting a general rage across the South and a slow-burning rage in Booth, and propelling the defenders to Canada.

Evidence of Booth's anger was demonstrated at the hanging of John Brown, who had laid plans to overthrow slavery in different areas of Canada West when he borrowed a uniform and posed as a member of the elite Richmond Grays, who were among the security detail.[23] Booth would later boast that "I may say I helped to hang John Brown and while I live, I shall think with joy upon the day when I saw the sun go down upon one trator [sic] less within our land."[24]

Martin Delany — now Major Delany — who had once been one of John Brown's confidantes, was quick to make his feelings known, calling the assassination:

> a calamity such as the world never before witnessed — a calamity, the most heart-rending, caused by the perpetration of a deed at the hands of a wretch, the most infamous and atrocious — a calamity as humiliating to America as it is infamous and atrocious — has suddenly brought our country to mourning by the untimely death of the humane, the benevolent, the philanthropic, the generous, the beloved, the able, the wise, great, and good man, the President of the United States, Abraham Lincoln, the Just.[25]

Delany called upon every black person in the country to contribute one cent to raise funds to build a monument to Lincoln, which he hoped would be in Illinois near the late president's home. Assuming that there were four million blacks, the fund would grow to forty thousand dollars, and the small amount would not be burdensome to anyone.

Shortly thereafter, an organization was formed bearing the name "The Colored People's National Lincoln Monument Association." Agents fanned out across the re-united states and into Canada, where AME minister Benjamin W. Arnett was appointed agent.[26] Reverend Willis Nazrey, Bishop of the BME church of Canada, then stationed in Chatham, was appointed life director of the organization, as was that same city's former resident, Major Martin Delany, who was still in the service. Abraham Galloway, formerly from Kingston, Canada West, was a state officer on the committee.[27] This monument was to be "a SEAT OF LEARNING, dedicated to God, to Literature, and to the Arts and Sciences and shall be held and appropriated for the education of the Children of Freemen and Freedmen, and their descendants forever," and was to be located in Washington, D.C. "A monument not of marble nor of brass merely, but a Monument of Education. Marble may crumble, brass may tarnish, but the light of learning is as enduring as time."[28]

Emancipation Statue, Washington, D.C., shows President Lincoln holding the Emancipation Proclamation while a freed black man with broken shackles kneels at his feet. Since its unveiling in 1876, the statue has been the subject of intense criticism because it appears to depict a subservient black man who has done nothing to contribute to the cause of his own freedom. *LC-D4-9090. LOC.*

The death of the "great emancipator" did not signal the end of the war. Although General Lee had surrendered to Ulysses S. Grant at Appomattox on April 9, 1865, with the other Southern generals and the Confederate navy soon following, there were still some skirmishes that took place in Georgia, Alabama, and South Carolina later that month. Black Union regiments, including the 28th USCI, were merged together and sent to the area of Brownsville, Texas to put an end to the rebellion by Confederate troops there, and to prevent an invasion from Mexico onto American soil. Many of the men were outraged, desperately wishing to return home to loved ones. Many had not been paid in months and knew that their families were suffering. Conditions both travelling to and camping in Texas were horrific: venomous snakes, scanty rations, shortages of drinking water, scorching heat, and outbreaks of scurvy were just part of the adversity.[29]

Of course, the families that the soldiers had left behind were giddy with the anticipation of the return of their loved ones. Priscilla Atwood could not wait to be reunited with her husband, Alexander. Although the distance was great between Canada West and Louisiana, she was determined to make the trip. On March 11, 1865, Alexander wrote to the adjutant a request from Camp Shaw, Louisiana for a seven-day furlough, "for the purpose of visiting New Orleans to get transportation for my wife to return home." It was granted for March 15–19. Their brief reunion after a separation of more than eighteen months can only be imagined. It was more of a blessing than they could have imagined after she departed again for home.

Five months later, his regiment had still not been mustered out, nor were the men allowed to go home. On August 5, Alexander requested another furlough to travel to New Orleans for personal business. Soon after, he was taken ill and, fearing the worst, penned a letter to his wife:

> It has been a good many days since I started this letter. I have been very near death's door. I am only a little better this morning. Oh, love, how I thought of you! The only earthly thing I thought of, was just to be at home a little while, and see you, and then die. I feel all right, for God is with me. My trust is in God, and feel sure that my peace is made. I am very ill, and may die soon; but grieve not for me; meet me in heaven.[30]

On August 29, 1865, William H. Chenery wrote to Priscilla with the news that every wife dreaded to hear:

> Dear Madam,
>
> It is with feelings of pain and regret, that I am compelled to announce to you the awful intelligence, that your late beloved husband is no more. He expired yesterday at 2 o'clock p.m. He had been ill two or three weeks before his death. He was conveyed to the Hospital about 10 days ago. While there everything was done for him that could be done by our good Surgeon, the Hosp. Attendants, and his brother soldiers. But our efforts

were of no avail. God has seen fit in his kind Providence, to call him home, to that world where the "wicked cease from troubling and the weary are at rest."

He had not an enemy in this Battalion; on the contrary, he was universally beloved respected and esteemed by all who knew him, from the officer to the private down. His gentlemanly qualities, kind arts and soldierly deportment, endeared him to all. As a soldier, he was ever ready and willing to perform everything that was laid down for him to do. In the death of Sergt. Atwood, the Country has lost a most worthy patient soldier. He died in the service of his Country, and his name with hosts of other martyred heroes of this war, will be recorded in that glorious record, which will be read by coming generations with pride, veneration and respect.

I am aware that my poor sympathy and consolation will not recompense and assuage the anguish and heartfelt sorrow of those who were connected with him in bonds of relationship; but let us remember always, that God is a protector and comforter to the widowed and fatherless; — and that not a sparrow falleth to the ground without His notice.

I was with the Sergt. when he died, but he was then unconscious. In conversing with one of his comrades, he expressed a desire to have his clothing be sent home. As soon as I can collect everything together, I will send every article that belonged to him, to you. I counted over his money, and found that he had $16.00 and some scraps about him. I understand that he owed Private Jacob Smith of this Co. (who is now at Pleguemine) $20.00. I will write and inquire about it: — and in the meantime, I will keep the money till I hear from you. His watch, clothing, knife, jacket, books etc., I shall send to you immediately by Express. His funeral took place this morning at 10 A.M. It was largely attended by the members of this Battalion. His remains I have had interred in the burying-ground at this place; so that if you wish at any time to have them conveyed home, you can send for them. I shall have a neat head-board put up over his grave and distinctly marked.

Any information that I can give you, concerning your late beloved husband, will be cheerfully given by

Your sincere friend,
Wm. H. Chenery
1st Let 11th U.S.C.A. (Hy)[31]

The doctor who shared the details of Atwood's death and the contents of the letter to his wife with the readers of *The Christian Recorder* was similarly touched by both, eulogizing the late soldier by saying:

So devoted was he to the cause of freedom, that he seemed willing to become a martyr. The death of Sergt. Atwood was truly lamentable for both white and colored citizens of this town; but we are happy to say, from the tone of his last letter to his wife, that he died happily ... Comment is useless, and we can only say that the cause of liberty made him bold on the field of battle, whilst the love of our Saviour made him valiant on the bed of death. Now to the God of victory Immortal thanks be paid, Who made him conqueror while in Death, Through Christ his living head. Far from this world of toil and strife, He's present with the Lord: His labors of this mortal life Ends in a blessed reward.[32]

Many other families would have painful memories of the war's end, when loved ones who were buried in distant graves did not return. William Stephens, one of the Buxton men who enlisted in the 102nd, survived the war only to suffer one of life's ultimate tragedies. He was mustered out by Dr. Alexander Augusta earlier than the rest of his regiment because of illness and a lengthy stay at the L'Ouverture General Hospital in Alexandria, Virginia. After being discharged and returning to Detroit, he sent for his wife, Mary, and large family — Almira, thirteen; Harriet, twelve; William, nine; Sarah, seven; Mary, six; Lucretia, three; and infant, Stalkden — to join him. Mary's excitement at the prospect of being reunited with her husband can be easily imagined, as can the hardships that she must have endured as a single parent to so many children. As she waited at the Chatham train station for the jubilant first leg of the trip to Detroit, William Junior went to the nearby Thames River to bathe and drowned, cruelly robbing the reunion of its joy.[33]

Many others would have more joyous memories to hold on to. At the end of the war Abbott was placed in charge of the Freedman's Village Hospital in Arlington, Virginia, ironically and purposely founded on the estate where Confederate General Robert E. Lee once lived. The village was intended to be a model colony for freed slaves. Also on the grounds is the Arlington National Cemetery, where many of America's honoured dead are buried.

Canadian surgeon Anderson Abbott had charge of the Freedman's Village in Arlington, Virginia following the war. *LC-DIG-ppmsca-34829. LOC.*

Upon leaving the service, and just before returning to his home in Toronto, Abbott was presented "with a very elegant sword, sash and belt, by the soldiers and residents at Arlington, Virginia, as an expression of the high regard they entertain of the kindness and skill with which he has discharged his duties as surgeon in charge of that post."[34] He also came away with flattering testimonials, including one from the chief medical officer from the Bureau of Refugees, Freedmen and Abandoned Lands, who praised Abbott's efficiency both before and after the latter was surgeon in charge of the Contraband Camp and Freedmen's Hospital.[35] Robert Reyburn, the Bureau's Surgeon in Chief for the District of Columbia, also gave commendations for Abbott's "professional ability & gentlemanly deportment."[36] Brevet Major G.B. Carse echoed similar sentiments.

Just as Canada had been the Underground Railroad's end for thousands, the conclusion of the Civil War permanently signalled that Railroad's end for all. While many like Abbott returned to Canada to resume and build their lives, there was an exodus of Canadian blacks back to the United States. They were filled with optimism that they would be reunited with loved ones, and that the country of their birth would now extend to them the rewards of citizenship, which so many of them had recently fought and died for.

CHAPTER 10

War's Aftermath

The historian's pen cannot fail to locate us somewhere among the good and the great, who have fought and bled upon the altar of their country.

— Garland H. White

Reverend Thomas Kinnard's prediction that "there would be one eternal black streak reaching from here to the uttermost parts of the South" if freedom was established in the United States, had a certain degree of accuracy, albeit vividly overstated for effect.[1] Anderson Abbott recorded that after the Civil War, the membership of the coloured Wesleyan Methodist Church in Toronto, which had been founded in 1838, declined to such an extent that it was impossible to support a minister. As a result, blacks stopped using it for religious services and rented the building out to several other groups to use for meetings.[2] Other black communities experienced a similar drain of their population.

Despite the fact that there was a significant exodus back to the United States after the Civil War, there continued to be some northerly movement as well. The late Niagara-area historian, Frank H. Severance, shared a glimpse of Thomas Banks, a Virginia-born slave who was sold to the deep South but was "freed by the bayonet" at Natchez, Mississippi.

This recruiting poster for the 24th USCT, stating "LET SOLDIERS IN WAR BE CITIZENS IN PEACE," was the hard-fought prayer for blacks. Canadian-born John Lewis, William Fitgyles, William Stratton, and Paul Western all served in the 24th. *Gladstone Collection, LOT 14022, no. 208, LOC.*

Severance reported that Banks then joined the 102nd USCI and fought until the end of the war, following which he moved to Fort Erie, Ontario.[3] Although the name "Thomas Banks" does not appear on the roster of the 102nd, nor does a Thomas Banks fitting his age or description appear in the ranks of the other coloured regiments, it is possible that he either enlisted under an alias and/or that Severance was mistaken about which regiment Banks served in.

Junius B. Roberts, a veteran of Indiana's 28th USCI, became a minister at the BME churches in Guelph, Oakville, and Hamilton, Ontario.[4] Plagued by illness throughout much of the two years his military service, and with lifelong after-effects, Reverend Roberts applied for an invalid pension on April 4, 1887. As his health continued to deteriorate, he returned to Indiana, and on October 12, 1893, while still the relatively young age of fifty-four, he was admitted to the U.S. National Home for Disabled Volunteer Soldiers in Marion, Grant County, where he died on June 13, 1894.[5] His wife, Francis, remained in Canada and applied for a widow's pension on May 9, 1895.[6]

Isaac Smith had quite a different story. Born into slavery in Richmond, Virginia, Smith had a close relationship with his master. When war was declared and his master joined the Confederate army, Smith accompanied him as his servant, even though he was given the choice to remain at their home. Three years after the war ended, he became a Baptist minister and had congregations in Virginia, West Virginia, Ohio, Kentucky, and Michigan, before taking over the pastorate at the First Baptist Church in Windsor, Ontario. Smith's last charge was at the Baptist church of North Buxton, where he died on January 19, 1906.[7]

Interestingly, Canada also remained a draw for certain white Southerners. Jacob Carvell of the 10th Virginia Infantry fought the entire four years of the war. Disgusted by the Confederate defeat, and unwilling to remain in the Union, he moved to Canada and joined the Royal Canadian North West Mounted Police, rising to the rank of superintendent.[8]

Some black veterans, even though they had moved back to the United States, never forgot the importance of Canada to them and to their people. When there was a pronounced fear in Canada of Fenian raids in 1866, one hundred black veteran troops who were then living in Philadelphia offered to march to the Canadian border to help defend it against a group of Irish-American veterans who called themselves "the Fenian Brotherhood," and who threatened to capture Canada and take it hostage from Britain as a tactic to achieve Ireland's independence. Speaking of Canada as it related to this, a black newspaper correspondent, writing on behalf of the black volunteers, pledged:

> "Fenian I spare that land;
> In slavery it sheltered me,
> And I'll protect it now."[9]

Some veterans had a difficult time deciding which county they would prefer to live in. In a November 5, 1865 letter, teacher and Civil War chaplain Samuel Lowery expressed that he quickly realized that the end of slavery in the United States did not ensure quality of life. Disillusioned, Lowery wished to return to his farm and to his three-room frame house in Canada. Scores of other blacks would agree with Lowery's sentiments "to Return to the Land of my Adoption & enjoy the freedom of British Law & Liberty" in Canada.[10] Lowery, however, soon had another change of heart, and decided not to remain in Canada. He returned to his home state of Tennessee and enrolled in college to study law. Despite the fact that the Ku Klux Klan broke up the school, Lowery eventually received his law degree and practiced in Tennessee, and later in Alabama, where he also preached. At the request of his daughter, he took up the vocation of raising silkworms, which were nourished in white mulberry trees. It became a thriving enterprise, and Lowery hoped that silk would replace cotton as a fabric.[11]

As Lowery's case suggests, all was not always well in Canada, and many blacks continued to find that they were unwelcome guests. As had happened in earlier years, some reported that prejudice in Canada was more insidious and hurtful than in the States because it was subtler, as opposed to their experiences in the States, where it was clearer. Some reported an increase in discrimination after the war, because there was a feeling that now that there was no longer slavery south of the border, there was no longer any reason for blacks to remain north of the border. After having read a newspaper article about abuse that American blacks were suffering, Ezekial Cooper responded that despite Canadian laws that safeguarded against it, his race was also oppressed and unfairly treated. Citing comparisons between the two countries, Cooper begrudged that blacks were not always allowed to ride on public transportation, were denied attendance at public schools even though they paid taxes, and were sometimes refused to be accepted as jurors. His opinion was that although prejudice had subsided in Canada after the Civil War, conditions were improving more in the United States.[12]

Of course, the fight against prejudice and discrimination continued and continues. Just as Garland H. White did in Toledo, Ohio when he brought a suit against the Board of Education for refusing to allow his daughter to attend the local school, so too did Windsor's James Dunn in launching the suit *Dunn v. the Board of Education of the Town of Windsor*. In White's case, he was forced to hire a tutor to come to his home.[13] James Dunn, whose father had been a slave and whose brothers had fought in the Civil War, was equally disappointed, as his daughter, Jane Ann, was refused admittance to the white school since there was a coloured school that she could attend.[14]

Elijah Willis, who is also credited as being a recruiter during the war, fought his local school board in Canada during the war, and repeated the fight in the United States after. During the winter of 1863–64, the Willis children — Charles, Maria, Margaret, and Robert — were treated so badly in the otherwise all-white school that they were forced to leave. At the next meeting of the householders in the district, Elijah Willis attended along with the other parents and taxpayers who supported the school, who offered him five dollars to keep his children away. Willis refused the money and sent his children back to school. They were denied entry and suspended on the grounds that they had been absent for reasons other than sickness or other urgent reasons.[15]

The Willis family moved to Detroit after the war, and the children, including young Robert, tried to attend the Duffield Union School, but were not allowed in because they were "Negroes." An angry Elijah filed a complaint and took the case to court; however, he was forced to withdraw because of a technicality regarding his citizenship, presumably because he had previously lived in Canada. Undeterred, Willis gave the necessary funds to pursue the case to another man named Workman, who agreed to aid him and to test their case in court. The case went to the Michigan Supreme Court, which ruled that separate schools for blacks were illegal. In 1870, Robert Willis began his studies at Duffield, and eventually became a lawyer.[16]

For many, there could be no justice. Amaziah Payton, originally from South Carolina, who had spent part of the war years working as a bricklayer in Chatham, met a tragic end when he returned to his home state. On one mid-July morning in 1866, Payton, who had always been free and was well regarded in the district, was shot without any provocation by a heavily armed desperado named Reuben L. Golding, whose only mission that day was to shoot a negro. Payton's offense was that after disembarking from a train he approached an eating establishment to purchase dinner. Golding told him that he was not allowed. The latter then demanded to know the time. When Payton pulled out his watch to reply, Golding grabbed the chain, trying to take it out of the owner's grasp. When he did not succeed, Golding stepped back a few paces, drew his gun, fired a shot into Payton's groin, then leisurely walked away.

Horrified spectators rushed to the wounded man's aid, but finding no doctor in the vicinity, transported Payton to the nearby town of Anderson, where he was met by his relatives and friends. However, their reunion only lasted for moments, as Payton soon died of his wounds. Governor James Orr of South Carolina offered a $250 reward for the arrest of the shooter, who slipped across the Savannah River into Georgia. Lacking a cavalry to give chase, the post commander of the region's Bureau of Refugees, Freedmen and Abandoned Lands was helpless to pursue.[17] However, both the Governor and the Bureau remained committed to justice, tracking Golding's trail through Florida, where he was arrested, but escaped, and investigating the possibility that he was hiding out in Louisiana or Texas. The Commissioner of the Bureau ordered all of the assistant commissioners, officers, and agents throughout the south to "make every possible exertion to discover and arrest" Golding, promising further military aid if necessary.[18]

Emancipation did not mean the end of the labours of many of the human rights activists who worked to help achieve it. Laura Haviland remained an active advocate for Southern blacks for most of the remainder of her life. After the war, The Freedmen's Aid Commission took over the River Raisin Institute, which had been renamed the "Haviland Home for Homeless and Destitute Children," which Laura and her husband had established on their Michigan farm. In 1867, Laura added to the population of the Home when she brought fifteen Southern orphans with her. The children's comfort, however, was short-lived, as the County Superintendent of the Poor, who was driven by racial prejudice, admonished Haviland that many of the children that she had brought had become an unbearable burden to the taxpayers, therefore making it necessary to prosecute anyone who brought a child or impoverished person into the county. Haviland fought back, replying that the home was primarily operated with the financial support of the long-time philanthropic American Missionary Association, as well as donations from community groups and from sympathetic individuals. After a temporary reprieve, the county authorities closed the Home, turning the orphans out into the streets, shipping eight of them — all unfed and under the age of eleven — to the New York City steps of the American Missionary

Association. An aging but determined Haviland refused to forsake her humanitarian principles or the plight of those children and all like them who suffered the cruelties of fate, and continued to come to their rescue and devote her life to what she considered to be God's work.

Mary Ann Shadd Cary continued her life as an activist for social justice and to encourage pride, independence, and opportunities for her people. In the final year of the war, she had moved to Detroit and taught school in a church basement. The gushing minister described her as an

> ... indefatigable worker in all reforms and education ... She is one of the few who never say "die" or "I can't" when any thing is to be done for the elevation of her people. Her school was thriving handsomely until the opening of the Public Schools, when most of her pupils left to attend them, "not that they loved Mrs. Carey [sic] less" but the Public Schools more, because attended with less expense.[19]

Cary soon moved to Washington, where she continued to speak up on equal rights for blacks and women, taught, and became principal of a black grammar school. She later received a law degree from Howard University.[20]

After serving in the military, Cary's younger brother, Abram W. Shadd, also received a law degree from Howard and practiced in both Arkansas and Mississippi. When he died, the Greenville, Mississippi newspaper was effusive in its praise:

> All nations and people justly pride themselves in individuals who by their superior virtues or abilities, raise themselves to such a height in the social scale as to reflect credit on those of their race or nationality.... The white people join their colored fellow-citizens in mourning for one who was alike an ornament to his race, and a beloved and highly respected citizen of the community in which he lived.[21]

Their brother, Isaac, who had worked on the *Provincial Freeman* with Mary Ann, and was a founding member of the African Civilization Society of Canada, became a member of the Mississippi House of Representatives and served as Speaker from 1874 to 1876.[22] During that time period, known as the "Reconstruction," Thomas Stringer, a contemporary of the family while living in Canada, also became a member of the Mississippi House of Representatives.[23]

In early July 1865, shortly after the cessation of the conflict, Dr. Alexander Augusta was sent to the area of Savannah, Georgia to care for the freedmen who clustered together on land in the Ogeechee District, which was primarily used for the cultivation of rice. By September 1, Augusta was placed in charge of the Lincoln General Hospital, which operated under the jurisdiction of the Bureau of Refugees, Freedmen and Abandoned Lands, which was established to spearhead the effort for constructing a new social order post-war and post-slavery. The Bureau's mandate included providing food, education, medical care, and jobs, and dealing with racially related challenges and confrontations. Augusta remained there until he resigned on March 27, 1867.

Following his departure from service, Augusta took up residence and returned to medical practice in Washington. There, he also became one of the instructors of the medical department at Howard University.[24] On occasions such as the grand celebration for the corner stone laying of Wilberforce University in Ohio, Augusta was praised as an example to young blacks as to what could be achieved with education and perseverance.[25]

Augusta, however, did continue to face social and professional hardships because of his race. On one occasion, he tried to help champion the cause of another when he was interviewed at a Senate committee hearing about the forcible removal of a black female employee of the Senate, who was thrown off a train in Alexandria, Virginia for refusing to give up her seat in the car designated for white ladies only. The woman, Kate Brown, was severely injured with sprains, bruising all over her body, torn ligaments, and internal injuries in the altercation, and as a result required daily medical treatment from Dr. Augusta. He also continued to face disappointments of his own when he was refused admission and membership to the Medical Society of Washington.[26]

Despite all of the challenges he faced in life, Augusta was granted final tributes upon his death in December 1890, when he was interred at Arlington National Cemetery, where members of his old regiment, the 7th USCI, held a special memorial tribute to their honoured comrade.[27]

Anderson Abbott would use the skills that he honed as an army surgeon as he practiced medicine in Chatham, Dundas, Oakville, and Toronto. While in Chatham, he was also the president of the Wilberforce Educational Institute for black students, and later the coroner for the County of Kent. Twenty-five years after the war ended, Abbott was elected a member of the Civil War veteran's society James S. Knowlton Post No. 532 Grand Army of the Republic (GAR). Profoundly touched by his experiences, for the remainder of his life Abbott would often reflect philosophically on the conflict. On one occasion, he opined that "it became a struggle between beautiful right and ugly wrong — it determined whether civilization or barbarism should rule, whether freedom or slavery should prevail upon this continent."[28] His praise for the soldiers who had died was profuse and deeply felt:

> Therefore we do not mourn for the departed heroes; their passports have been signed by the Great commanding officer of the Universe. The bugle has sounded at the assembly of the Grand Army of Heaven and they have responded to the call.[29]

There were several GAR posts in Canada. According to historian Scott A. MacKenzie, they were: the William Winer #77 in Hamilton, the Hannibal Hamlin #652 of NY in London, the W.W. Cooke #472 of NY also in Hamilton, and the J.S. Knowlton #532 of NY in Toronto. Quebec had three: the Joseph Bernard #77 of New Hampshire, the General Hancock #73 of Vermont in Montreal, and the Quebec #117, also of Vermont, in Quebec City.[30]

London's Hamilton Hamlin post was named after Abraham Lincoln's vice-president from his first term in office. Hamlin was a staunch anti-slavery senator and former governor of Maine. Opponents referred to Lincoln's party as "Black Republicans" and sought to render disdain on the swarthy-skinned Hamlin in the public's view by claiming that he was a mulatto, giving them the opportunity to use the pejorative term "nigger."[31]

There appeared to be no such racial animosity at the Hamlin GAR post, which met every second Tuesday in the Duffield Block on Dundas Street. Black members George W. Duncan, formerly of the 107th USCI; Oliver Fountain of the 12th USCI; London barber James Charles (alias James Marble) of the 6th USCI; and Canadian barber Richard Williams, who travelled to the meetings from St. Thomas, of the 26th USCI, all appear with their thirty-one white comrades on the "Muster Roll," all having joined in 1891.

Richard Williams was only eighteen and already a barber when he enlisted at Dunkirk in New York State on January 5, 1864. Declaring his birthplace as Canada, he had no trouble solemnly swearing "that I will bear true faith and allegiance to the United States of America, and that I will observe them honestly and faithfully against all their enemies or opposers, whomsoever; and that I will observe and obey the orders of the President of the United States."[32]

Oliver Fountain, who was born in Richmond, Virginia, was an officer in the GAR Post, serving as quarter master sergeant, a far cry from when, as a twenty-two-year-old, he first enlisted at Elk River, Tennessee on July 19, 1863. At that time, he gave his occupation as "servant" — the more genteel Southern term for "slave." Fountain quickly rose in the ranks, being promoted from private to corporal in just over two months from the time of his enlistment. He endeavoured to exert his newfound independence, but just as quickly learned the uncompromising nature of army discipline when he was reduced to the ranks by the colonel for disobedience to orders. Thus chastened, and both smarter and forgiven, he rose to the lofty position of sergeant on February 6, 1865. Perhaps Fountain received some valuable training for his future position as quarter mastersergeant to look after supplies at the Hamlin GAR when he was placed on detached service as a guard for the commissary at White Bluff, Arkansas.[33]

The issue of aliases, as used by James Charles and George Duncan, is an interesting topic. This was frequently done with runaway slaves as they sought to make their trail more difficult to follow. James Charles served as James Marble when he enlisted as a substitute in St. Louis,

Missouri on January 3, 1865. He gave his place of birth as Mississippi, as opposed to his GAR records, which give it as Virginia.[34] George Duncan's story is even more curious.

In his GAR registration on October 27, 1891, he gave his name as George W. Duncan, alias George English, born in Stevensburg, Harding County, Kentucky, and his regiment as the 107th. His compiled military service records cover the time from when he enlisted at Elizabethtown, Kentucky on June 22, 1864 to when he was mustered out on November 22, 1866, and including a request for a thirty-day furlough to visit his family in Kentucky in August of 1865, all are under the alias George English.[35] The intriguing part from that same set of records is that they show that there was a George Duncan in that regiment who died of pneumonia at the general hospital at Fort Monroe, Virginia on October 27, 1864. A century and a half later, we are left to wonder at English's later choice of names.

The use of aliases also raised trouble for veterans who applied for pensions. Those who had been wounded or who had suffered long-term ill effects from their involvement in the war could apply to the U.S. government for a modest pension to help support them. William Henry Bannister, alias Benjamin Franklin Hanson, was a twenty-nine-year-old sailor at the time he enlisted on August 6, 1864 at Bergen, New York in the 6th Regiment USCI, Company C. He gave his place of birth variously as Mississippi and Michigan, and collected one hundred dollars, which was the first installment of his bounty. In the final year of the war he was sick in the hospital from January through June before being mustered out at Fort Monroe, Virginia on June 23, 1865.

One of his descendants, Lorraine Hanson Johnston, a great-great-niece, shared the story that her uncle, who is buried on the Hanson farm on the fifth concession of Chatham Township, enlisted in 1863 as Frank Hanson, deserted, and re-enlisted as William Henry Bannister.

Actually getting a pension was a difficult and drawn-out affair. The smallest irregularities in the paperwork exchanges could cause big problems. Francis Johnson of Otterville gave his age as twenty when he went to New York State to enlist in the 26th USCI. However, in his pension application, he wrote that he was just short of his nineteenth birthday, and was "born in 1800 and 45." This inconsistency added to the delay in finalizing the paperwork, as did the many medical reports and affidavits from acquaintances that testified as to his inability to work because of physical disabilities, which began in South Carolina during the war.

Although Priscilla Atwood was only thirty-one years of age at the time of her husband, Alexander Atwood's, death, the grieving widow never remarried, living out her life in her King Street East home in Chatham, with only the occasional trip back to the United States to visit relatives in Ohio. She survived in part by receiving a widow's pension, which she was entitled to as the survivor of a soldier who died during the war. She applied for the pension within three weeks of her husband's death, having the appropriate papers and affidavits notarized by a Kent County Justice of the Peace and witnessed by her spouse's late business partner, Henry Jackson. In her application, Priscilla had to show proof of where, when, and by whom she was legally married, and that she had not remarried after her husband's death, which she said was caused by "inflammation of the bowels caused by Camp life, the heat of the weather and fatigue." The application process was never easy and never quick. In addition to a sworn statement from Brown County, Ohio's Probate Court, confirming all details of the marriage, Priscilla tried to move the process along on March 22, 1866 by having two people who had been in attendance at her wedding, Sarah Pearson and Amelia Robinson, sign sworn affidavits that they witnessed it.

She reported that she had no children.

The documents had to be submitted and reviewed by the U.S. Department of the Treasury and the Adjutant General's Office in Washington, who also had to check the details of each soldier's service. It was not until May 19, 1866 that her pension of eight dollars per month was approved. On April 22, 1879, following the passage of new legislation to increase the rate, Priscilla again went to the Clerk of the Peace for Kent County to submit the proper paperwork to receive twelve dollars per month. Once again, the process was complicated. In a supporting letter, notarized on September 5, 1879, Alexander's daughter and Priscilla's stepdaughter, Sarahfine, relayed the melancholy story of her own past. She wrote that her father used to tell her about her birth mother, who she could not remember, having died before her daughter was old enough to speak. She was told that her parents had married in Mobile, Alabama and that they lived there until her mother died. Following the death, she and her father moved to Ripley, Ohio, where he married Priscilla, with whom Sarahfine continued to live and be supported by to the present date. (Sarahfine, or at least Priscilla, must have known that these details were not true. Both women gave Sarahfine's birthdate as June 30, 1854 — which would have been seventeen days after Priscilla and Alexander were married. Also, Alexander was taken by his master to Ohio in the 1830s at about nine years of age, and contemporary records suggest that he never returned to Alabama.

Unfortunately, and inexplicably, the issue of Alexander's first marriage and the daughter from that union was problematic for pension officials, as they demanded further confirmation of those details which Priscilla was unable to provide, stating that she did not know anyone from Mobile, nor any relatives of her husband that might exist who could provide them.

Challenges related to her continued to arise throughout Priscilla's life, as they did for many Canadian veterans and their widows. In a letter dated July 20, 1893, the Bureau of Pensions advised her that her benefits were cut off following an Act of Congress that stated: "no pension shall be paid to a non-resident, who is not a citizen of the United States," and that her husband's citizenship would determine her own. She then had the difficult task of proving that her husband had been born in the United States — a request that was particularly oppressive for anyone who had been born in slavery for whom no official state or county records existed. Partially coming to the rescue on the thorny issue was Lucy Overstreet of Chatham, who, on August 1, 1893, claimed to have been born on the Bluff plantation in Alabama. Unable to write, she dictated her affidavit that she knew Alexander, as well as his parents, who informed her that he had been born on the same plantation. Delia Lawson of Albion, Michigan was also sought out, and she too came to Chatham and dictated that she had been born on that same Bluff plantation and could testify that Alexander had been as well. A determined Priscilla Atwood added her own statement that she knew her husband had been born in Bluff Prairie because he had written it in their family bible. Wishing to distinguish herself from her supporters, a literate Priscilla proudly included, "this statement is written by my Self and not dicated by eny one." She also added that, "I have not Renounced my CitizenShip of the united States." Satisfied at the response, Priscilla's pension was reinstated on September 8, 1893.

Still feeling that it was a struggle to get by, an aged and sickly Priscilla finally wrote in desperation to the Washington, D.C. pension agent on April 22, 1911:

> Now as I have become a Burdon on others also Helpless with many weeknesses, my only help has been in the care of me the Little Girl that my Husband Alexander Atwood left with me. She has been with me in all my afflictions now she is Broken in health not able to give me Care, I have had to divide all this many years with this wooman. Now what is best for me to Do in regards to a home for me, Please let me know Just as Soon as you can what you think best for me in this Sad State.
>
> If it should be the Soldiers Widow's Home what will be the Charges.
>
> Please Send me the particulars.
>
> I am as ever a well wisher to thos that rule this Great-work for the Soldiers Poor widows.
>
> Priscilla J. Atwood

Her request was responded to in a letter that stated that the pension bureau had no jurisdiction with the various Homes that were provided in different states of widows, and that she was already receiving the maximum pension allowed for the widow of a sergeant. She received her final pension cheque for twelve dollars to cover the period to December 11, 1911.

She waited many years for the hoped-for reunion that her husband had written her about in his final letter. At 6:45 a.m. on March 3, 1912, the effects of senility, apoplexy, heart disease, and paralysis on her left side took her, aged seventy-eight years, nine months, and eight days. A dutiful Sarahfine, now sixty years of age and never married, informed the pension bureau about her stepmother's (who she called Aunt) passing, and asked for the last quarterly cheque for thirty-six dollars that Priscilla would have been entitled to had she lived for two more days, so she could pay for expenses that had already been incurred. Fanny Atwood, a relative from Ripley, made the trip to Canada and assisted in making preparations to deliver Priscilla's body for burial in what had been the free city of her youth in Ripley, Ohio.[36] The Chatham funeral directors submitted their invoice:

$60.00 for a black cloth casket and box
$10.00 for arterial embalming
$5.00 for hearse and personal service
$2.50 for a hack
$21.70 for two train tickets to Ripley, Ohio.

In addition to the undertaker's total of $99.20, Doctor George McKeough, who had attended to Priscilla in her final illness, requested $17.50 for medicine and his visits. There was an additional $48.75 for funeral expenses in Ripley. The pension bureau rejected those requests on the grounds that Priscilla had assets of cash and debentures worth two thousand dollars. In Maplewood Cemetery in Ripley, a modest tombstone marks her final resting place.

While the collective experiences of all of the soldiers left meaningful footprints on the larger maps of history, some inadvertently left substantial personal tracks in an indirect way. Noteworthy among this group is Joshua Dunbar, a Garrett County, Kentucky slave who had escaped to Canada. During the Civil War, soon after blacks were allowed to enlist, he volunteered for the 55th Massachusetts. Judging his age to be between forty and forty-five years, the five-foot-ten-inch man, who made his living as a plasterer, was much older than most of his comrades in the regiment — indeed, in all of the army. Perhaps his age contributed to his early release from the regiment. On October 28, 1863 at Folly Island, South Carolina, he was discharged by reason of physical disability caused by injuries received by heavy lifting while on fatigue duty. He had been unfit for more than two months at the time. Demonstrating remarkable determination after physically recovering, Joshua re-enlisted into the 5th Regiment, Massachusetts Colored Cavalry on May 9, 1864. Well respected and capable, he was promoted to corporal by October 30, 1864 and to sergeant on May 1, 1865, before being mustered out in Clarksville, Texas on October 31, 1865.[37] His contributions in the field were significant, but his most lasting legacy was through his son.

Six years after the war, Joshua married the widowed Matilda Murphy, and a few months later, Paul Laurence Dunbar was born to the couple. Although the couple divorced four years later, and Joshua was soon thereafter admitted to the U.S. National Home for Disabled Volunteer Soldiers in Dayton, Ohio. Joshua's father and his experiences in the war had a profound impact on the son. In a short lifetime of only thirty-three years, Paul became the first nationally acclaimed literary celebrity, authoring many poems, essays, short stories, and novels. Several of his striking works were inspired by personal stories of the Civil War that his father shared with him.

Like Dunbar Sr., the National Homes housed many other men who had once made Canada home. Ex-soldiers who applied to the Homes had to present proof that they were honourably discharged from service, and medical proof that they were disabled and that the disability was clearly traced to that service. If the manager was satisfied and granted admission, the man was assigned to a barracks and given a suit of clothes that resembled a uniform. Men who received a military invalid's pension had to buy their own clothes thereafter, as well as purchase their own tobacco. The treasurer at the Home acted as banker, but allowed the men to maintain the right to their income, except when it might be squandered. If the inmate had a wife and/or children, money orders were occasionally sent to them from these funds. The men were encouraged to supplement their income by taking paying jobs at the Homes, in a variety of employment opportunities at onsite workshops.

The Homes maintained a military atmosphere. There were strict rules about order, cleanliness, and respect for fellow inmates, and against bad language, drunkenness, and being absent without leave. Day passes or furloughs for thirty, sixty, or ninety days had to be applied for, along with proof that the inmate was able to pay for his return transportation. The latter was made somewhat more affordable, as the board of managers had made a deal with railroad companies in both the United States and Canada that fares would be at one-half the usual rate.[38]

Joshua Dunbar of the 5th Massachusetts Colored Cavalry was the father
of famous poet Paul Lawrence Dunbar. *Courtesy of St. Clairsville (Ohio)
Public Library.*

Coloured soldiers were entitled to the same benefits of the Homes that their white comrades were granted. It was felt that the blacks would be more comfortable in the climate of a southern location. This branch was constructed at a picturesque location on the Chesapeake River near Fort Monroe at Hampton, Virginia. Here, as in the other locations, they could attend the chapel, participate in special programs and work activities, and make use of the libraries as they learned or fine-tuned the fundamentals of reading and writing, many for the first times in their lives.[39]

On November 30, 1876, William Johnson, a forty-year-old widowed veteran from Brantford, Canada West, who had fought with the 5th Massachusetts Colored Cavalry from April 30, 1864 to May 31, 1865, was placed in the Togus, Maine's branch of the National Home for Disabled Volunteer Soldiers. His closest relative, sister Angelina Miller from Hamilton, was unable to care for her brother, who had been shot in the knee and was partially paralyzed. On August 8, 1887 Johnson became one of the men who were transferred to the Southern Branch of the National Home in Hampton, Virginia.[40]

Michigan Soldiers' Home in Grand Rapids, Michigan was the final home for many Civil War veterans. *LC-DIG-det-4a23406. LOC.*

Lorenzo Rann of Buxton served in the 102nd USCT. After the war he married his first wife, but she tragically died several months later, at age nineteen. His second marriage ended in separation. By 1902, Rann had lost all contact with his four children, and ill health forced him to move into the Soldier's Home in Grand Rapids, Michigan, where he remained until his death on December 4, 1922. *Courtesy of BNHS&M.*

An aged James Newby, formerly of the 3rd USCT, and his wife Eliza (whose brother Lorenzo Rann fought with the 102nd) with their home and farm buildings in the background. *Courtesy of great-great-granddaughter Dalyce Newby.*

On April 15, 1901, Lorenzo Rann, another former Buxton resident who was in the 102nd USCI, applied for admission to the state-run Michigan Soldier's Home in Grand Rapids. Sixty-five and married, he was unable to support himself, a condition exasperated by an injury to his leg. During a battle in South Carolina, a shell burst, causing a broken ankle on his right leg and the loss of part of his middle toe.[41] Rann died on December 4, 1922 and is buried in the Veteran's Home Cemetery.

Charles Henry Griffin, the veteran of Illinois's 29th USCI who had been hospitalized after the Battle of the Crater "for fatigues, nerves and everything unstrung," returned to Chatham Township after being mustered out, later moved to Port Huron, and finally settled in Grand Rapids, Michigan. After seven years there, and after his wife's death, he moved into the Northwestern Branch of the National Home for Disabled Volunteers Soldiers in Milwaukee so he could be close to his sister, Emma Chandler, who lived in Chicago. At the time of his admission, he was forty-nine and suffered from pleurisy, neuralgia, varicose veins in his right leg, and chronic diarrhea.[42] He remained there until 1902, when he moved to San Diego, where one of his daughters lived. He died in the Pacific Branch National Home in Sawtelle, in what is now part of Los Angeles, California, in 1925. In one of those interesting twists of fate, years later, Charles Griffin's grandson would establish a funeral home in Chicago on part of the land where Camp Douglas — where over six thousand Confederate prisoners died of disease and exposure — once stood. According to Griffin's descendants, this was also the location where Charles Henry Griffin had enlisted.[43]

Henry Williams was born in Chatham and had been a barber up until the time of his enlistment in the 102nd. Following the war he lived in Windsor, where Reverend Augustus Green performed his marriage to Elizabeth Myers Wyatt. Like Lorenzo Rann, he too was compelled to move into the Soldier's Home in Grand Rapids, incapacitated from "double rupture and chronic Rheumatism contracted near Charleston, S.C." Williams spent his last days at the Central Branch National Home in Dayton, Ohio. While living there, the Home's treasurer forwarded half of Williams's pension to Windsor for his wife, Elizabeth. Upon his death in December 1817, that pension ceased. Elizabeth had been married to another soldier during the war. That husband had also joined the Union army, but was supposed dead, as she never heard from him again after he enlisted.

Camp Douglas was a Chicago prison camp for captured Confederate soldiers. In later years, descendants of Canadian USCT veteran Charles Griffin established a funeral home on these grounds. *LC-USZ62-15612. LOC.*

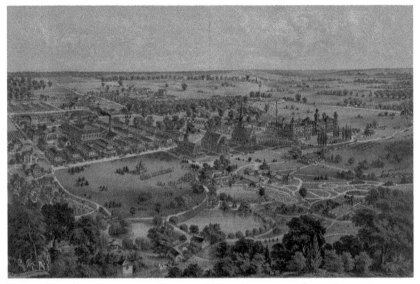

National Soldiers' home near Dayton, Ohio, where many Canadian veterans spent their final years. *LC-DIG-pga-01825. LOC.*

As was the case with most pension applicants, Elizabeth was required to supply an endless stream of documentation: records of her marriage, affidavits describing her husband's past, his occupation, places of birth and residences, and his physical description — which she described as "middling tall, rather heavy, of a light brown complection, black eyes and black hair." At age eighty-one, and being separated from her husband for years, on account of his living in the Soldier's Home, she did not recall if he had any scars or marks on his body. She also had to prove that the couple had never been divorced, nor were there any rumours of them having been separated. To do this, she had to convince three men, whom she and her husband had known, to write notarized letters supporting her statements. Unable to read or write, she was dependent upon a friend from Detroit, who periodically visited, to write on her behalf.

One melancholy and unexpected piece of information surfaced during the investigation of her eligibility for a pension. It was discovered in the files of the Department of War that Elizabeth's first husband, William Wyatt, who fought with the 17th USCI, was killed in Nashville, Tennessee on December 15, 1864. It is unclear from her pension application file if she was ever granted a pension.

Alice Williams, the widow of the other Henry Williams in the 102nd (the fourteen-year-old who was tricked into service) had many similar challenges in getting her widow's pension. She had a large number of friends and acquaintances write detailed affidavits about her husband, all stating that he suffered greatly both during and after the war. Some distinctly remembered him contracting disease of his lungs and kidneys, caused from exposure to the cold at Honey Hill, South Carolina, at the end of November 1864. After his discharge from service, he was rarely able to do any manual labour because of the pain in his back and chest. An acquaintance remarked that Henry's physical condition was worse than that of a seventy-five-year-old. He did become a Baptist minister and was stationed in Toronto at the time of his death from congestion of lungs and kidneys on November 7, 1888 at age thirty-eight. In 1892, after many months of trying, Alice, who supported herself by sewing dresses, was given a widow's pension of eight dollars per month.[44]

Following the war, there was a renewed effort for people to seek loved ones who had been left behind in slavery. The October 6, 1866 edition of *The Christian Recorder* published the following advertisement:

Willis Fant, raised in Galliten County, Kentucky, wishes information from his brother and sister, Washington and Mary Fant. At the time I left, about twenty-five years ago, they belonged to W.B. Fant. Information wanted also of James and Robert Smith, who, at that time, belonged to Wat Civil. Address, Willis Fant, Newbury Post Office, Canada West.

Over the years, *The Christian Recorder* carried many more such articles, all heart wrenching and all vital for remembering the most basic reason for the war:

- Sept 24, 1870. Information wanted — Of my brothers Thomas and Aminger Moton, sons of Polly Parker, of Washington City. When last heard of they were in Canada. They lived at Fredericksburgh, and belonged to Lewis Halton, but escaped by Underground Railroad. Any information will be gladly received by their sister. Francis Parker, St. Joseph, Mo.

- July 14, 1866. Lewis Wade wishes to learn the whereabouts of his wife, Lucy, and three children, named respectively, Benjamin, Harriet and Charlotte. He left them in 1850, they then being in Rockbridge County, Virginia. He belonged to Wm. Thompson, while his wife and children belonged to James Watts. Any information respecting them will be thankfully received by the subscriber at Chatham, Canada West, — and Heaven will bless the hand that guides the wanders home. Chatham, Canada West.

- August 25, 1866. (By Maria Gibbs) of Joseph Gibson, her son, who formerly resided near Chatham, Canada West. Any information in regard to him can be sent to Maria Gibbs, in care of Dr. J.F. Holt, 1139 Pine Street, Philadelphia.

- December 16, 1865. Fanny Frazer wishes to ascertain the whereabouts of her six children, who were owned by a family of the name of Bailey, who lived at Clarksville. Va. Some years ago the children assumed the name of their owners, and are known by the following names: Nelson Bailey, Hannah Bailey, Maria Bailey, Charlotte Bailey, Norah Bailey and Amie Bailey. Any information respecting them will be thankfully received by Fanny Frazer, Buxton, Canada West.

- Sept 16, 1865. Of Eliza McDowell, who lived in Savington, Mo. and was engaged on the packet "Edward Brass." She was owned by one Capt. Chammon, and left for Canada, in 1848. Any information will be most thankfully received by her son. Benj. Coates, Care of Amos Fosset, Hannibal, Mo.

- June 12, 1869. Information wanted of my mother, Deborah Brown, of Chestertown, Kent Co. MD. She was a slave of Daniel Collins, but escaped from him in 1854. Five years ago I heard she was in Canada. Any information of her whereabouts will be thankfully received. Address Sarah Elizabeth Brooks, Chester, Pa.

- July 30, 1870. Information wanted of John Barclay, who went from Charleston, S.C. to Canada with Prof. Andrew Miller to be educated in the 12th year of his age, about the year 1854 or '55, is now if living about 28 years old. When last heard from, about eleven years ago, he was in England on board of an American vessel, Capt. Richards, Liverpool. Any information concerning him will be thankfully received by his mother. Address, Meriah Johnson, Morrisons's Mills, Orange Creek, Alachna Co. East Florida.

- March 7, 1863. Mr Editor. — Please have the kindness to grant the following a place in your valuable paper. I have a son somewhere up north, and I take this method of trying to ascertain his whereabouts. John Terry is his name. It has been three years since I received a letter from him. He was then in Chicago, Illinois, having made his escape from slavery in St. Louis, Mo. The last I heard of him was that he left Chicago for Canada, at the time so many of our people went from there for fear of the enforcement of the fugitive slave law, &c. The first time we were all sold together to the widow Beck at Plattsburgh, Mo. The last time we were separated, my other son was sold south. Thank the good Lord, since then I have obtained my freedom. I am now living in Leavenworth city, Kansas. Any information respecting this inquiry will be thankfully received. Eliza Beck

- August 5, 1865. Can any one inform me of the whereabouts of Emily Wilson, the mother of Amanda Jane Wilson? She belonged to John K. Wilson, who lived in Montgomery County, Tennessee, four miles from Clarsville. She was sold and taken to Mississippi, in 1856;

or of Eveline Wilson, who belonged to the same John K. Wilson, who, after selling my mother, removed from Montgomery County, Tennessee, to Marshal County, Kentucky, eighteen miles from Paducah. Harriet Wilson, another sister, was sold to Joseph Dear, and taken to Texas. My name was Amanda Jane Wilson. I left Kentucky in 1861 or 1862. My name now is Amanda Jane Bass. Any information of the above named persons will be thankfully received. Amanda Jane Bass, Hamilton, C.W.

- September 26, 1868. Notice — Information wanted of my relatives, Louisa, Henrietta, and Eliza Woods. Belonged to the widow Bailey of Shepherstown, Va. Address, Mary A. Glancford, Hamilton, Ont, C.W.
- September 26, 1868. Notice — Information of my brothers, Archey, Felix, Joseph and James Goodler; also, my sisters Rachel, Caroline and Sinty, children of David and Daphney Goodler, formerly of Morefield, Hardy co., Ky. Address, David Goodler, Hamilton, Ont, C.W.
- January 11, 1868. Information is wanted of my son, Joseph Sipple. When last heard of, in 1863, he was in Toronto C.W. Any information of his whereabouts will be thankfully received by his mother. Address Mary Ann Sipple, 1229 Arch Street. 1624 Barclay Street. Or, Care Bethel AME Church, Philadelphia, Pa.
- August 29, 1868. Information Wanted. Of the children (sons) of Julia Graham, from Louisville, Ky. When she left Louisville, they belonged to James Golden. Address information to Julia Thomas, Windsor, Ca.
- September 26, 1868. Information of my son, Merryman Gray, known as Peter Hicks, of Baltimore county, Md., he lived with Aaron Sparks, also America Eli Gray. Address, Ruth Gray, Hamilton, Ont., May Street.
- September 26, 1868. Information is wanted of my mother, Sucky Boone, of my brothers Jordon, William, and Frederick; of my sisters Matilda, and Harriet.

Belonged to Capt. Samuel Boone, Callamy county, Missouri. Address, Peter Boone, Hamilton, Ont., care of Josiah Cochran, King St.

Mary Brown, also from Canada, returned to the United States in late 1867 to retrieve two of her children who had been left behind in slavery when she escaped. One daughter, Dinah, remained a slave in Nicholasville, Kentucky, and the other daughter, Mary Jane, was still enslaved in the same state in Fleming County. Neither former master would agree to release the girls and the stricken mother was forced to seek the help of the Freedmen's Bureau.[45]

Many blacks who had educational advantages over their American brethren shared the skills that they had received in Canadian classrooms to teach at the various schools that were established for blacks throughout the south. Charles Spencer Smith, who was born on March 16, 1852 in Colborne, was among them. Moving to the U.S. at about twelve years of age, he was employed in various occupations before becoming a teacher near Lexington, Kentucky through the Freedman's Bureau. Acutely embittered at the new social reality, the Ku Klux Klan broke up the school and ordered Smith to leave within forty-eight hours. Smith was reassigned to Hopkinsville, Kentucky, where his fortunes — and those of his students — were much better. After a religious conversion, Smith was licensed to become an AME minister, serving first in Mississippi, then Alabama, and eventually in many other states, as well as parts of Africa. In 1874, he was elected to the House of Representatives for Alabama. In 1900, he was appointed a bishop of the AME church and assigned the huge Twelfth Episcopal District, composed of Ontario, Nova Scotia, Bermuda, Windward Islands, and the South American Annual Conferences. In 1911, he returned to his home province, and, while at a conference at Victoria College in Toronto, was conferred the degree of Doctor of Divinity, the first such honour bestowed on a person of colour.[46]

Smith's sister, Lucy Smith, was equally dynamic. She and her siblings were inspired by the example of their remarkable father, Nehemiah, who had been born in 1812 in Queenston, Upper Canada, a military hotspot at the time. During the Rebellion of 1837, Nehemiah served as a sergeant

Many Canadians taught at Freedmen's schools such as this one in Edisto, South Carolina. *Photograph taken between 1862 and 1865 by Samuel A. Cooley, Gladstone collection, LOT 14022, no. 168. LOC.*

for Canada's segregated coloured corps, and later worked as a steward on a British man-of-war. He had a passion for studying natural history and was able to speak several native Indian languages, as well as German and French. He was also credited with being a great friend of fugitive slaves who came to Canada. Rising from that foundation, and fortified with a good education, at the end of the Civil War, at age seventeen, Lucy went to Maryland to teach. During those early days in the United States, Lucy became acquainted with and further inspired by former anti-slavery champions Frederick Douglass and William Wells Brown. As she settled in to American life, she became alarmed at the negative effects of alcohol abuse and became active in the temperance movement. She joined the Woman's Christian Temperance Union and eventually became the super-intendent of the organization, and an eloquent and much sought-after lecturer to both white and black audiences across the United States and in England. Lucy was twice married, first to Reverend Henry Simpson, and, after his death, to Frank Thurman, who had been raised by an uncle in Essex County, Canada West, where he had been sent from Indiana to avoid being sold into slavery, and under whose surname she became internationally known. Interested in other social causes, including women's voting rights and educational opportunities, Lucy was instrumental in organizing the Michigan State Association of Colored Women's Club in 1900, serving as its first president, a position she later held in the national association. In 1931, the Detroit Young Women's Christian Association named one of its branches the "Lucy Thurman YWCA," in her honour.[47]

Anderson Abbott recalled that seven hundred children of former slaves and free blacks had attended the Buxton school by the time the Civil War ended. Many went south and served as teachers in the schools for freedmen. John Riley was among those young people that Abbott referred to. Riley was too young to serve in the army, but wished to become involved in other ways when he came of age. As a child he had been carried away from slavery in Missouri by his parents and had been raised and educated in Canada, now offering his services as a teacher. Writing to the American Missionary Association from Knox College in Toronto, where he was studying theology and approaching graduation, Riley complimented the organization for having "taken upon yourselves of educating my fellow countrymen from whose necks the yolk of Slavery has recently fallen … notwithstanding the horrors and vicissitudes of war."

John Riley was among the Canadian-raised ministers who returned to the U.S. to minister to the freedmen. *Courtesy of Western Archives, Western University, Annie Straith Jamieson fonds, Box B4192.*

Considering that it would be a "privilege of communicating to my brethren in the south some of the knowledge which in the Providence of God I have been favoured with," Riley offered to go to Maryland to either teach or preach. After graduating in 1867, and being ordained in London, he kept good his pledge and taught school in Tennessee and Missouri. Later he went into mission work in Leavenworth, Kansas and Louisville, Kentucky, and after being ordained again by the Louisville Presbytery in 1870, preached for years in Washington, Indianapolis, and Knoxville. In 1904, the state university in Louisville conferred upon him the degree of Doctor of Divinity.[48]

John's younger brother, Jerome, was born in St. Catharines — his parent's first Canadian destination after their flight from slavery. Jerome left Canada while John was still attending college. He attended medical school in Chicago, where it was said that he was the first colored person to matriculate in Illinois, graduating in 1869. He opened a practice in Chicago, and later took graduate courses at Howard University in Washington, D.C. He moved to Arkansas in 1873, where he opened a medical practice and held several political positions, including becoming the first enrolling clerk of the Arkansas State Legislature. However, Jerome made a politically unwise decision that haunted him for the rest of his life by attaching himself to the Democratic Party, thus alienating him from blacks who clung to the late Abraham Lincoln's Republicans, and who refused to patronize his practice. Seeking better prospects, Jerome went to Washington and was hired to work for the attorney general. While there, he also wrote a widely discussed and controversial book on the political status of blacks, *Philosophy of Negro Suffrage*, which credited his upbringing in an integrated area of Canada for some of his education on the subject. However, he became involved in a contractual dispute with a publisher, and in a civil suit against a woman who had called his wife, Agnes, "unchaste," and the legal fights drained him of all of his money. Discouraged and widowed at the beginning of the New Year in 1903, he moved to New York City, where he began to publish a number of medical articles and two more books: *Reach the Reached Negro* and *Evolution and Racial Development*. In the former, he pointed to Reverend King as a man that leaders should be patterned after, for his "character, virtue, morality and truthfulness, which he taught and practiced." Of his childhood memories, he wrote: "The pulpit, school room and fireside teaching in that community was in keeping with the eternal fitness of things."[49]

Jerome also held the office of president of the Colored National Anti-Imperialist League. Although he was labelled "one of the best known negroes in the United States," as well as "the greatest thinker, writer and philosopher of his race," and was widely known for his gift for oratory, black ministers refused to allow him to use their churches to deliver addresses because of his political affiliation. He desperately tried to get his fellow blacks to consider that national and state Republican administrations had taken away many of their rights that were hard-earned during and immediately after the Civil War. Never compromising on his beliefs, he philosophically answered his critics: "That I was, I am; and from present reckoning I hope to be to the end, God willing, and when I go hence, looking into the deep, I desire no more fitting epitaph than, 'I sought the right as I understood the right.'"[50]

Sarah Thomas, first cousin of Dr. John Rapier, was considered to be one of the brightest pupils of the Buxton School.[51] An admirer wrote to her: "all who pay you compliments do not speak idle words for your keen and quick perception, affable manners, good sense and kind heart make you a charming and an agreeable companion."[52] In May of 1865, Sarah was in Washington, waiting for a position. By August 1865, she was teaching in Washington at the Theodore-Parker Freedmen's Aid school.[53] Sarah went on to teach for several years, and also became an accomplished writer; she lived her later years in Chicago.

John Rapier's younger brother, James, who also attended school in Buxton as well as in Toronto, returned to the United States after the war and became a congressman in Alabama. John Rapier continued to provide medical care for the District of Columbia's black community, and assisted Sarah in getting a teaching position. Unfortunately, he died at age twenty-six of bilious fever on May 17, 1866, one year following the war's end.[54]

Thirty-two-year-old Ezekial C. Cooper Jr., who had been a Buxton classmate of the Rapiers, Rileys, Sarah Thomas, Anderson Abbott, and Solomon King, who we met earlier in this book, also applied to become a teacher. Cooper had come as a teen with his parents to Canada from

Northampton, Massachusetts after the passage of the Fugitive Slave Law, at a time his father described as "when men of my complexion used to come to Canada on a keen trot, by broad day light, when we used to love to sing of the lion's paw."[55] He had conducted prayer meetings, was a vocal teacher, and was the superintendent of the Sabbath School at the Presbyterian Church. Writing to the American Missionary Association in New York on three different occasions in the autumn of 1865, Cooper expressed his desire to work in that field and requested more information. In one letter, he wrote: "As it has pleased God in his providence to bestow upon me the blessings of a tolerable education, I am willing to be made an instrument in His hands for doing good anywhere it may please Him to cast my lot."[56] The recipients were more than pleased at his qualifications and quickly accepted him, sent him details for the school where he would be stationed, and a cheque for travel expenses. However, Cooper had second thoughts as he explained that he was needed at the church in Buxton, being one of two people who were capable of handling its business. He felt that although the other elders, most of whom had been slaves, were pious, possessed common sense, and able to read, they were best "fit for the Positions they occupy." Cooper consulted with them, as well as two ministers and others in the community, who "argued that should I go South I would leave a Mission field where my labours were nearly as much needed as they in Tennessee amongst the recently freed people." However, he would be glad to refer a request to Reverend King to supply a list of names of qualified and experienced teachers who might be anxious to find a job in the South.[57]

Many people from other parts of Canada went South during and soon after the closing weeks of the war. Among them was Mrs. Sarah Ann Armstrong, who taught and was the principal in one of the government schools in Chatham for eight years. In 1861, she sailed to Africa and spent two years there as a missionary. When that time elapsed, she was forced to return to her childhood home in New Bedford, Massachusetts to care for her ailing mother, but soon thereafter was requested to go to Rhode Island to teach. "She remained there until the Macedonia cry came up from the South, 'Come and help us' when she and few others, hastened to the South." For the next three years she taught at the Freedmen's school in Easton, Maryland, where she served both parents and children.[58]

Among the black Canadians who went to teach at the newly formed Freedmen's schools that were scattered throughout the south, was a Mr. Hamborough, who taught at Louisville, Kentucky. He may very well have been the same teacher who was reported to have

> ... no idea of the difference which a Kentuckian holds to exist between a white and colored man, made himself obnoxious by what they called his "airs" and was notified to depart instantly ... The burden of his offense was that he refused to give up more than half the side-walk to a white lady.

He was driven out of the town, and was placed at another school elsewhere, where he prospered.[59]

Many of the ministers who had served in Canadian black churches before and during the war were also moved to preach among the freedmen. Among them were BME ministers who returned to their AME roots, George W. Brodie (who had also previously recruited for the USCT) and Charles H. Pearce. Brodie was first assigned to Raleigh, North Carolina and Pearce to Tallahassee, Florida.[60] BME minister William H. Jones had lectured in Britain from 1865 to 1868 to raise money for the newly freed slaves, and did missionary work in Tennessee.

Many other ministers who had served in Canada also returned to the Northern states. Thomas Wesley Cooper, who had been licensed to preach by the BME church in 1864 at Otterville, moved to Brooklyn following the war, where he became part of the AME conference. His appointments in the United States, which required him to frequently move, included Oswego, Freehold, Buffalo, Melrose, Coxsackie, and Albany, all in New York State, as well as Camden, Salem, Princeton, Bridgeport, New Brunswick, Cape May, Trenton, Plainfield, Atlantic Highlands, South Camden, Morristown, Woodbury, Rahway, Fair Haven, and Riverton, New Jersey.[61] Likewise, Cooper's colleague, Reverend Thomas Kinnard, who had in the not-too-distant past been arrested for stepping into the state of Delaware, also returned north to Philadelphia in 1866. He too became a minister for the AME church, but also resumed his dentistry and medical practice. Three years later, he was appointed by the American University of Philadelphia to act as their agent to travel across the United States and invite black men who wanted to study medicine to enrol, "free of all expense."[62]

Reverend Theodore Crosby of Colchester joined the Indiana Conference in 1869 and served in Chicago and Detroit. He died in the pulpit in the latter city, uttering his final words, "I will lay aside my Bible and preach the word no more." By the time that ninety-three-year-old Reverend Jermiah G. Bulaugh died, he had "been the instrument in the hand of God in forming many churches, and laboring in the Baltimore and New York Conferences, in Canada, and lastly in the Philadelphia Annual Conference." Popular minister William Stewart, of the First Baptist Church of Windsor, moved to Alton, Illinois.[63]

By the 1870s, Garland White was a pastor at a Halifax, North Carolina church. However, after proclaiming his support for the Democratic Party, his congregation dismissed him. Threats were made against his life, but White was unwavering in his beliefs. To illustrate that point, after reading that his old master, Robert Toombs, had voted for Democratic presidential candidate Grover Cleveland, White could not resist writing to him to share their similar political tastes.

White's old companion and fellow minister in Canada, Augustus Green, after years of battling with the older-established Canadian BME conference, served briefly as the bishop for the renamed Independent Methodist Episcopal Church (IME). At the September 4, 1875 annual conference of the IME church, held in Detroit, Bishop Green was authorized to meet with the general conference of the AME church in Atlanta, Georgia the following year to unite the AME and IME conferences. The mission was successful, and at the 16th Annual Conference of the IME Church, held at Liberty Chapel in Colchester, Ontario on July 29, it was unanimously decided that the AME and IME would unite. The newly formed conference would have an international makeup, composed of churches from Washington, D.C., Lansing, Mason, Fon Du Lac, Fox Lake, Grand Haven, Windsor, Chatham, Dover, Colchester, and Detroit.

Bishop Nazrey of the BME had already showed that his conference had extended its boundaries and influence even further. On June 11, 1870, at his annual conference held at the London Chapel, Nazrey reported that "the Nova Scotia District is in a prosperous and flourishing state, and large numbers have been added to the Church since the last conference; and a nice, neat Chapel has been built in St. John, New Brunswick." Nazrey had received a request for membership from the Bermuda Islands and had received inquiries from Central America and Demarar in South America.

With the end of the war, funds from international sources for fugitive slave missions in Canada began to dry up. Missionaries who had been supported by Britain's Colonial and Continental Church Society begged for reconsideration, as the need was still great. They argued that …

> the numbers, position, circumstances, and prospects of the coloured population in British North America, for whose benefit this Mission was instituted, have not been materially affected by the close of the war. They are still as numerous, as poor, as much a separate people, as before. If such an agency as that which this Mission endeavours to supply was ever needed, it is needed now; more so perhaps, now that the efforts of former years, by God's blessing, have produced their effect, and marks of progress encourage us to further exertions.[64]

In response to the request, Reverend John Hurst from the Society was sent on a three-month tour of the principal black settlements in Canada West, and asked to report. The missionaries believed that his findings confirmed that much of the black population would remain in the province. Reverend Hurst reported from Windsor that although his parishioners rejoiced at the Union victory, the expected exodus back to the U.S. had not occurred. As of June 30, 1865, he commented that:

> … beyond the departure of a few turbulent spirits and low characters brought amongst us by the war, there is no visible change. The same faces are present at our meetings and on the streets; the same children are in the schools; and I receive the same friendly greetings everywhere.[65]

However, he also stated that although there were no longer fugitive slaves coming to the city, there were some destitute blacks arriving that needed assistance.

His fellow missionaries concurred, gratefully acknowledging the funding that the Diocese of Toronto (which included the town of Barrie) had received, but they also pointed out that the Diocese of Huron in the southwest, in which places like London, Chatham, Windsor, Dresden, and Amherstburg contained large coloured populations, still desperately needed clergymen, teachers, scripture readers, and student catechists, as well as "colporteurs" who would travel and sell bibles and religious tracts. Reverend Hurst also argued that it would be a grave mistake to remove coloured agents from the field, as, he stated: "I firmly believe that no permanent good can be accomplished for the race except through their agency."[66] He was convinced that in order to elevate the race, blacks must become the ministers and teachers and hold other positions of leadership that required formal education. Hurst also observed that in some ways, blacks were now more hated than before and more discriminated against. Reverend Thomas Hughes, the Anglican missionary stationed at Dresden and Dawn Mills, was cautiously optimistic about his charge, reporting that an English family had recently moved nearby and frequently attended services with their black neighbours — the first time this had happened. Despite this gesture of hope, Hughes admitted that prejudice was increasing, and some of it "to a more disagreeable extent than native-born Americans." However, as the years went by, a discouraged Hughes noted in his diary on May 28, 1871:

Felt very much depressed in spirit today. Sometimes think that my work is done in this mission.... The unchristian prejudice against color seems to be ineradicable and as various denominations positively refuse to admit colored members, they absorb sooner or later the white church people, few of whom remain long proof against the popular feeling against the colored people. This tries at times, both my faith and patience. Frequently I am led to ask — can men be really the disciples of Christ who refuse to worship in company with any of their fellow sinners, though their skins may be of a different complexion …

On a more personal level that hints at his love for his flock, Reverend Hughes shared the heart-wrenching story of a veteran of the war who he identified only as "F.T.," who was well respected by both black and white, and a man of quiet and gentlemanly manners, who, Hughes believed, foolishly enlisted in the Union army. He had been defrauded out of his bounty, as were countless others, and his health was ruined while serving. Reverend Hughes painted a picture of the family's lot:

> It is impossible for me to describe the wretched state in which this poor sick man and his family are living. Their shanty is the most miserable hovel imaginable, consisting only of one room of about twelve feet square, with a sort of shed behind. In this room, which is but just high enough to stand upright in, live, how I cannot tell, the man, his wife, and five daughters. The sick man lies on one side on a dirty mattress, supported by rickety chairs; and as to the poor girls, some of whom are growing up into womanhood, they are either shapeless bundles of rags or almost in a state of nudity.[67]

In his next letter to the society, Reverend Hughes reported that this same man had suffered for many weeks, being unable to lie down either day or night. As his end grew nearer, he embraced religion and requested a family worship service, after which "he conversed cheerfully for a few minutes, told his family that he was going home, laid his head upon his wife's shoulder, and breathed his last."

Stories of other men whose health was ruined when they returned from the war are plentiful. In but one example, after having triumphantly returned from the Civil War, a twenty-two-year-old man named Thomas brought small pox home to Buxton with him. Reverend King suspected that the contagion was in his clothing. Within a few days he fell sick

Reverend Thomas Hughes was an Anglican missionary to blacks in and around the Dawn Settlement. *Courtesy of BNHS&M.*

with a fever. King knew enough about medicine to insist that the family remain quarantined until the disease abated. A woman who had already had the disease, and was therefore immune, was found nearby to serve as a nurse. No other visitors were allowed, and all of the family members were cautioned to remain inside. All five of the other children, including a six-month old baby, contracted the disease; however, the mother miraculously escaped it and the father was still in the South where he had gone during the war. The fourteen-year-old brother unfortunately suffered the most severely. King graphically describes how the pox rose on his flesh until they covered his entire body. The sores ran with a thick yellow fluid, and he died after ten days. The rest of the family recovered, but despite everyone's precautions to remain isolated, the disease spread to several other families. Eighteen people fell ill to the disease before it ran its course. Many of the settlement's inhabitants were quickly vaccinated, and the homes of those who had been sick were cleaned and fumigated.[68]

Some interesting legal cases related to slavery emerged in the aftermath of emancipation, none more so than that of the son of a former Richmond, Virginia slave named John Harris. John lived somewhat independently, despite being someone's chattel, renting his own home, and having the occupation of a painter, giving most of his earnings to his master. His wife Sarah worked as a washerwoman, giving most of her pay to her mistress. Their 1825 marriage, with both blacks and whites in attendance, occurred in the home of Sarah's master, Major Halloway, under the auspices of a Baptist minister. Although the ceremony was the same as would have been performed for whites, there was no license issued, thereby not making it legally recognized, because it was considered to be only a slave wedding. The couple produced three children. John escaped from slavery in 1833, leaving Sarah and the children behind and assuming the new name of "George Johnstone." Sarah remained a slave until the fall of Richmond in 1865. After her husband left her, she married another man named Brown, and lived in freedom until her death in 1869 or 1870.

John Harris first fled to New York, where, considering his first marriage not to be valid, he met and married another woman, also named Sarah. Feeling unsafe in the North, this couple moved to Toronto in the spring of 1834. In 1847, the "Johnstones" were well enough established to buy a three-acre farm just east of the Don River, in York Township; they purchased the farm from John Beverley Robinson, Chief Justice of the Court of Queen's Bench of Upper Canada, and a defender of the rights of blacks. John Harris died in February 1851, without leaving a will. His widow then sold the land and later remarried. Sometime thereafter, his eldest son, who had been born in slavery from Harris's first marriage, claimed it should have been his right to his father's farm as the legal heir-at-law. Twenty years later, Harris Jr. took the case to the Court of Queen's Bench.

The high profile court case was intriguing. Three blacks who had attended the slave wedding in Virginia — including the woman who had served as bridesmaid — testified that they had witnessed the ceremony. One of these gave the matter-of-fact testimony that he knew that slaves could get no license for a legal marriage. A fourth witness, Philip Anderson, who was himself a runaway slave and had known John Harris in both Virginia and in New York, testified that both he and John Harris did not consider the first marriage to be valid. To further drive home the point, Anderson said that in his own case, he had been married to a woman in Virginia but when they got to a free state "I married her again in New York, to make the former marriage valid; I was bound by Heaven by the first marriage, but not by the law of the land."

Most damning of all was the evidence given by William Crump, a lawyer from Richmond, Virginia and former Judge of the Circuit Superior Court of Law. Crump stated that according to the laws of Virginia, up until the end of the Civil War, no marriage of slaves was legal. By the same token, there could be no consideration of bigamy if a slave "married" more than one spouse. Likewise, there could never be any argument about the legitimacy of slave children, because they absolutely belonged to the master and not to either enslaved parent. Furthermore, biological children of a slave had no rights to inherit any property that their parents might have possessed.

Crump's evidence sealed the case. The judgment of the Court was that Canada was bound to respect the laws of foreign jurisdictions. In this case, since neither the marriage nor the rights of inheritance were valid in the State of Virginia, they could not be valid elsewhere. The disappointed son of John Harris could take no comfort at the Justice's sympathetic tone as the ruling was read, which decreed in part:

> This is no doubt an unfortunate conclusion, for the plaintiff is undoubtedly the child of John Harris and of Sarah, who were made man and wife in form and by all of the usual solemnities of real matrimony. The parents were of mature age, of sound sense, reason, and understanding. The father had a trade, which he followed by the permission of his master for a yearly sum which he paid to him for the privilege, or, as it is said, "he hired his own time." He rented a house for himself; he was married with the consent of those who could give it by a minister in orders and in form at least under the sanction of religion; he lived with the woman he had taken as his wife, and had children by her, and left her only to gain his freedom; yet it is manifest, by the force of positive human law, there was no marriage and no legitimate issue.[69]

The results of this case, along with thousands of other examples, can only hint at the profound challenges that were so much a part of the lives for so many people. So deeply ingrained are those experiences that even now — generations later — black Canadians join with other former British colonies to celebrate Emancipation Day on August 1 of every year since the Slave Emancipation Act came into effect on that day in 1834. It is fascinating to read accounts of blacks in various cities in the United States, regularly celebrating that day as a symbol of freedom in their own communities, or crossing the border to join with their Canadian brothers and sisters.[70]

Those celebrations serve as a living monument to freedom. Sprinkled throughout some Canadian cemeteries are the granite monuments of Canadian veterans who fought with the United States Colored Troops, and who did their part to put an end to slavery.

African-American Civil War memorial, "The Spirit of Freedom," in Washington, D.C. by Ed Hamilton of Louisville, Kentucky. The names of Canadian men are included in the rosters of the USCT on the wall that surrounds the monument. *LC-DIG-highsm-04880. LOC.*

On June 20, 2009, the descendants of Robert Dudley celebrated the unveiling of his official Civil War tombstone in Oungah, Ontario. Dudley had briefly served in the 1st Michigan Colored Infantry, before enlisting in New York in the 20th U.S. Colored Infantry. As a lasting tribute to Civil War veterans, the U.S. Department of Veterans Affairs will provide a headstone — free of charge, even to Canada — to mark the final resting place for those heroes who served. *Courtesy of James and Judy Dudley.*

ACKNOWLEDGEMENTS

Many individuals and organizations have graciously contributed to the publication of this book and it is my pleasure to recognize and to thank them.

This undertaking would not have been possible without the financial support of the Canada Council for the Arts.

There are several people who gave so much of their talents and their time during the various stages along the way. My wife, Shannon, helped in a myriad of ways — from assisting on research trips during the early stages to tracking down and doctoring old photographs that appear within the book. My daughter Rebecca helped with some of the time-consuming tasks that are a part of completing this work.

Some of the most gratifying experiences related to the pursuit of history are the people that you meet along the way. Several of those who we have had the good fortune to meet, to learn from, and hopefully at least in a minor way to share new information were and are authorities in this field. Two of them, Tom Brooks of Gravenhurst, Ontario, and Norman McRae of Detroit, Michigan, are no longer with us, but their incredible work, encouragement and inspiration outlives them. Cut from that same cloth is Benny McRae Jr. from Ohio whose "Lest We Forget" website is a treasure trove of information. Our friend, Charles Brewer, was always eager and helpful in pulling compiled military service records, pensions, and other documents from Washington, D.C's National Archives, Library of Congress and other institutions. My respect for these men is enormous and their generosity and friendship remain in a special place.

On many occasions, we have enjoyed watching and meeting several Civil War re-enactment groups, including the 102nd USCT, 10th Louisiana Infantry, 54th Massachusetts, 6th New York Volunteer Cavalry, 4th Michigan Infantry, 2nd Louisiana Medical Brigade, and Donaldsonville Louisiana Artillery. Dennis Watson, Donna and Wayne Elliot, Larry and Jacqui Reynolds, Donald Vest, Ross Fowler, Tim and Teresa Warnick are just a few of those many members who have worked to bring that history to life and who have participated in events that celebrate the memories of those who fought in the Civil War.

It has been a special treat to meet with descendants of Civil War soldiers. Dalyce Newby and Irene Moore Davis, both historians, work to chronical their lives and both shared family photographs for this book. A unique memory was watching the Dudley family celebrate the unveiling of an official Civil War tombstone at the resting place of their ancestor. Historians and friends Kate Clifford Larson from Boston, Karolyn Smardz Frost from Wolfville, Nova Scotia, Donna Ford from St, Catharines, Wilma Morrison from Niagara Falls, and genealogist Tony Burroughs from Chicago have always freely shared information and advice and given help along the uncertain paths of research.

Professor Loren Schweninger from the University of North Carolina, Chapel Hill, has done remarkable work over the years, including chronicling the lives of the various members of Rapier/Thomas family. I am indebted to him for his research which he has shared both publicly and privately. I would also like to thank the staff, particularly Esme Bhan, Jean Currie Church and Joellen El Bashir, from the Moorland-Spingarn Research Center, Howard University in Washington D.C. for their guidance and cheerful help in sharing the Rapier Papers and the Shadd Papers in the collection which is housed in their care.

Digitizing projects are a god-send to researchers. Particularly useful are "Documenting the American South" (University of North Carolina, Chapel Hill); "American Memory" (Library of Congress); the "Samuel J.

May Anti-Slavery Collection" (Cornell University), which freely offers books and documents that have long since been out of print; Canadian abolitionist newspapers of the 1850s at "OurOnatrio"; and American newspapers at "AccessibleArchives" and "GenealogyBank." "Ancestry," "fold3" and the U.S. National Parks Service's "Civil War Soldiers and Sailors System" are of special importance to Civil War researchers.

My favourite repositories while researching this (as well as other black history projects) are "The Burton Collection" at Detroit Public Library; Western Archives at University of Western Ontario in London; Houghton Library, Harvard University; Library of Congress and National Archives Record Administration in Washington D.C.; Buxton National Historic Site & Museum in North Buxton; and Library and Archives Canada in Ottawa. I am grateful to all of the staff members there, and to those at all of the other libraries and archives I have visited or corresponded with, who helped me.

And as is all-too-often the case and too-seldom expressed, my thanks go to my family, Chris, Justin, Melanie, Rebecca, Shannon, and dad, who filled in my missing place on the farm and at other places while I wrestled with the manuscript — a pretty tough customer. I do wish to acknowledge that there were scores of men from Canada East, Canada West and the other British North American provinces who served in the Union navy. They too are deserving of recognition and praise for their service — and perhaps an in-depth tribute for another time.

The staff at Dundurn Press are amazing to work with and I thank them for their guidance, their help and particularly for their patience. I expect that they were reminded of the phrase that "the road to Hell is paved with good intentions" and I appreciate that they never suggested that I take that particular exit. Shannon Whibbs, Carrie Gleason, Britanie Wilson, Sheila Douglas, Allister Thompson, Synora Van Drine, Caitlyn Stewart, Karen McMullin, Barry Penhale, Jane Gibson, president Kirk Howard, and everyone on the team, please accept my sincerest thanks.

NOTES

Chapter 1: One Soldier's Story

1. Civil War widow's pension file for Sarah King, widow of Solomon King, deposition of Milton Grant, December 29, 1890, National Archives Records Administration (NARA).
2. Historian Tom Brooks from Gravenhurst, Ontario, was undoubtedly the foremost authority on British North America's role in the Civil War. He identified over fifty thousand individuals from what is now Canada who joined the Northern and Southern armies.
3. In the 1840 Federal Census for East Feliciana Parish, John Phares is listed as having thirty-three slaves.
4. Freedman's Bank Records, South Carolina, March 21, 1871, *http://search. ancestry.ca/iexec?htx=View&r=5543&dbid=8755&iid=SCM816_23-0045&f-n=Solomon&ln=King&st=d&ssrc=&pid=161744*. Accessed January 28, 2013.
5. John E. Phares married Mary Cobb on January 14, 1830. Ancestry.com, *Louisiana Marriages to 1850* [database online] (Provo, UT: Ancestry.com Operations Inc, 1997); He married widow Lucetta Adelaide Robinson Pennyman or Penniman on November 10, 1834. William Henry Egle, ed., *Historical Register, Notes and Queries, Historical and Genealogical, relating to Interior Pennsylvania, for the Year 1883*, Volume 1 (Harrisburg, PA: Lane S. Hart, 1883), 101; At the time of writing his will, a copy of which is at the Buxton National Historic Site & Museum, John Phares was married to Francis Evaline Phares.

6. Bill of Sale for twenty-two-year-old slave Jacob by John Moore of Virginia to John Phares, agent for William King, December 28, 1843. Copy courtesy of Victor Ullman Collection, Buxton National Historic Site & Museum.

7. Reverend William King to the Clerk of Toronto Presbytery, June 21, 1848, William King Papers, Public Archives Canada (PAC).

8. William King to Reverend Gale, February 23, 1849, William King Papers, PAC.

9. William King Papers, PAC.

10. Reverend A.M. Coll, list of marriages submitted to the Clerk of the Peace in Sandwich on January 4, 1851. Photocopy in author's collection.

11. Civil War survivors pension application by Jacob King concerning his son Cornelius King.

12. Unpublished autobiography of William King, William King Papers, PAC.

13. Civil War widow's pension file for Sarah King, widow of Solomon King, deposition of Alexander D. Cook, fellow member of 102nd USCT, October 21, 1897.

14. Norman McRae, *Negroes in Michigan During The Civil War* (Michigan Civil War Centennial Observance Commission, 1966), 58, 59. The quote is from *Detroit Advertiser and Tribune*, December 28, 1863.

15. Norman McRae, *Negroes in Michigan During The Civil War* (Michigan Civil War Centennial Observance Commission, 1966), 58.

16. Deposition of Assistant Adjutant General, August 2, 1893 and deposition of 1st Lieutenant of 9th Cavalry, October 28, 1884, NARA, original widow's pension, #302.253

17. Civil War widow's pension file for Sarah King, widow of Solomon King, deposition by 1st Lieutenant Davenport, 9th Cavalry, Adjutant General's Office of the Department of War, October 28, 1884.

18. Compiled Military Service Record for Solomon King, NARA.

19. Civil War widow's pension file for Sarah King, widow of Solomon King, deposition of Alexander D. Cook, fellow member of 102nd USCT, October 21, 1897, and of Thomas Weaver (sp?), October 21, 1897.

20. 1870 Census of Fourth Ward, Saginaw, Michigan, 121.

21. Civil War widow's pension file for Sarah King, widow of Solomon King, deposition of James Stewart, December 2, 1897.

22. Civil War widow's pension file for Sarah King, widow of Solomon King, deposition of Sarah King, dated July 12, 1883.

23. Marc. R. Matrana, *Lost Plantations of the South* (University Press of Mississippi, 2009), 62.

24. Ibid., 66, 67.

25. South Carolina Jockeys Club, *History of the Turf in South Carolina* (Charleston: Russell & Jones, 1857), 188.

26. Emily Wharton Sinkler, *Between North and South: The Letters of Emily Wharton Sinkler, 1842–1865*, Edited by Anne Sinkler Whaley LeClercq (Columbia: University of South Carolina Press, 2001), 29.

27. Ibid., 32

28. *Elizabeth Sinkler Coxe's Tales from the Grand Tour, 1890–1910*, Edited by Anne Sinkler Whaley LeClercq (Columbia: University of South Carolina Press, 2006), 4.

29. Elizabeth Sinkler Richardson Manning, *Recollections of the "Sand Hills" In the Olden Days*. Richard Manning's obituary identifies him as a senator in the South Carolina Legislature. Ancestry.com, *Columbia, South Carolina Obituaries, 1859–77* [database online] (Provo, UT: The Generations Network, Inc., 1998). Original data: Holcomb, Brent Howard, *Record of Deaths in Columbia and other places as recorded by John Glass, 1859–1877* (Columbia, SC: SCMAR, 1986).

30. Life of Elizabeth Sinkler Richardson, *http://freepages.genealogy.rootsweb. ancestry.com/~cathcart/SourceDocs/WillsDeedsOtherDocumentTrans/ LifeElizSinkRichManning.htm.* Accessed January 2, 2013.

31. 1860 Census Slave Schedules for Sumter County, SC, p. 204, 205.

32. Life of Elizabeth Sinkler Richardson, *http://freepages.genealogy.rootsweb. ancestry.com/~cathcart/SourceDocs/WillsDeedsOtherDocumentTrans/ LifeElizSinkRichManning.htm.* Accessed January 2, 2013.

33. *Elizabeth Sinkler Coxe's Tales from the Grand Tour, 1890–1910*, Edited by Anne Sinkler Whaley LeClercq (Columbia: University of South Carolina Press, 2006), XXV.

34. *Journal of the Senate of South Carolina: Being the Sessions of 1861* (Columbia: Charles P. Pelham, 1861), *http://docsouth.unc.edu/imls/ scsess61/scsess61.xml.* Accessed January 12, 2013.

35. Evaluation of slaves of the late Richard I. Manning as transcribed, *http:// emilyevaughn.com/pineland.htm.* Accessed January 22, 2013.

36. Elizabeth Sinkler Richardson, *Life of Elizabeth Sinkler Richardson*, *http://freepages.genealogy.rootsweb.ancestry.com/~cathcart/SourceDocs/ WillsDeedsOtherDocumentTrans/LifeElizSinkRichManning.htm.* Accessed January 11, 2013.

37. Elizabeth Sinkler Manning Richardson, *Recollections of the "Sand Hills" in the Olden Days, http://freepages.genealogy.rootsweb.ancestry.com/~- cathcart/SourceDocs/WillsDeedsOtherDocumentTrans/Recollections_ ElizabethSinklerManningRichardson.htm.* Accessed January 11, 2013.

38. As related to Anne Sinkler Fishburne and reported in the *Columbia*

Star, *http://www.thecolumbiastar.com/news/2008-07-11/Travel.* Accessed January 21, 2013.

39. Civil War widow's pension file for Sarah King, widow of Solomon King, deposition of Sarah King; No. 296.592; September 3, 1897, NARA.

40. *http://www.archives.gov/exhibits/featured_documents/emancipation_proclamation/.* Accessed January 11, 2013.

41. *Elizabeth Sinkler Coxe's Tales from the Grand Tour, 1890–1910*, Edited by Anne Sinkler Whaley LeClercq (Columbia: University of South Carolina Press, 2006), 6.

42. U.S. Interviews with Former Slaves, 1936–1938, Project #1655, Interviewer Martha S. Pinckney, Charleston, South Carolina; U.S. Interviews with Former Slaves, 1936–1938, *http://search.ancestry.ca/Browse/view.aspx?dbid=1944&path=South+Carolina.Eddington%2c+Harriet+-+Hunter%2c+Hester.297&sid=&gskw.* Accessed January 26, 2013.

43. *Elizabeth Sinkler Coxe's Tales from the Grand Tour, 1890–1910*, Edited by Anne Sinkler Whaley LeClercq (Columbia: University of South Carolina Press, 2006), 7.

44. Mary Rhodes Henagan, *Reminiscences of Mrs. Mary Rhodes (Waring) Henagan.* This is part of the University of North Carolina's Documenting the American South online publication, *Two Diaries from Middle St. John's, Berkeley, South Carolina, February–May, 1865, Journals Kept by Miss Susan R. Jervey and Miss Charlotte Ravenel, At Northampton and Pooshee Plantations, and Reminiscences of Mrs. (Waring) Henagan with Two Contemporary Reports from Federal Officials* (St. John's Hunting Club, 1921), 36, 37, 41, 42. *http://docsouth.unc.edu/fpn/jervey/jervey.html.* Accessed January 17, 2013.

45. Ibid., 49.

46. *The North Star*, May 26, 1848.

47. *Charleston News and Courier*, January 20, 1874.

48. Civil War widow's pension file for Sarah King, widow of Solomon King, deposition of Milton Grant, September 6, 1897.

49. Civil War widow's pension file for Sarah King, deposition of Sarah King, September 3, 1897.

50. Undated note in Civil War widow's pension file for Sarah King, widow of Solomon King.

51. Civil War widow's pension file for Sarah King, widow of Solomon King, deposition of Joseph A. Robinson, June 16, 1866.

52. 1880 United States Census, Charleston, South Carolina, Enumeration district 55, p. 7.

Chapter 2: Canada and the Civil War

1. Howe Family Papers, Houghton Library, Harvard University, b MS Am 2119, item 1536.
2. *Northern Draft of 1862, http://www.etymonline.com/cw/draft.htm.* Accessed April 16, 2014.
3. *Douglass' Monthly,* October 1862.
4. Henry Wilson to the President, November 30, 1863, Abraham Lincoln Papers, *http://memory.loc.gov/.* Accessed May 14, 2014.
5. Samuel Small to "Thomas Lincoln," undated, Abraham Lincoln Papers, *http://memory.loc.gov/.* Accessed May 14, 2014.
6. *Southern Bivouac, Landon Papers,* Regional Collection, Weldon Library, University of Western Ontario: 571.
7. *The Christian Recorder,* November 21, 1863.
8. Kennedy's confession appeared in *Albany Journal,* March 27, 1865.
9. W. Preston to Francis P. Blair Sr., January 30, 1865, Abraham Lincoln Papers, *http://memory.loc.gov/.* Accessed May 14, 2014. The refusal to allow Margaret Preston and her son and daughter to land in Boston appears in *The Daily Picayune* (New Orleans), January 14, 1865.
10. Peter J. Sehlinger, *Kentucky's Last Cavalier: General William Preston, 1816–1887* (Lexington: Kentucky Historical Society, distributed by The University Press of Kentucky, 2004), 182–191.
11. Lewis Chambers to George Whipple, November 18, 1862, American Missionary Association Papers: Canada.
12. Freedmen's Inquiry Commission, Canadian Testimony: 76, 77.
13. P. Jertius Kempson to Abraham Lincoln, February 25, 1863, Abraham Lincoln Papers, Library of Congress, *http://memory.loc.gov/.* Accessed May 14, 2014.
14. Augustus Watson to Abraham Lincoln, March 20, 1861. Abraham Lincoln Papers, Library of Congress, *http://memory.loc.gov/.* Accessed May 14, 2014.
15. *Wisconsin Patriot,* January 18, 1862.
16. *Wisconsin Patriot,* January 18, 1862 (quoting article that originally appeared in the *New-York Tribune*).
17. *Wisconsin Patriot,* January 18, 1862 (quoting article that originally appeared in the *Chicago Post*).
18. George Whipple To Lewis Tappan, January 10, 1861, American Missionary Association records: Canada.
19. Pennsylvania State Archives, Bureau of Archives and History, Pennsylvania Historical and Museum Commission, 39th Regiment, 10th

Reserves, Company H, p. 51, *http://www.phmc.state.pa.us/bah/dam/rg/di/ r19-65RegisterPaVolunteers/r19-65%20Reg23-39Interface.htm.* Accessed May 5, 2014.

20. David Hotchkiss to Reverend George Whipple, May 21, 1861. American Missionary Association records: Canada.
21. *Chatham Planet*, January 16, 1862.
22. A. Dingman to Abraham Lincoln, June 17, 1863, The Abraham Lincoln Papers, *http://memory.loc.gov/.* Accessed May 14, 2014.
23. A. Lincoln to General A. Dingman, June 18, 1863, *The Papers And Writings Of Abraham Lincoln, Volume Six, http://www.gutenberg.org/.* Accessed May 14, 2014.
24. *http://www.angelfire.com/tx4/oneida/page9.html.* Accessed March 28, 2013
25. *http://collectionscanada.gc.ca/pam_archives/index.php?fuseaction=genitem. displayEcopies&lang=eng&rec_nbr=2063207&title=WESTERN.* Accessed February 10, 2014.
26. J. Grant to Captain Hall, April 6, 1864, War Office Fonds, Public Archives of Canada, R 25147 (13).
27. H. Sabin to Colonel, April 4, 1864, War Office Fonds, Public Archives of Canada, R 25147 (9); R. 24019; R 24513; R 24541. Note: the three men were Peter Quin, Dennis Cleary, and John Doyle. John Day was their co-conspirator in Detroit. The Canadian War Office had also recently announced that the reward for apprehending American Crimps or agents had been increased from fifty dollars to two hundred dollars.
28. *Christian Advocate*, January 28, 1863: 2.
29. *The Globe* (Toronto), January 30, 1863.
30. Library and Archives Canada, online exhibit, *A Nation's Chronicle: The Canada Gazette, http://www.collectionscanada.gc.ca/databases/canada-ga-zette/.* Accessed April, 13, 2014, pp. 152–155 (online pagination).
31. For a further look at crimping, see William F. Raney, *Recruiting and Crimping in Canada for the Northern Forces, 1861-1865*; photocopy of article is in Fred Landon Papers, Weldon Library, University of Western Ontario, and is "Reprinted from the Mississippi Valley Historical Review, Vol. X, No. 1, June 1923.
32. *The Journal of Education for Upper Canada: Volume XVII — for the year 1864*, Edited by Adolphus Egerton Ryerson, John George Hodgins, Adam Crooks (Toronto: Lovell and Gibson, 1864), 30.
33. *Evening Union* (Washington, D.C.), December 24, 1864.
34. *Daily National Intelligencer*, December 30, 1864.
35. *Daily National Intelligencer*, December 28, 1864.
36. *Chatham Weekly Planet*, August 8, 1861.

37. *Christian Advocate*, August 24, 1861: 2.
38. *Christian Advocate*, March 12, 1862: 2.
39. The late Tom Brooks accumulated this list, which was published in a 1993 commemorative newspaper, *Winchester Republican: Winchester, Va.*, May 25, 1862.
40. Information provided in part by Arthur Purnell, late Civil War historian from Burlington, Ontario.
41. Arlington National Cemetery Website, *http://www.arlingtoncemetery.net/jcronan.htm.* Accessed April 14, 2014.
42. For more on Cooke's life, see Steve Arnold and Tim French's biography, *Custer's Forgotten Friend: The Life of W. W. Cooke, Adjutant, Seventh U.S. Cavalry* (Howell, MI: Powder River Press, 1993).
43. *The Raleigh Register*, December 10, 1862.
44. Reprinted in Massachusetts's *Springfield Republican*, October 4, 1862.
45. Reprinted in Massachusetts's *Springfield Republican*, October 4, 1862.
46. Article from *Lambton Observer* was reprinted in part in *The Daily Globe*, January 21, 1863.
47. *The Daily Globe*, January 21, 1863.

Chapter 3: Recruiters

1. Lewis Chambers to George Whipple, December 31, 1862. American Missionary Association Papers: Canada.
2. Transcript of letter from Parker T. Smith to Jacob C. White Jr., in possession of author.
3. *The Christian Recorder*, October 11, 1862.
4. Sarah A. Lester to William Still, April 21, 1863. Reprinted in C. Peter Ripley et al, eds., *The Black Abolitionist Papers: Canada, 1830–1865* (Chapel Hill and London: The University of North Carolina Press, 1986), 515, 516.
5. *The Christian Recorder*, September 14, 1861.
6. *Chatham Weekly Planet*, August 15, 1861.
7. William Still, *The Underground Railroad* (Chicago: Johnson Publishing Company, Inc, 1970), 144–147. Reprint of Philadelphia: Porter & Coates, 1872.
8. John David Smith, *Black Soldiers in Blue: African American Troops in the Civil War Era* (Chapel Hill, University of North Carolina Press, 2002), 405.
9. David S. Cecelski, *Waterman's Song: Slavery and Freedom in Maritime North Carolina*, (Chapel Hill: University of North Carolina Press, 2001), 36, *http://books.google.ca/.* Accessed June 29, 2014.

10. North Carolina Museum of History, *http://moh.ncdcr.gov/exhibits/civil-war/explore_section4d.html*. Accessed June 29, 2014.

11. Lewis Chambers to George Whipple, November 18, 1862, American Missionary Association Papers: Canada.

12. *The Telegraph and Messenger* (Macon, Georgia), November 30, 1884, and *Cleveland Daily Leader*, March 28, 1866.

13. *http://www.fold3.com/image/263479587/*. Accessed March 8, 2014.

14. *http://www.gilderlehrman.org/sites/all/themes/gli/panels/civilwar150/ Civil%20War%20Reader%204%20(single-page%20version).pdf*. Accessed November 22, 2013.

15. *The Christian Recorder*, May 16, 1863.

16. Frank Preston Stearns, *The Life and Public Services of George Luther Stearns* (Philadelphia and London: J.B. Lippincott Company, 1907). Reprinted in 1969 in New York by Kraus Reprint Co., 285–289. Also, Charles E. Heller, *Portrait of an Abolitionist: A Biography of George Luther Stearns, 1809–1867* (Westport, CT and London: Greenwood Press, 1996), 147.

17. *Sandusky Daily Commercial Register*, June 6, 1863, submitted by Ms. Elaine Lawson, *http://www.coax.net/people/lwf/sandusky.htm*. Accessed April 8, 2000.

18. Russell Duncan, ed., *Blue-Eyed Child of Fortune: The Civil War Letters of Colonel Robert Gould Shaw* (Athens, GA: University of Georgia Press, 1999), 292, 296, 298.

19. *The Black Abolitionist Papers, Volume V, The United States, 1859–1865*, Edited by Ripley et al. (Chapel Hill and London: The University of North Carolina Press, 1992), 125, 126

20. Reverend A.R. Green and Samuel Venable, *A Brief Account of the Re-organization of the B.M.E. Church in B.N.A.* (Detroit: O.S. Gulley's Steam Printing House, 1872), 106–107.

21. Ibid., 106, 130.

22. *Detroit Free Press*, September 18, 1863. The recruiter was Alfred J. Works.

23. *Detroit Free Press*, September 17, 1873.

24. *The Christian Recorder*, March 26, 1864.

25. William H. Chenery, *The Fourteenth Regiment Rhode Island Heavy Artllery (Colored) In the War to preserve the Union, 1861–1865* (Providence: Snow & Farnham, 1898), 66.

26. A. Lincoln to Hon. Charles Sumner, May 19, 1864, Abraham Lincoln Papers, Library of Congress, *http://memory.loc.gov/*. Accessed November 9, 2006.

27. *http://memory.loc.gov/mss/mal/mal1/231/2316400/001.gif*. Accessed January 30, 2004.

28. *Report of the Select Committee on Emancipation and Colonization* (Washington: Government Printing Office, 1862), 37–59.
29. Mary Ann Shadd papers, Moorland-Spingarn Research Center, Howard University, Washington, D.C.
30. *New York Times*, April 9, 1864
31. *Hartford Daily Courant*, March 31, 1864. Versions of this story appeared in Massachusetts's *Springfield Daily Union* of April 1, 1864; *The Connecticut Courant*, April 2, 1864; *Newport Mercury* (Rhode Island), April 9, 1864; *Newark Daily Advertiser* (New Jersey), April 9, 1864; *The Troy Weekly Times* (Troy, New York), April 16, 1864; *Liberator*, May 6, 1864.
32. Original held in Mary Ann Shadd Carey papers in Public Archives Canada, Ottawa, Ontario.
33. Barbara Blair, *Women in the American Civil War: Volume 1*, Edited by Lisa Tendrich Frank (Santa Barbara, CA: ABC-CLIO. Inc., 2008), 157; this from Barbara Blair's *An Encyclopedia of American Women at War: From the Home Front to the Battlefields* (Santa Barbara, CA: ABC-CLIO. Inc., 2013), 128.
34. William Wells Brown, *The Rising Sun: Or, the Antecedents and Advancement of the Colored Race* (Boston: A.G. Brown & Co., 1874) 539–540.
35. Compiled Military Service Record, NARA.
36. *Provincial Freeman*, June 20, 1857.
37. *The Christian Recorder*, November 25, 1865.
38. *The Black Abolitionist Papers: Canada, 1830–1865*, Edited by C. Peter Ripley et. al. (Chapel Hill and London: University of North Carolina Press, 1986), 338.
39. Hondon B. Hargrove, *Black Union Soldiers in the Civil War* (Jefferson, North Carolina and London: McFarland & Company, 1988), 3.
40. *Muskegon Daily Chronicle*, April 20, 1897.
41. Harris's appointment is online at *http://digital.ncdcr.gov/cdm/ref/collection/ p15012coll8/id/10708*. Accessed June 28, 2014.
42. Among the sources are C. Peter Ripley, *The Black Abolitionist Papers: Canada, 1830–1865* (Chapel Hill and London: University of North Carolina Press, 1986), 40. Thus far, efforts to find documentation of his Civil War service have been unsuccessful.
43. *Patriot* (Harrisburg, Pennsylvania), December 14, 1872.
44. *Detroit Free Press*, November 24, 1863.
45. Note that Henson had four autobiographies, the earliest being *The Life of Josiah Henson, Formerly a Slave, Now an Inhabitant of Canada, as Narrated by Himself* (Boston: A.D. Phelps, 1849); "Dictated by themselves,"

Narratives of the Sufferings of Lewis & Milton Clarke, among the Slaveholders of Kentucky (Boston: Bela Marsh, 1846).

46. *Massachusetts Weekly Spy*, June 24, 1863.

47. Henry Greenleaf Pearson, *The Life of John A. Andrew, Governor of Massachusetts, 1861–1865*, Volume 2 (Boston and New York: Houghton, Mifflin and Company, 1904), 91.

48. *The Christian Recorder*, February 27, 1864.

49. *The Daily Globe*, July 18, 1863.

50. Charles H. Middleton to Abraham Lincoln, December 30, 1861, The Abraham Lincoln Papers, *http://memory.loc.gov/*. Accessed May 14, 2014.

51. Frederick W. Seward, *Seward at Washington as Senator and Secretary of State: A Memoir of His Life, With Selections From His Letters 1846–1861* (New York: Derby and Miller, 1891), 118.

52. *Newark Daily Advertiser*, July 1, 1864.

53. William H. Seward to the President, June 25, 1864, and Edwin M. Stanton to the President, June 27, 1864, *The war of the rebellion: a compilation of the official records of the Union and Confederate armies, Series 3 — Volume 4*: 455–458, *http://ebooks.library.cornell.edu/*. Accessed June 29, 2014.

54. Kent County Police Court Records held at Chatham Kent Municipal Police Office. Cases dated November 1 and 30 and December 2, 1864.

55. Kent County Police Court and Compiled Military Service Record, NARA.

56. *Local Court's & Municipal Gazette, Volume I*: 157, 158.

57. *The Canadian Law Journal, Volume 1: From January to December 1865*, Edited by W.D. Ardagh, Robt. A. Harrison & Henry O'Brien (Toronto: W.C. Chewett & Co., 1865), 241, 242.

58. *Chatham Weekly Planet*, September 5, 1861.

59. Elizabeth Nugent to Your Excellency, July 22, 1862, Public Archives of Canada, R 20302 (337).

60. Anne Aide to His Excellency the Governor General, July 29, 1862, Public Archives of Canada, R 20318.

61. Francis Retattack to Sir, July 31, 1862, Public Archives of Canada, R 20302 (318).

62. Samuel Waller to Abraham Lincoln, November 8: 186? (illeg), The Abraham Lincoln Papers, Library of Congress.

63. Compiled Military Service Record for Henry Hugh Williams and pension file for his widow, Alice Williams, NARA.

Chapter 4: Soldiers

1. Adline Dyer to Dear Sir, *Letters Received Relating to Recruiting*, NARA, Washington, D.C., RG94, box 346, entry 366.
2. Adline Dyer to the Department of War, *Letters Received Relating to Recruiting*, NARA, Washington, D.C., RG94, box 346, entry 366.
3. 1871 Canadian census for Stamford, Welland County, Ontario.
4. Compiled Military Service Record for George M. Lucas.
5. Mary C. Gillett, *The Army Medical Department, 1818–1865* (Washington: U.S. Government Printing Office, 1987), 229.
6. Compiled Military Service Record for Jacob Hicks.
7. Pension file for widow Nancy Johnson Matthews Merrill.
8. Paternity confirmed by biography of Alexander's brother, William Q. Atwood, in William J. Simmons's *Men of Mark: Eminent, Progressive and Rising* (Cleveland: Geo. M. Rewell & Co., 1887), 651–655. This was further confirmed by testimony of Alexander's sister Ann's husband, William J. Anderson, in Benjamin Drew's *A North-Side View of Slavery: The Refugee: or the Narratives of Fugitive Slaves in Canada* (Boston: John P. Jewett and Company, 1856), 254–256.
9. The handwritten will can be seen in its entirety at The University of Alabama's website, *http://acumen.lib.us.edu*. Accessed April 28, 2014.
10. Incidentally, Henry made similar provisions for two other mulatto children who belonged to his slave woman Mary, who lived on another plantation six miles away, which raises the suspicion that he may have also fathered those children. He also granted a twenty-year-old male named Seaborn, his wife, Milly, and their four small children their freedom. Also, as was the case with Candis, both Mary and Seaborn were to receive two thousand dollars.
11. Henry Stiles Atwood's will.
12. *Cases Argued and Determined in The Supreme Court of Alabama, during the June Term, 1852. Vol. XXI*, Reported by J.W. Shepherd (Montgomery: Brittan and De Wolf, 1853), 590–625.
13. William J. Simmons, *Men of Mark: Eminent, Progressive and Rising* (Cleveland: Geo. M. Rewell & Co., 1887), 652.
14. 1860 census for Ripley, Brown County, Ohio, p. 48.
15. William H. Chenery, *The Fourteenth Regiment Rhode Island Heavy Artillery (Colored) in the War to Preserve the Union, 1861–1865* (Providence: Snow & Farnham, 1898), 134.
16. *The Christian Recorder*, October 26, 1867.
17. National Parks Service, *Soldiers and Sailors* database, *http://www.nps.gov/civilwar/soldiers-and-sailors-database.htm*. Accessed April 29, 2014.

18. *Saginaw News* (Michigan), December 21, 1910.
19. Francis H. Warren, *Michigan Manual of Freedmen's Progress* (Detroit: Freedmen's Progress Commission, 1915), 111.
20. Lewis Tappan to "My dear Sir," December 10, 1852, *The Tappan Papers*, Library of Congress; Paul McGrath, *Hiram Denio: Court of Appeals: 1853–1865*, https://www.nycourts.gov/history/legal-history-new-york/luminaries-court-appeals/denio-hiram.html. Accessed June 30, 2014.
21. Benjamin Drew, *A North-Side View of Slavery. The Refugee: or the Narratives of Fugitive Slaves in Canada*, (Boston: John P. Jewett and Company, 1856), 333.
22. Compiled Military Service Record for Touissant Delany.
23. Records of the 54th Massachusetts, NARA.
24. Thomas P. Lowery, *Tarnished Scalpels: The Court-martials of Fifty Union Surgeons*, (Mechanicsburg, PA: Stackpole Books, 2000), 76–78.
25. Compiled Military Service Record for Henry Cosby.
26. W.D. Ardagh, Robt. A. Harrison & Henry O'Brien, eds. *The Canadian Law Journal, Volume 1: From January to December 1865* (Toronto: W.C. Chewett & Co., 1865), 272.
27. Freedmen's Inquiry Commission, Canadian Testimony, 93.
28. Ibid.
29. Ibid.
30. Cuyahoga County Archive; Cleveland, Ohio; *Cuyahoga County, Ohio, Marriage Records, 1810–1973*, Vol. 3–4, Oct. 1832– Sept. 1849, p. 338; Ancestry.com, *Cuyahoga County, Ohio, Marriage Records and Indexes, 1810–1973* [database online] (Provo, UT).
31. Compiled Military Service Record for Thomas Kennedy.
32. Compiled Military Service Record for Louis Labrush.
33. Courtesy of Tom Brooks.
34. Rita L. Hubbard, *African Americans of Chattanooga: A History of Unsung Heroes* (Charleston: The History Press, 2007), 56–57.
35. Lois E. Darroch, *Four Went to the Civil War* (Willowdale, ON: Ampersand Press, 1985), 268.
36. *The Christian Recorder*, March 12, 1864.
37. *The Christian Recorder*, April 16, 1864.

Chapter 5: "They also serve ..." Doctors, Nurses, and Chaplains

1. Anderson Ruffin Abbott Papers, file Misc. 3, Special Collections, Toronto Reference Library, Toronto, Canada.
2. Compiled Military Service Record for Albert J. Ratliff, NARA.

3. Abraham D. Shadd diary, Buxton National Historic Site & Museum.
4. Compiled Military Service Record for Alexander T. Augusta.
5. *The New York Times*, March 30, 1863.
6. *The Liberator*, May 8, 1863 (Copying article that originally appeared in *Baltimore Clipper*, May 2, 1863).
7. *The New York Herald*, May 20, 1863.
8. A.T. Augusta to General W.A. Hammond, December 31, 1863. Compiled Military Service Record for Alexander T. Augusta.
9. Anderson Ruffin Abbott Papers, Volume 9, S.90, Special Collections, Toronto Reference Library, Toronto, Canada.
10. A.R. Abbott to Hon. E.M. Stanton, April 30, 1863.
11. Typed transcript of article written by Anderson Ruffin Abbott entitled *Civil War* in the Anderson Ruffin Abbott Papers, Volume 9, S.90, Special Collections, Toronto Reference Library, Toronto, Canada.
12. Jill L. Newmark, *Contraband Hospital, 1862–1863: Health Care for the First Freedpeople*, http://www.blackpast.org/perspectives/contraband-hospital-1862-1863-heath-care-first-freedpeople. Accessed July 2, 2014.
13. Typed transcript of article written by Anderson Ruffin Abbott entitled *Civil War* in the Anderson Ruffin Abbott Papers, Volume 9, S.90, Special Collections, Toronto Reference Library, Toronto, Canada.
14. Personal papers of medical officers, RG 94, NARA.
15. Newspapers that included the article in the first two weeks of January 1864 were *Salem Register* (Massachusetts), *Wisconsin Daily Patriot, Plain Dealer* (Cleveland), *Providence Evening Press, Daily Illinois State Register, Newark Daily Advertiser, Alexandria Gazette*, and *Rocky Mountain News* (Colorado).
16. *The Christian Chronicle*, December 31, 1864.
17. *Evening Star*, November 2, 1864.
18. Dr. John Rapier to Surgeon C.W. Horner, November 28, 1864, RG 94, Entry 561, medical officer's files, John H. Rapier file, National Archives, Washington, D.C.
19. *The Christian Recorder*, June 16, 1866.
20. John Rapier Sr. to John Rapier Jr., September 15, 1856, Rapier family papers, Moorland Spingarn Library, Howard University.
21. John H. Rapier Jr. to James Thomas, February 23, 1861, Rapier papers.
22. John H. Rapier Jr. to James Thomas, March 6, 1862, Rapier papers.
23. *The Christian Recorder*, June 16, 1866, obituary of John H. Rapier.
24. John H. Rapier Jr. to James Thomas, July 8, 1863, Rapier papers.
25. Ibid.
26. John Rapier Jr. to James Thomas, February 25, 1861, Rapier papers.

27. RG 94, Entry 561, medical officer's files, John H. Rapier file, National Archives, Washington, D.C.

28. This petition from 1865 appears in *The Black Military Experience: A Documentary History*, edited by Ira Berlin, Joseph P. Reidy and Leslie S. Rowland (New York: Cambridge University Press, 1982).

29. *Provincial Freeman*, March 8, 1856.

30. Martin R. Dalany, *Official Report of the Niger Valley Exploring Party* (1861), unpaginated, *http://archive.org/stream/officialreportof22118gut/22118.txt*. Accessed July 4, 2014.

31. Victor Ullman, *Martin R. Delany: The Beginnings of Black Nationalism* (Boston: Beacon Press, 1971), 284–285.

32. *http://www.bowdoindailysun.com/2012/10/whispering-pines-the-medical-school-of-maine-liberia-and-the-american-civil-war/*. Accessed April 9, 2014.

33. *Chatham Weekly Planet*, August 20, 1863.

34. Laura was also a co-founder of a Lewanee County Female Benevolent and Antislavery Society. *The Signal of Liberty* (Ann Arbor, Michigan), October 10, 1846.

35. Letter from Thomas K. Chester, February 7, 1847 as published in Laura S. Haviland, *A Woman's Life Work, Labors and Experiences of Laura S. Haviland* (Cincinnati: Waldron and Stowe, 1882), Chapter 3, unpaginated. E-copy of this book is online at *http://www.gutenberg.org*. Accessed April 1, 2014.

36. For a look at Elizabeth Comstock's life, see *Life and Letters of Elizabeth L. Comstock*, compiled by her Sister, Caroline Hare (London: Headley Brothers, 1895 and Philadelphia: J.C. Winston & Co., 1895).

37. Kate Clifford Larson, *Bound for the Promised Land* (New York: Ballantine Books, 2004), 208.

38. *The Freedmen's Record*, Vol. 1, No. 3 (Journal of the New England Freedmen's Aid Society, Boston: March, 1865), 34, 37. Note that the anonymous author gives credit for some of the contents to another article that appeared in *The Commonwealth*, July 17, 1863. Larson credits Ednah Dow Cheney as the author of the *Freedmen's Record* article, noting that Franklin B. Sanborn authored the piece in *The Commonwealth*.

39. *Douglass' Monthly*, August 1863.

40. Kate Clifford Larson, *Bound for the Promised Land* (New York: Ballantine Books, 2004), 227.

41. *The Christian Recorder*, April 6, 1865.

42. Kate Clifford Larson, *Bound for the Promised Land* (New York: Ballantine Books, 2004), 228–229.

43. Reverend William J. Simmons, *Men of Mark: Eminent, Progressive and Rising* (Cleveland: Geo. M. Rewell & Co., 1887), 144–145.

44. E. Williams M.D. et al to Captain C.H. Potter, Publication #M345, Union Provost Marshal's File Of Paper Relating To Individual Civilians, NARA, Record Group 109, Catalog ID 2133278. Fold3. Accessed March 24, 2014.

45. Compiled Military Service Records, NARA, catalog ID 300398.

46. http://ww2.tnstate.edu/library/digital/lowery.htm. Accessed July 7, 2014.

47. C. Peter Ripley et al., eds., *Black Abolitionist Papers: Canada, 1830–1865* (Chapel Hill and London: University of North Carolina Press, 1986), 487.

48. *The Christian Recorder*, January 30, 1864.

49. Ibid.

50. Reverend A.R. Green and Samuel Venable, *A Brief Account of the Re-organization of the B.M.E. Church in B.N.A.* (Detroit: O.S. Gulley's Steam Printing House, 1872), 132–133.

51. Garland H. White to Hon. Wm. H. Seward, May 18, 1864, Compiled Military Service Record for Garland H. White.

52. *New York Herald*, September 14, 1860.

53. Compiled Military Service Record of Garland H. White.

54. *The Christian Recorder*, May 6, 1865.

55. U.S. National Parks Service, http://www.nps.gov/nr/twhp/wwwlps/lessons/11andersonville/11andersonville.htm. Accessed July 4, 2014.

56. Garland H. White to Hon. Wm. H. Seward, Compiled Military Service Record for Garland H. White.

Chapter 6: Battles

1. Anderson Ruffin Abbott Papers, file Misc. 3, Special Collections, Toronto Reference Library, Toronto, Canada.

2. Compiled Military Service Record.

3. Luis F. Emilio, *A Brave Black Regiment* (New York: Johnson Reprint Company, 1968), 62.

4. Lieutenant James W. Grace to Brigadier General R.A. Pierce, July 22, 1863, http://54th-mass.org/2010/07/. Accessed July 8, 2014.

5. George E. Stephens to the Editor of *Weekly Anglo-American*, July 21, 1863, http://54th-mass.org/2010/07/. Accessed July 8, 2014.

6. For a complete list of those missing after the battle of Fort Wagner see National Archives Records Administration, http://www.archives.gov/exhibits/american_originals/54reg.jpg. Accessed July 8, 2014.

7. Luis F. Emilio, *A Brave Black Regiment* (New York: Johnson Reprint Company, 1968), 413–415.

8. Ibid., 420–421

9. *The Christian Recorder*, August 1, 1863.

10. Arthur W. Bergeron Jr. (author), John David Smith (editor), *Black Soldiers in Blue: African American Troops in the Civil War Era* (Chapel Hill: University of North Carolina Press, 2002), 144.

11. *Boston Journal*, March 4, 1864.

12. Rufus S. Johns to *The Christian Recorder*, published April 16, 1864.

13. Ibid.

14. Gregory J.W. Urwin, ed., *Black Flag Over Dixie: Racial Atrocities and Reprisals in the Civil War* (Carbondale: Southern Illinois University Press, 2005), 83.

15. Rufus Sibb Jones to *The Christian Recorder*, published May 7, 1864.

16. Edwin S. Redkey, ed., *A Grand Army of Black Men: Letters from African-American Soldiers in the Union Army, 1861–1865* (Cambridge: Cambridge University Press, 1993), 111.

17. Bryce A. Suderow, "The Battle of the Crater: the Civil War's worst massacre," *Civil War History*, v43 n3, September 1997, 222.

18. Hondon B. Hargrove, *Black Union Soldiers in the Civil War* (Jefferson, NC and London: McFarland & Company, 1988), 185.

19. Ibid. For a full account see pages 219–224.

20. Civil War pension for Charles Henry Griffin.

21. Information provided to author in part by the late Arthur Purnell, Civil War historian from Burlington, Ontario. Robert Fulton Dodd is buried in Hillside Cemetery, in Portage La Prairie, Manitoba and his tombstone bears the image of the Medal of Honor. Image available at *http://geneofun. on.ca/names/photo/1268683*. Accessed April 4, 2014.

22. Information provided by Tom Brooks.

23. James M. Paradis, *Strike the Blow for Freedom: The 6th United States Colored Infantry in the Civil War* (Shippensburg, PA: White Mane Books, 1998), 76.

24. Anderson Ruffin Abbott papers, pages 17–18 of transcription entitled "Civil War," Baldwin Room, Toronto Reference Library.

25. Ibid.

26. Thank you to Katherine Dhalle for sharing her *An Examination of Alfred S. Hartwell and the 55th Massachusetts Volunteer Infantry During the Civil War and His Public Life Thereafter*, unpublished historical research paper submitted in partial fulfillment of the requirements for the degree of Master of Arts, State University of New York, Empire State College, 1995: 18.

27. Soldier to *The Christian Recorder*, May 21, 1864 and P.C.H.K to *The Christian Recorder*, June 11, 1864.

28. *The Christian Recorder*, November 12, 1864.
29. Papers of the 102nd in Lansing State Archives.
30. Will of William Fields and land records for north half of the south half of Lot 9, Concession 8, for the township of Raleigh, Kent County, housed at Registry Office, Chatham, Ontario. Note that Mary Fields was a spinster but used the surname Saunders at the time of her visit to Buxton. Also, William's wife Hardinia, who is mentioned in the will, was Mary's stepmother.

Chapter 7: The War at Home

1. *The New York Herald*, January 5, 1863.
2. C. Peter Ripley et al, eds., *The Black Abolitionist Papers: Canada* (Chapel Hill and London: University of North Carolina Press, 1986), 465.
3. Special thanks to Don Papson of Saranac, New York for sharing this article from *Canadian Gleaner*, December 4, 1863.
4. G.C. Porter, *The Model Negro Colony in Kent* (handwritten copy at Buxton National Historic Site & Museum).
5. American Missionary Association Papers: Canada.
6. *Liberator*, July 4, 1862; William Still, *The Underground Railroad* (Chicago: Johnson Publishing Company, Inc., 1970), 251–255. Reprint of Philadelphia: Porter & Coates, 1872.
7. Macdougall, 120–125. See also Patrick Brode, *The Odyssey of John Anderson* (Toronto: University of Toronto Press, 1989), 291. For an account almost contemporary with the case, see Harper Twelvetrees, *The Story of the Life of John Anderson, The Fugitive Slave* (London, U.K.: William Tweedie, 1863). Also, *The Christian Recorder*, February 23, 1861.
8. The article which originally appeared in the *Chatham Planet* was reprinted in Toronto's *Daily Globe*, April 20, 1863; in Kingston's *The Daily News*, April 21, 1863; and in New York's *Herald-Tribune*, April 29, 1863.
9. Ferdinand Fitzgerald to Abraham Lincoln, January 4 and 8, 1861. *The Abraham Lincoln Papers*, Library of Congress, *http://memory.loc.gov/*. Accessed February 2, 2014.
10. Donald G. Simpson, *Under the North Star* (Trenton, New Jersey: Africa World Press, 2005), 338–339.
11. *Douglass' Monthly*, September 1862.
12. *Douglass' Monthly*, August 1861.
13. *Douglass' Monthly*, May 1859.
14. John R. McKivigan, *Forgotten Firebrand: James Redpath and the Making of Nineteenth-Century America* (Ithaca, New York: Cornell University Press, 2008), 71–72.

15. *Chatham Weekly Planet*, January 31, 1861, reprinting from *Maple Leaf.*
16. *The Christian Recorder*, September 7, 1861.
17. John Brown Jr. to the editor. Letter dated Chatham, August 15, 1861. Appeared in *Chatham Weekly Planet*, December 26, 1861.
18. David Hotchkiss to George Whipple, September 20, 1861. American Missionary Association Papers: Canada.
19. David Hotchkiss to George Whipple. American Missionary Association Papers: Canada.
20. Reverend Thomas Hughes Diary, entry for October 22, 1861.
21. *The Christian Recorder*, March, 8, 1862.
22. John M. Green, *Negroes in Michigan History* (Detroit: John M. Green, 1985), 120.
23. Surrogate Court of the County of Kent record for George Jacobs. Archives of Ontario, Toronto, reference #1-514 (GSI-213), #310.
24. Arlie C. Robbins, *Legacy To Buxton* (Chatham: Ideal Printing, 1983), 87–88
25. *The Christian Recorder*, May 23, 1863.
26. This article was reprinted in Boston's *Liberator*, March 27, 1863.
27. For a scholarly account of the riot, see Matthew Kundinger, *Racial Rhetoric: The Detroit Free Press and Its Part in the Detroit Race Riot of 1863, http://www.umich.edu/~historyj/pages_folder/articles/Racial_ Rhetoric.pdf.* Accessed March 28, 2013.
28. *Chicago Tribune*, March 9, 1863, and *The Liberator*, March 13, 1863.
29. Anonymous, *A Thrilling Narrative from the Lips of the Sufferers of the Late Detroit Riot, March 6, 1863, with the Hair Breadth Escapes of Men, Women and Children, and Destruction of Colored Men's Property, Not Less Than $15,000* (Detroit: Published by Author, 1863), 2, 3, 7, 11, 16, 19.
30. *Douglass' Monthly*, April 1863.
31. Anonymous, *A Thrilling Narrative from the Lips of the Sufferers of the Late Detroit Riot, March 6, 1863, with the Hair Breadth Escapes of Men, Women and Children, and Destruction of Colored Men's Property, Not Less Than $15,000* (Detroit: Published by Author, 1863), 12.
32. *Report of the Committee of Merchants for the Relief of Colored People, Suffering from the Late Riots in the City of New York* (New York: G.A. Whitehorne, 1863), 29.
33. Hallie Q. Brown, *Homespun Heroines and other Women of Distinction* (Xenia, OH: The Aldine Publishing Company, 1926) 75–78.
34. Letter dated Aug. 15 1861 from Parker T. Smith to *The Christian Recorder*, Sept 7, 1861.
35. *The Christian Recorder*, December 22, 1862.

36. J. Wilson et al. to His Excellency, November 8, 1864. *The Abraham Lincoln Papers*, Library of Congress, *http://memory.loc.gov/*. Accessed February 2, 2014.
37. *The Christian Recorder*, December 17, 1864.
38. Ibid.
39. Ibid.
40. John W. Taylor, *The Christian Recorder*, March 4, 1865.
41. *The Christian Recorder*, May 9 and July 25, 1863. The writer of the articles was Reverend W.H. Jones.
42. Reverend A.R. Green and Samuel Venable, *A Brief Account of the Re-organization of the B.M.E. Church in B.N.A.* (Detroit: O.S. Gulley's Steam Printing House, 1872), 67–105.
43. *Massachusetts Spy*, August 27, 1862 and *Liberator*, August 22, 1862.
44. *Liberator*, May 13, 1864.
45. Parker T. Smith to Jacob C. White, Jr., November 1861, January 17, 1862. Smith had arrived in Dresden in late July 1861 and occasionally submitted articles for publication in *The Christian Recorder.*
46. *The Christian Recorder*, March 7, 1863.
47. *Evening Star* (Washington, D.C.), September 3, 1864.
48. *Daily National Intelligencer*, September 5, 1864.

Chapter 8: Freedmen's Inquiry Commission

1. *Springfield Republican*, February 6, 1864.
2. S.G. Howe, *Report to the Freedmen's Inquiry Commission, 1864: The Refugees from Slavery in Canada West* (New York: Arno Press and the New York Times, 1969), 1.
3. American Freedmen's Inquiry Commission Records, Houghton Library, Harvard University. bMS AM 702, Item 102.
4. Frederick Douglass to Commissioners, July 24, 1863, American Freedmen's Inquiry Commission Records, Houghton Library, Harvard University. Series 1, box 1, Folder 35.
5. Broadwater's testimony, p. 1–3. Note that all of the interviews are available on microfilm roll #201, National Archives microfilm publication M-619 at the National Archives in Washington, D.C. as a part of Record Group 94, War Department, Letters Received by the Adjutant General (Main Series), 1861–1870, part of file 328-0-1863.
6. Howard's testimony, 4–9.
7. Ridley's testimony, 10–12.
8. Geddes testimony, 13–15.

9. Canadian testimony, Freedmen's Inquiry Commission, 16–17.
10. Kinnard's testimony, 16, 17.
11. *The Christian Recorder*, June 25, 1864.
12. Cochrane's testimony, 19–21.
13. McCullum's testimony, 22–26.
14. Buchanan's testimony, 27.
15. Brown's testimony, 27–28.
16. Henning's testimony, 28.
17. Butler's testimony, 30–35.
18. Smallwood's testimony, 34–38.
19. Workman's testimony, 39–40.
20. Ryerson's testimony, 40–43.
21. Barber's testimony, p. 44.
22. Cary's testimony, 45–50.
23. Simpson's testimony, 51–61.
24. Richardson's testimony, 62_63.
25. McCaul's testimony, 64–66.
26. Allen's testimony, 66.
27. Dunn's testimony, 67.
28. Mayor and police chief's testimonies, 67–68.
29. Webb's testimony, 69; Boyle's 69–70; Gurd's 70–71; Yates's, 71.
30. Proudfoot's testimony, 71–78.
31. McBride's testimony, 78–79.
32. Jones' testimony, 79–83.
33. Clark's testimony, 84–87.
34. Bissell's testimony, p. 88.
35. Cross's testimony, 88–93.
36. Paynes's testimonies, 93–95.
37. Sinclair's testimony, 95–102.
38. Starks's testimony, 102–103.
39. Shadd's testimony, 104.
40. Jackson's testimony, 105.
41. McColl's testimony, 106–108.
42. King's testimony, 110–124.
43. Green's testimony, 125–130.
44. Bartlett's testimony, 131–132.
45. Whipper's testimony, 133.
46. Jailers' testimonies, 134.
47. Fisher's testimony, 135–136.
48. Meigs's [Meek's] testimony, 138–139.

49. Park's testimony, 139–140.
50. Averill's testimony, 141.
51. Brush's testimony, 142–144.
52. Foster's testimony, 145–155.
53. Trip to Colchester, 156–158.
54. Camp's testimony, 159.
55. Freedmen's Inquiry Commission records at Houghton Library, Harvard University; bMS Am 702, Item 172.
56. Kinney's testimony, 167–168.
57. Brown's testimony, 169–172.
58. Gibson's testimony, 72–73.
59. Stephenson's testimony, 172–178.
60. Mack's testimony, 178–183.
61. Perry's testimony, 183–184.
62. Brown's testimony, 184–185.
63. *The Milwaukee Sentinel*, November 18, 1863.
64. Conclusions appear on pages 101–104 of Samuel Gridley Howe's *The Refugees from Slavery in Canada West* (Boston: Wright & Potter, 1864).
65. Ibid., 102.
66. Samuel Gridley Howe as quoting Reverend Proudfoot in *The Wisconsin Daily Patriot*, March 12, 1864. The quote also appears in S.G. Howe, *The Refugees from Slavery in Canada West* (Boston: Wright and Potter, 1864), 40.
67. Samuel G. Howe to Hon T.D. Eliot, *The Liberator*, January 15, 1864.
68. S.G. Howe, *Report to the Freedmen's Inquiry Commission, 1864: The Refugees from Slavery in Canada West* (New York: Arno Press and the New York Times, 1969), preface to IV.
69. Robert Dale Owen, *The Wrong of Slavery, The Right of Emancipation, and the Future of the African Race in the United States* (Philadelphia: J.B. Lippincott & Co, 1864), 196–197.

Chapter 9: The War's End

1. Anderson Ruffin Abbott Papers, file Misc. 3, Special Collections, Toronto Reference Library, Toronto, Canada.
2. Reprinted in *The Daily Age* (Philadelphia), January 24, 1865.
3. *Harper's Weekly*, March 4, 1865.
4. Katherine Dhalle, *An Examination of Alfred S. Hartwell and the 55th Massachusetts Volunteer Infantry*, unpublished Historical Research Paper for State University of New York, Empire State College, 1995, 52–53.
5. Luis F. Emilio, *History of the Fifty-Fourth Regiment of Massachusetts*

Volunteer Infantry (Boston: The Boston Book Company, 1894), 284.

6. Robert J. Zalimas, *Black Soldiers in Blue: African American Troops in the Civil War Era*, Edited by Jr. John David Smith (Chapel Hill and London: University of North Carolina Press, 2002), 361–365.

7. Charles B. Fox, *Record of the Service of the 55th Regiment of Massachusetts Volunteer Infantry* (Freeport, New York, Books for Library Press, 1971), 135.

8. *The Christian Recorder*, April 8, 1865.

9. *Richmond Examiner*, April 3, 1865.

10. *Alexandria Gazette*, April 3, 1865.

11. *Alexandria Gazette*, April 7, 1865.

12. *Alexandria Gazette*, April 4, 1865.

13. National Park Service, *Black Soldiers on the Appomattox* Campaign, *http:// www.nps.gov/apco/black-soldiers.htm*. Accessed July 13, 2014.

14. *Alexandria Gazette*, April 10, 1865.

15. This letter published in *The Christian Recorder*, April 29, 1865 was simply signed "A Canadian."

16. *The Christian Recorder*, April 29, 1865.

17. Anderson Ruffin Abbott, *The Anglo-American Magazine, Volume 5, 1901 Some Recollections of Lincoln's Assassination*, 397–402, *http://archive.org/ details/angloamericanma02unkngoog*. Accessed April 2, 2013.

18. Interview with Mrs. William Henry Chase, *Windsor Daily Star*, July 25, 1942.

19. *New York Tribune*, reprinted in *Jackson Daily Citizen* (Jackson, Michigan), April 27, 1865.

20. *Detroit Advertiser and Tribune*, April 17, 1865.

21. *New York Herald*, May 4, 1865.

22. John Wilkes Booth, *Right or Wrong, God Judge Me: The Writings of John Wilkes Booth*, Edited by John Rhodehamel and Louise Taper (Urbana: University of Illinois Press, 2001), 64, 68.

23. Ibid., 67.

24. Ibid., 60.

25. *The Christian Recorder*, May 20, 1865.

26. Ibid., September 9, 1865.

27. Ibid., July 15, 1865.

28. Ibid., July 15, 1865.

29. Joseph T. Glatthaar, *Forged In Battle: The Civil War Alliance of Black Soldiers and White Officers* (New York: First Merridian Printing, 1991), 218–220.

30. *The Christian Recorder*, November 4, 1865.

31. Widow's pension file of Priscilla J. Atwood, NARA.
32. *The Christian Recorder*, November 4, 1865.
33. *Chatham Weekly Planet*, June 15, 1866.
34. *The Christian Recorder*, April 21, 1866.
35. Caleb W. Hornor, May 14, 1866. Major R.O. Abbott also lent his personal endorsement, May 15, 1866.
36. Robert Reyburn, May 12, 1866.

Chapter 10: War's Aftermath

1. Freedmen's Inquiry Commission, Canadian Testimony, p. 16, 17.
2. Anderson Ruffin Abbott Papers, file labelled "Coloured Weslyian Methodist Church," Special Collections, Toronto Reference Library, Toronto, Ontario.
3. Frank H. Severance, *Old Trails on the Niagara Frontier* (Buffalo: The Matthews-Northrup Co., 1899), 197.
4. *http://freepages.genealogy.rootsweb.ancestry.com/~methodists/bmechurch.htm*. Accessed April 1, 2013.
5. *http://search.ancestry.ca/browse/view.aspx?dbid=1200&iid=MIUSA186 6_113836-00596&pid=514249&ssrc=&fn=Junius+B&ln=Roberts&st=g*. Accessed April 1, 2013.
6. Junius B. Robert's pension application, #604 950, certificate #690 784; Francis A. Robert's widow's application, #614 172.
7. Reverend D.D. Buck, *The Progression of the Race in the United States and Canada* (Chicago: Atwell Printing and Binding Co, 1907), 394–395.
8. Note there is a photo of Carvell at *http://www.collectionscanada.gc.ca/nwmp-pcno/025003-1200-e.html*.
9. *The Christian Recorder*, June 16, 1866.
10. "The Township Papers" for Raleigh Township, Kent County. A microfilm is available at the main Chatham-Kent Public library within the Kent Branch Genealogical Society's research room.
11. William J. Simmons, *Men of Mark: Eminent, Progressive and Rising* (Cleveland: Geo. M. Rewell & Co., 1887), 145–148.
12. Ezekial C. Cooper, writing from Chatham, April 13, 1866, which appeared in *The Christian Recorder*, May 12, 1866.
13. *The Louisianian*, March 2, 1871.
14. Christopher Robinson, ed., *The Ontario Reports: Volume VI. Containing Reports of Cases Decided in the Queen's Bench, Chancery and Common Pleas Divisions, of the High Court of Justice for Ontario* (Toronto: Rpwse;; & Hutchison, 1885), 126–128.

15. *Chatham Weekly Planet*, February 11, 1864.
16. Details provided by late historian Norman Mcrae.
17. The Freedmen's Bureau Online, *http://freedmensbureau.com/southcarolina/ scoperations7.htm*. Accessed April 2, 2013. Canadian census of Chatham, County of Kent (1861), *The Anderson Intelligencer* (S.C.), July 26, 1866.
18. Records of the Field Offices for the State of Virginia, Bureau of Refugees, Freedman, and Abandoned Lands, 1865–1872.
19. *The Christian Recorder*, October 7, 1865.
20. *Black Abolitionist Papers: Canada*, 192.
21. *The Christian Recorder*, December 5, 1878 published the article that had originally appeared in Greenville, Mississippi's *Local and Advertiser*.
22. *Black Abolitionist Papers: Canada*, 369.
23. *The Christian Recorder*, December 17, 1870.
24. *The Christian Recorder*, October 17, 1868.
25. *The Christian Recorder*, July 14, 1866.
26. *The Christian Recorder*, July 3, 1869.
27. *The Freeman* (Indianapolis), February 21, 1891.
28. Anderson Ruffin Abbott Papers, Special Collections, Toronto Reference Library, Toronto, Ontario.
29. Ibid.
30. *http://theslaveholderswar.blogspot.ca/2012/02/grant-army-of-republic-in-canada.htm*. Accessed April 5, 2014.
31. Charles Eugene Hamlin, *The Life and Times of Hannibal Hamlin* (Cambridge: Riverside Press, 1899), 354.
32. Compiled Military Service Record for Richard Williams, NARA
33. Compiled Military Service Record for Oliver Fountain, NARA.
34. Compiled Military Service Record for James Marble, NARA.
35. Compiled Military Service Record for George English, NARA.
36. Ontario, Canada, Deaths, 1869–1938 and Deaths Overseas, 1939–1947, *www. ancestry.ca*. Accessed April 25, 2014.
37. Bennie McRae, *http://www.bjmjr.net/special/dunbar_legend.htm*. Accessed March 30, 2013.
38. J.C. Gobrecht, *History of The National Home for Disabled Volunteer, Soldiers: with a Complete Guide-Book to the Central Home, at Dayton, Ohio* (Dayton: United Brethren Printing Establishment, 1875), 32, 51–61.
39. Ibid., 135.
40. *http://search.ancestry.ca/iexec?htx=View&r=5543&dbid=1200&i-id=MIUSA1866_113820-00156&fn=William&ln=Johnson&st=d&ss-rc=&pid=136134*. Accessed April 1, 2013.
41. Scanned copies of these documents, courtesy of Marcie Beck from Grand

Rapids Public Library.

42. http://search.ancestry.ca/iexec?htx=View&r=5543&dbid=1200&i-
id=MIUSA1866_113878-00386&fn=Charles+H&ln=Griffin&st=d&ss-
rc=&pid=209967.

43. Chicago Sun Times, November 12, 2007.

44. Compiled military service record for Henry Hugh Williams and widow's
pension file for Alice Williams, NARA.

45. Wilbert L. Jenkins, Climbing Up To Glory: A short history of African
Americans During the Civil War and Reconstruction (Wilmington,
Delaware: Scholarly Resource Inc., 2002), 146.

46. Richard R. Wright, 1816–1916 Centennial Encyclopaedia of the African
Methodist Episcopal Church (Philadelphia: Book Concern of the A.M.E.
Church, 1916), 205–207.

47. Hallie Quinn Brown, Homespun Heroines and Other Women of Distinction
(New York: reprinted by Oxford University Press, 1988), 176–177; Virginia
Law Burns, Bold Women in Michigan History (Missoula, MT: Mountain
Press Publishing Company, 2006), 47–54.

48. J.R. Riley to Mrs. Anna S. Jamieson, March 5, 1909, The Jamieson Papers,
Regional Collection, Weldon Library, University of Western Ontario.

49. Jerome R. Riley, Reach the Reached Negro (Atlanta: Byrd Printing Co.,
1903), 72–73.

50. The Brooklyn Daily Eagle, January 5, 1906; Springfield Daily News, April
15, 1912; The News and Courier, (Charleston, South Carolina), April 7,
1902; Morning Republican (Little Rock, Arkansas), July 25, 1873; Evening
Star (Washington, D.C, January 4, 1882; Jerome R. Riley, The Philosophy
of Negro Suffrage, (Washington, D.C: Self-published, 1897) 77–79; Also,
Jerome Riley to Anna Jamieson, Jamieson Papers, Regional Collection,
Weldon Library, University of Western Ontario.

51. Ezekial C. Cooper to Mrs. Jamieson, February 24, 1909, Jamieson Papers,
Regional Collection, Weldon Library, University of Western Ontario.

52. Letter to Sarah Thomas from Detroit in May [?]. [Page with signature
is missing and much of the letter is so faded as to be illegible.] Rapiers
Papers, Moorland-Spingarn Research Center, Howard University,
Washington, D.C.

53. The Freedmen's Record, May, 1865, p. 136; The Freedmen's Record, August,
1865, p. 150.

54. Evening Star (Washington), May 19, 1866.

55. The Christian Recorder, May 12, 1866.

56. Ezekial C. Cooper to Rev. S. Hunt, November 15, 1865, American
Missionary Association Papers, F1-737.

57. E.C. Cooper to Rev. Geo. Whipple, October 23, 1865, American Missionary Association Papers, F1-734; Ezekial C. Cooper to Rev. Samuel Hunt, November 2, 1865, American Missionary Association Papers, F1-735.

58. *The Christian Recorder*, August 28; *The Christian* Recorder, September 11, 1869.

59. J.W. Alvord, *First Semi-Annual Report on Schools and Finances of Freedmen (Bureau Refugees, Freedmen and Abandoned Lands —1866)* (Washington: Government Printing Office, 1868), 53.

60. Theophilus G. Steward, *Fifty Years in the Gospel Ministry* (Philadelphia: A.M.E. Book Concern, 1921), 34.

61. Richard R. Wright, *Centennial Encyclopaedia of the African Methodist Episcopal Church* (Philadelphia: Book Concern of the A.M.E. Church, 1916), 73.

62. *The Christian Recorder*, June 9, 1866; *The Christian Recorder*, May 25, 1867; *The Christian Recorder*, September 11, 1869.

63. *The Christian Recorder*, May 7, 1874.

64. (Annual Report) *Mission to the Coloured Population in Canada: Late Fugitive Slave Mission: Being A Branch of the Operations of the Colonial and Continental Church Society* (London, England: Society's Offices, 1866), A2.

65. Ibid., 12.

66. Ibid., 6.

67. Ibid., 8–9.

68. Unpublished autobiography of Reverend William King; the King Collection, National Archives of Canada.

69. *Queen's Bench, Hilary Term, 34 VIC., 1871*, 182–199.

70. As an example, *The Christian Recorder*, August 20, 1870, reported on a pleasant day on August 1, morning trains from Ypsilanti, Pontiac, Adrian, and Toledo brought people to Detroit where they crossed the river to celebrate with Canadians at a grove near Sandwich, where the celebration had been held annually for several years.

BIBLIOGRAPHY

Adams, Virginia M. *On the Altar of Freedom: A Black Soldier's Civil War Letters from the Front. Corporal, James Henry Gooding.* Amherst, MA: University of Massachusetts Press, 1991.

Bacon, Margaret Hope. *Rebellion at Christiana.* New York: Crown Publishers, 1975.

Berlin, Ira, Barbara J. Fields, Steven F. Miller, Joseph P. Reidy, and Leslie S. Rowland. *Free at Last: A Documentary History of Slavery, Freedom, and the Civil War.* New York: The New Press, 1992.

Blackett, R.J.M. *Thomas Morris Chester Black Civil War Correspondent: His Dispatches from the Virginia Front.* Baton Rouge and London: Louisiana State University Press, 1989.

Brown-Kubisch, Linda. *The Queen's Busy Settlement: Black Pioneers 1839–1865.* Toronto: Natural Heritage Books, 2004.

Collison, Gary. *Shadrach Minkins: From Fugitive Slave to Citizen.* Cambridge and London: Harvard University Press, 1997.

Drew, Benjamin. *The Narratives of Fugitive Slaves (The Refugee: or the Narratives of Fugitive Slaves in Canada: Related by Themselves, with an Account of the History and Condition of the Colored Population of Upper Canada).* Toronto: Prospero Books, 2000.

Duncan, Russell. *Blue-Eyed Child of Fortune: The Civil War Letters of Colonel Robert Gould Shaw.* Athens, GA: The University of Georgia Press, 1992.

Eisenschiml, Otto and Newman, Ralph. *The Civil War: The American Iliad as Told by Those Who Lived It.* New York: Mallard Press, 1956.

Emilio, Luis F. *A Brave Black Regiment.* Boston: Boston Book Company (The Basic Afro-American Reprint Library), 1894.

Emilio, Luis F. *A Brave Black Regiment: The History of the Fifty-Fourth Regiment of Massachusetts Volunteer Infantry 1863–1865.* New York: Da Capo Press, 1995.

Forbes, Ella. *But We Have No Country: The 1851 Christiana, Pennsylvania Resistance.* Cherry Hill, NJ: Africana Homestead Legacy Publishers, 1998.

Gibbs, C.R. *Black, Copper & Bright: The District of Columbia's Black Civil War Regiment.* Silver Spring: Three Dimensional Publishing, 2002.

Gladstone, William A. *United States Colored Troops: 1863–1867.* Gettysburg: Thomas Publications, 1990.

Glatthaar, Joseph T. *Forged in Battle: The Civil War Alliance of Black Soldiers and White Officers.* New York: Penguin Group, 1990.

Gordon-Reed, Annette. *The Hemingses of Monticello.* New York: W.W. Norton & Company, 2008.

Green, John M. *Negroes in Michigan History.* Detroit: John M. Green, 1985.

Gutman, Herbert G. *The Black Family in Slavery and Freedom, 1750–1925.* New York: Pantheon Books, 1976.

Hamer, Marguerite B. "Luring Canadian Soldiers into Union Lines during the War Between the States." *Canadian Historical Review* 27, no. 2 (1946): 150–62.

Hargrove, Hondon B. *Black Union Soldiers in the Civil War.* Jefferson, NC, and London: McFarland & Company, 1988.

Haviland, Laura Smith. *A Woman's Life Work: Labors and Experiences of Laura S. Haviland.* London, U.K.: Forgotten Books, 2008.

Hepburn, Sharon A. Roger. *Crossing the Border: A Free Black Community in Canada.* Urbana and Chicago: University of Illinois Press, 2007.

Higginson, Thomas Wentworth. *Army Life in a Black Regiment.* Cambridge: University Press, 1869.

Holzer, Harold. *Hearts Touched by Fire: The Best of Battles and Leaders of the Civil War.* New York: Modern Library, 2011.

Howe, S.G. *Report to the Freedmen's Inquiry Commission 1864: The Refugees from Slavery in Canada West.* New York: Arno Press, 1969.

Hoy, Claire. *Canadians in the Civil War.* Toronto: McArthur & Company, 2004.

Jamieson, Annie Straith. *William King: Friend and Champion of Slaves.* Toronto: Missions of Evangelism, 1925.

La Lancette, Thomas E. *A Noble and Glorious Cause: The Life, Times and Civil War Service of Captain Elijah W. Gibbons.* Middletown, CT: Godfrey Memorial Library, 2005.

Larson, Kate Clifford. *The Assassin's Accomplice: Mary Surratt and the Plot to Kill Abraham Lincoln.* New York: Basic Books, 2008.

Larson, Kate Clifford. *Bound for the Promise Land: Harriet Tubman, Portrait of an American Hero.* New York: Random House, 2004.

Long, Richard A. *Black Writers and The American Civil War: Black Involvement and Participation in the War Between the States.* Secaucus, NJ: The Blue & Grey Press, 1988.

Luck, Wilbert H. *Journey to Honey Hill.* Washington: Wiluk Press, 1985.

Mabee, Carleton. *Sojourner Truth: Slave, Prophet, Legend.* New York and London: New York University Press, 1993, 1995.

Markle, Donald E. *Spies and Spymasters of the Civil War.* New York: Barnes and Noble, 1994.

Mayers, Adam. *Dixie & the Dominion: Canada, the Confederacy, and the War for the Union.* Toronto: Dundurn, 2003.

Miller, Edward A. Jr. *The Black Civil War Soldiers of Illinois: The Story of the Twenty-ninth U.S. Colored Infantry.* Columbia: University of South Carolina Press, 1998.

Miller, Edward A. Jr. *Lincoln's Abolitionist General: The Biography of David Hunter.* Columbia: University of South Carolina Press, 1997.

Newby, Dalyce M. *Anderson Ruffin Abbott: First Afro-Canadian Doctor.* Markham, ON: Fitzhenry & Whiteside, 1998.

Paradis, James M. *Strike the Blow for Freedom: The 6th United States Colored Infantry in the Civil War.* Shippensburg: White Mane Books, 1998.

Quarles, Benjamin. *The Negro in the Civil War.* New York: Da Capo Press, 1953.

Ramold, Steven J. *Slaves, Sailors, Citizens: African Americans in the Union Navy.* DeKalb: Northern Illinois University Press, 2002.

Redkey, Edwin S. *A Grand Army of Black Men: Letters from African-American Soldiers in the Union Army, 1861–1865.* Cambridge: Cambridge University Press, 1992.

Redpath, James. *The Roving Editor, or Talks with Slaves in the Southern States.* University Park: The Pennsylvania State University Press, 1996.

Renehan, Edward J. Jr. *The Secret Six: The True Tale of the Men Who Conspired with John Brown.* New York: Crown Publishers, 1995.

Ripley, C. Peter. *The Black Abolitionist Papers: Volume I The British Isles, 1830–1865.* Chapel Hill and London: The University of North Carolina Press, 1985.

Ripley, C. Peter. *The Black Abolitionist Papers: Volume II Canada, 1830–1865.* Chapel Hill and London: The University of North Carolina Press, 1986.

Robbins, Arlie C. *Legacy to Buxton.* Chatham, ON: Ideal Printing, 1983.

Siebert, Wilbur H. *The Underground Railroad from Slavery to Freedom*. New York: The Macmillan Company, 1898.

Simpson, Donald G. *Under the North Star: Black Communities in Upper Canada Before Confederation (1867)*. Trenton, NJ: African World Press, 2005.

Slotkin, Richard. *No Quarter: The Battle of the Crater, 1864*. New York: Random House, 2009.

Smith, John David. *Black Soldiers in Blue: African American Troopers in the Civil War Era*. Chapel Hill and London: The University of North Carolina Press, 2002.

Sterling, Dorothy. *The Making of an Afro-American: Martin Robison Delany 1812–1885*. Garden City, NY: Doubleday & Company, 1971.

Still, William. *The Underground Railroad*. Chicago: Johnson Publishing Company, 1970.

Ullman, Victor. *Look to the North Star: A Life of William King*. Boston: Beacon Press, 1969.

Villard, Oswald Garrison. *John Brown 1800–1859: A Biography Fifty Years After*. Boston and New York: Houghton Mifflin Company, 1910.

Vinet, Mark. *Canada and the American Civil War: Prelude to War*. Vaudreuil-Sur-le-Lac, QC: Wadem Publishing, 2001.

Voegeli, V. Jacque. *Free but Not Equal: The Midwest and the Negro During the Civil War*. Chicago: University of Chicago Press, 1967.

Von Frank, Albert J. *The Trials of Anthony Burns: Freedom and Slavery in Emerson's Boston*. Cambridge, MA, and London: Harvard University Press, 1998.

Walton, Clyde C. "Civil War History." *Quarterly Journal by the State University of Iowa* 5, no. 4 (1959): 346–445.

Westwood, Howard C. *Black Troops White Commanders and Freedmen During the Civil War*. Carbondale and Edwardsville: Southern Illinois University Press, 1992.

Wheeler, Richard. *Voices of the Civil War*. New York: Penguin Group, 1976.

Wilson, Joseph T. *The Black Phalanx: African American Soldiers in the War of Independence, The War of 1812, and the Civil War*. New York: Da Capo Press, 1994.

Winks, Robin W. *Canada and the United States: The Civil War Years*. Baltimore: John Hopkins Press, 1960.

Woodford, Frank B. *Father Abraham's Children: Michigan Episodes in the Civil War*. Detroit: Wayne State University Press, 1961, 1999.

Further Reading at Library and Archives Canada

John Bell fonds. Toronto-born physician and naturalist served in Union Army Hospitals during the American Civil War.

Charles E. Riggins fonds. Canadian from Niagara Peninsula who joined the
   Union Army in February, 1862. Fought in several battles including Bull
   Run. After the war he became a pharmacist in Beamsville, Ontario.

Charles Edward Coons fonds. Coons was a Kentucky native and a Confederate
   soldier who was captured during the war and imprisoned at Camp Chase
   and Camp Douglas in Illinois, from which he escaped and took refuge in
   Canada.

Government Constabulary for Frontier Service fonds. This organization,
   known as the Frontier Police, was organized to patrol the border during
   the Civil War.

Samuel Edmour St. Onge Chapleau fonds. Educated in Terrebonne, Canada
   East, Chapleau served as an officer in the Union Army. He is buried in
   Arlington National Cemetery.

Abraham Lincoln fonds. Public and private papers on microfilm reels
   M-371-M464, M5894 to M-5898.

William Fenwick Williams fonds. Williams was a native of Annapolis Royal,
   Nova Scotia. During the Civil War, Williams was commander in chief of
   the forces in all of British North America. He particularly feared invasion
   by the United States and fought to have more troops brought from the
   mother country to defend against it.

INDEX

ALSO BY BRYAN PRINCE

One More River to Cross

In the early to mid-nineteenth century, Isaac Brown, a slave, was accused of the attempted murder of a prominent plantation owner, despite there being no evidence of his guilt. Brown, after enduring two brutal floggings, was shipped to a New Orleans slave pen. From there the resourceful Brown was able to make a daring escape to Philadelphia in the free state of Pennsylvania. His biggest error was writing a note informing his free wife and eleven children in Maryland of his whereabouts. The note was intercepted and led to his arrest and extradition back to Maryland. While engaged in researching an ancestor named Isaac Brown, Bryan Prince encountered the very high-profile case of what turned out to be a different Isaac Brown. The story of this slave, with its culmination in Brown's dramatic escape and ultimate success in crossing the border into Canada, is the riveting subject of historian Bryan Prince's latest book.

OF RELATED INTEREST

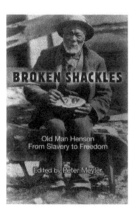

Broken Shackles
Old Man Henson from Slavery to Freedom
Edited by Peter Meyler

In 1889, *Broken Shackles* was published in Toronto under the pseudonym of Glenelg. This very unique book, containing the recollections of a resident of Owen Sound, Ontario, an African American known as Old Man Henson, was one of the very few books that documented the journey to Canada from the perspective of a person of African descent. Henson was a great storyteller and the spark of life shines through as he describes the horrors of slavery and his goal of escaping its tenacious hold. His times as a slave in Maryland, his refuge in Pennsylvania and New Jersey, and his ultimate freedom in Canada are vividly depicted through his remembrances.

The stories of Henson's family, friends, and enemies will both amuse and shock readers. His observations of life's struggles and triumphs are as relevant today as they were in his time.

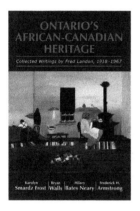

Ontario's African-Canadian Heritage
Collected Writings by Fred Landon, 1918–1967
Edited by Karolyn Smardz Frost, Hilary Bates,
Bryan Walls, and Frederick H. Armstrong

Ontario's African-Canadian Heritage is composed of the collected works of Professor Fred Landon, who for more than sixty years wrote about African-Canadian history. The selected articles have, for the most part, never been surpassed by more recent research and offer a wealth of data on slavery, abolition, the Underground Railroad, and more, providing unique insights into the abundance of African-Canadian heritage in Ontario. This volume, illustrated and extensively annotated, includes research by the editors into the life of Fred Landon. It is the Legacy Project for the Bicentennial of the Abolition of the Atlantic Slave Trade, an initiative of the OHS, funded by a "Roots of Freedom" grant received from the Ontario Ministry of Citizenship and Immigration.

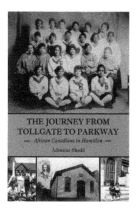

The Journey from Tollgate to Parkway
African Canadians in Hamilton
by Adrienne Shadd

When the Lincoln Alexander Parkway was named, it was a triumph not only for this distinguished Canadian, but for all African Canadians. *The Journey from Tollgate to Parkway* looks at the history of blacks in the Ancaster-Burlington-Hamilton area, their long struggle for justice and equality in education and opportunity, and their achievements, presented in a fascinating and meticulously researched historical narrative. Although popular wisdom suggests that blacks first came via the Underground Railroad, the possibility that slaves owned by early settlers were part of the initial community, then known as the "Head of the Lake," is explored.

Adrienne Shadd's original research offers new insights into urban black history, filling in gaps on the background of families and individuals who are very much part of the history of this region, while also exploding stereotypes, such as that of the uneducated, low-income early black Hamiltonian.

Available at your favourite bookseller

VISIT US AT

Dundurn.com
@dundurnpress
Facebook.com/dundurnpress
Pinterest.com/dundurnpress